VINO

GREAT WINE FOR EVERYDAY LIFE

HAMISH ANDERSON

C

CENTURY

Published by Century in 2003

1 3 5 7 9 10 8 6 4 2

First published in the United Kingdom in 2003 by Century
The Random House Group Limited
20 Vauxhall Bridge Road, London, SW1V 2SA

Random House Australia (Pty) Limited
20 Alfred Street, Milsons Point, Sydney
New South Wales 2061, Australia

Random House New Zealand Limited
18 Poland Road, Glenfield
Auckland 10, New Zealand

Random House (Pty) Limited
Endulini, 5a Jubilee Road, Parktown 2193, South Africa

The Random House Group Limited Reg. No. 954009

www.randomhouse.co.uk

A CIP catalogue record for this book
is available from the British Library

Papers used by Random House
are natural, recyclable products made from wood grown in
sustainable forests. The manufacturing processes conform to
the environmental regulations of the country of origin

ISBN 1 8441 3187 4

A HERE+THERE production for Century
Art Direction: Caz Hildebrand
Design: Mark Paton
Jacket design: Kate Marlow
Maps: Mark Lewis
Typesetting: Julie Martin Ltd

Cookery: Peter Begg

Printed and bound in China by C&C Offset Printing Co., Ltd

To my parents who have always encouraged me to do what I wanted to do, and to Celia with love.

CONTENTS

INTRODUCTION

This book can be read from cover to cover but is not designed to be. Rather think of it as something to be dipped in and out of.

On the simplest level you will be able to look up a wine and learn about it. In this sense it differs little from other wine books. However, at the end of each entry you will find a series of links to take you to other parts of the book. These will enable you to branch out from the usual tried and tested bottles safe in the knowledge that you are not just making a wild stab in the dark. The links to food work in a similar fashion and I hope they will provide some inspiration and help you to get pleasure out of the bottles you buy. The key sections are indicated by the following symbols representing the three main sections of the book:

   ⚫ Region

⚫ ⚫ The Grapes, red and white

   ⚫ Food

I have also included a list of my favourite producers for each region and grape variety. You'll find these listed in the margin.

At the back of the book is a glossary of wine terms. Not all of these words feature in the book, but they are common terms that are found on wine labels. Where words from the glossary appear in the text, they will be printed in **bold**.

Working at the Tate Gallery, whose cellar has been famous for years, I am able to indulge my own passion by choosing the wines to go on the list myself. After helping set up the restaurants at Tate Modern, however, I soon realised that whilst people's enthusiasm for food had increased hugely, their knowledge of wine had remained fairly static. Each and every one of us is drinking more and more wine each year, yet although we are prepared to try different foods without prompting, the same is not yet true for wine.

At present, there is an awful trend towards substituting the bland for the individual, as formulaic wines are made to fit a particular price bracket. Thus we now have a range of wines from around the world that all taste the same.

Just as food offers you more than just the basic fuel to walk around each day, so can wine. Wine should be riding on the back of the explosion of interest in cooking. Many people are now happy to slavishly follow cookbook recipes and have heated arguments over whether Delia or Nigella has a better béarnaise sauce, and yet we still go out to eat wonderful meals and drink wines with all the character of a pre-packaged frozen dinner.

The aim of this book is not to turn you into an underground organic wine activist or a crusader against the big wine sellers. What I really want is for you to get·the most out of wine, and I believe that all you need to achieve this is a small foundation of knowledge and the confidence to experiment.

I am often asked what my top tip is when buying a wine. There is, I am afraid, no holy grail; it is simply not possible to give you ten insider tips and solve all your purchasing problems. However, there is one thing I would ask you to remember above all: grape varieties or regions do not make fine wine, wine makers and producers do. Some areas and grapes have a head start and are predisposed towards making better wine; however, it is up to man to realise this potential.

Here is some other advice I would like to offer:

- Chardonnay is produced all over the world yet its quality ranges from abysmal to bland and finally sublime; the defining factor for which category the wine falls in is the maker. If you enjoy a wine, make a note of the producer and you'll be glad you did.

- Price will, of course, play a part in the equation but don't get sucked into comparing wines purely on price. Wine is made in a wealth of different circumstances all with varying economic conditions and geography. Even my limited mathematical and economic skills can work out that to produce a bottle of Syrah from the cliff-like vineyards of Côte-Rôtie is going to cost infinitely more than on the flat plains or Paarl in South Africa, where land and labour is cheap. Like everything in life, if you want to experience hand-crafted, small production goods, they will inevitably cost more.

- When purchasing wine remember that, while a shroud of mystery often surrounds this subject, day-to-day buying is straightforward. Wine is treated in the supermarket and high street as any other product might be. This is beneficial in the sense that wine has now been truly democratised, but it can be bad for individuality and excitement. Buy three-get-one-free might seem like a great deal, but don't for a minute think that the producer has suddenly had a wave of compassion and reduced their profit margin. Offers are funded by inflated retail prices for the other eleven months of the year.

- Look for wines with limited shelf space and poor labels. If you want to buy wine from someone with passion, though, find your local independent wine merchant. It might be sold by the case, but get a few friends together and this won't be a problem. You'll end up drinking interesting, individual wines and might even find yourself asked along to a few tastings in the process.

- The taxation laws in this country are such that at the bottom end even a small increase in a bottle's selling price can have a dramatic impact on quality. The example below will reinforce the point. First, let's take a £3.50 bottle of French wine and work out how much of this is the actual cost of the wine. The breakdown is as follows:
  - VAT: 0.52p
  - Duty: £1.16
  - Transport: 0.17p
  - Cork, capsule, bottle and label: 0.20p
  - Supplier's margin of 20%: 0.50p

  So for this £3.50 bottle the winemaker is left with £0.95 to produce the wine and make a profit.

  Now let's take a £5.00 bottle:
  - VAT: 0.75p
  - Duty: £1.16
  - Transport: 0.17p
  - Cork, capsule, bottle and label: 0.20p
  - Supplier Margin of 20%: 0.70p

  This producer suddenly has £2.02 to produce the wine. Because so many of the costs are fixed (the major one for cheaper bottles is government duty), the quality of the wine could have more than doubled in return for a 40% increase in outlay from your pocket.

- Gleaning the information required to make an informed choice from a wine label can be a tricky affair, as the Old and New Worlds take very different approaches in presenting this information to you. The fundamental difference is that in the New World the producer is more often than not selling you a grape variety, i.e. Cabernet Sauvignon. European wines, on the contrary, sell themselves not on what grapes the wine is made from but rather the region it is from, i.e. Chablis. There are, of course, exceptions to this rule, but the notion of a wine's regional identity is far more important in Europe than the New World. Overleaf are some tips and things to look for.

New World Label

First of all look for a grape variety; this will usually be displayed prominently. Grape variety is likely to be the defining factor in the wine's taste, so you should use this as your entry point to the book. If it is not immediately clear what grapes are being used, have a look at the back label – these are usually rammed full of information. You might also find information on whether the wine has been matured in oak barrels or not.

Turning to the front label, we can discover more about the region. Use the opposite label as an example. You'll be able to look up the Napa Valley in the USA section and learn that it is California's finest region. The producer is all-important. Using the example, unfortunately, it is not enough just to remember you have enjoyed a Zinfandel from the Napa Valley. I have tasted plenty of poor Zinfandels from the region; the reason this wine is good is because of Frog's Leap.

Old World Label

Europe is altogether more complicated, I am afraid, as regional identity is the key. Europe has thousands of geographically designated areas that taste different, yet helpful information like what grape the wine is made from is not placed on the label. This is incredibly frustrating in one sense as you, the consumer, are often making a blind guess. However, spend a little time getting to know what regions you enjoy and you'll be glad of this system. The diversity of taste on offer is vast.

The second spanner to throw into the works is the law that governs a wine's production. In the New World pretty much anything goes. In Europe, winemakers are restricted by a set of rules. For example, Pouilly-Fumé can only be produced from one grape and restrictions on production apply. Every country has a grading system; I will discuss each one more specifically in the country section. You need to be aware of the laws in place but generally, to my mind, they fail. Ever wondered why one Pouilly-Fumé tastes great and the next so poor? It is back to the producer I am afraid. Pouilly-Fumé is governed by France's strictest set of laws, yet much of the wine is poor; the reason the one adjacent is good is down to Domaine de Saint-Laurent-l'Abbaye, the producer.

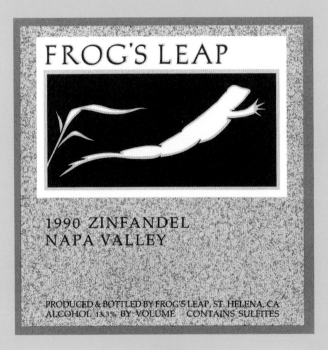

FROG'S LEAP

1990 ZINFANDEL
NAPA VALLEY

PRODUCED & BOTTLED BY FROG'S LEAP, ST. HELENA, CA
ALCOHOL 13.3% BY VOLUME   CONTAINS SULFITES

PRODUCT OF FRANCE

POUILLY-FUMÉ

APPELLATION POUILLY-FUMÉ CONTROLÉE

Domaine de Saint-Laurent-l'Abbaye

Mis en bouteille au domaine

e 75 cl   Jean-Claude CHATELAIN   12,5% vol.

PROPRIÉTAIRE A SAINT-ANDELAIN · POUILLY-S/-LOIRE

REGIONS

OLD WORLD

The nature of the way wine is sold to us in the Old World countries necessitates a far larger section than the New World. The essential difference is that within Europe, the majority of wine is sold off the back of its regional identity. Around the rest of the globe, far more emphasis is placed on the grape variety, e.g. Chardonnay. While there are thousands of different grapes, only a few have become prominent in the New World. Within Europe wine styles may vary widely across only a short distance. These various styles are protected by a set of laws that does not allow the wine growers to plant whatever plant they please and produce it in any way they fancy. Additionally, wine production in Europe is steeped in history. The famous regions have been exporting for hundreds of years, while lesser known ones have always produced wine of a distinctive taste to satisfy thirsty locals. This has in the past encouraged diversity as the consumer learned to find the style that suited them.

Contrast this to the New World where wine has only really started to be produced and exported seriously in the last thirty years. The basis for its success was founded on accessible wines that could be easily understood by the consumer. This situation does not encourage diversity. That is not to say all New World is the same. It is not, and indeed all the finest New World wines are now emphasising their regionality. Additionally, growing these grapes in hotter conditions blurs the differences that are more noticeable in the varied climate of Europe. This, coupled with a smaller palette of varieties, means that the New World will always be simpler to understand and thus require less space in a book such as this.

FRANCE

Within Europe there is a bias towards France. This is for two reasons; firstly, we drink more of this country's wine than any other; secondly, it has the most diverse production of sparkling, white and red in the world.

Recent reports suggest we now spend slightly more in total on Australian rather than French wine. Much as I love Australian wine, this is down to the brilliance of their marketing, and the ability of the French to shoot themselves in the foot, rather than the superiority of their wines. The diversity of wine on offer in France is unrivalled. The fine, expensive stuff has never been a problem to sell, regardless of its quality. It's the wine that we mortals can afford to drink every day that's been the cause for concern.

The competition on the export market has become greater than ever, though, and this has sent an unequivocal message to French producers: make decent wine at all price points or get on your *bicyclette*. Poor wines still hide behind the French classification systems, but generally the quality of winemaking has never been so high. For those of you whose tongues are weary with the homogeneity of many New World offerings, now is the time to return to the Manchester United of winemaking countries.

French wine law is divided into four basic categories. As you move up the levels, the laws on **yields**, grape varieties and production methods become increasingly strict.

Vin de Table

Table wine, the lowest level. These are usually only good for marinating food in, as the sole requirement is that they be fit for human consumption.

Vins de Pays

Usually translated as 'country wine'. Each named *Vin de Pays* will always specify a large swathe of land that the grapes must come from, i.e. Vins de Pays d'Oc from the Mediterranean side of Southern France. There has been an explosion in *Vins de Pays* made from single grape varieties such as Merlot or Chardonnay. This is not, though, what France does best – it produces competent if bland wines. Leave this method to the New World.

Vin Délimité de Qualité Supérieure

Thankfully shortened to VDQS on the label. This usually refers to a more specific site of higher quality than a *Vin de Pays*.

Appellation d'Origine Contrôlée

Usually shortened to *Appellation Contrôlée* (AC) on the label. At the top of the pile, these wines come from the best sites in France. However, there is still plenty of room for poor producers in the elite category, so remember that this is an indication of potential rather than absolute quality.

Nearly all the French regions I will be discussing are of AC quality. To make things more complicated, though, specific AC laws will apply to each region. I will highlight vagaries, where they exist, and point out the most important pieces of information to look for.

Alsatian wine should really be very easy to sell in this country. The wines are not expensive, the appellation system is easy to understand and – wait for it – the grape variety is actually written on the label. In short, not too much knowledge is required to be able to pick up a bottle and ascertain roughly what the wine inside will taste like. The wine press love them; the trade adore them so why aren't we all drinking them?

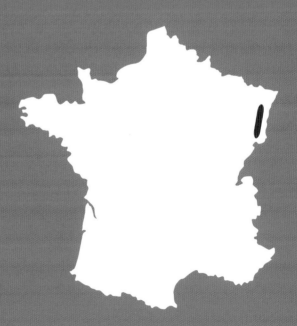

Hugel, Trimbach, Schofitt, Bott-Geyl, Schlumberger, Faller, Zind-Humbrecht, Bruno Sorg, Ostertag, Kientzler, Rolly-Gassmann, Ernest Burn

Well, things are never as they seem. The bottles are suspiciously Germanic in shape – as demanded by the region – and this immediately puts the consumer on guard. One of the major varieties grown there is Riesling, which has about as much selling power as writing 'cat's piss' on the label. Another variety, Gewürztraminer, also sounds like it comes from the other side of the Rhine.

Cast your inhibitions aside because Alsace has some hugely talented winemakers turning out products that are vastly undervalued. The range of white wine produced there is breathtaking.

Geographically, Alsace looks like a dead end for still winemaking as it is nearly as far north as Champagne, a region in which the grapes only ripen sufficiently to make sparkling wine. Indeed, it is further north than Chablis, yet the styles of wine couldn't be more different – the wines of Alsace taste far riper than their Burgundian and Germanic counterparts. The reason for this is the Vosges mountain range that runs to the east. They create a sheltered microclimate that is low in rainfall and thus high in the crucial sunshine hours.

*A fairly recent addition to the appellation laws has been the creation of a **Grand Cru** system. There are fifty designated vineyards at this level that have to conform to stricter production laws. To qualify to have **Grand Cru** on the label, a wine must be grown within one of these sites and must also be produced from one of the four noble varieties of the region; Riesling, Pinot Gris, Gewürztraminer or Muscat. In reality, the first three are of most importance.*

*The second round of vineyard classification was only finished in 1993, so a certain amount of bedding-in needs to take place. Fundamentally, this could have a major impact on how we perceive Alsatian wine, with a shift in emphasis from the grape variety to the site. Needless to say, with so many growers and vineyards to accommodate, the authorities' efforts have not met with universal approval. Many producers, such as the great Trimbach, have bypassed the system. He produces what I believe to be the finest expression of Riesling in the world from a vineyard called Clos Ste-Hune, yet he fails to declare that it lies within the **Grand Cru** of Rosacker.*

Of the minor grapes I find Pinot Blanc to be the most interesting, making crisp, refreshing aperitifs. Chasselas can be passable in the right hands. Sylvaner, with a few exceptions, is plain dull. Trying to ripen the red grape Pinot Noir in this region is a thankless task so I would avoid this variety. Even with its warmer climate, good-value fizz is produced under the guise of Cremant d'Alsace; as with all AC sparkling wine it is made by the **traditional method**.

For fizzy, try
Loire Valley p.72, **Italy** p.104, **Champagne** p.64

For Riesling try

🍷 **Germany** p.98, **Austria** p.96, **Loire Valley** p.72, **Australia** p.156, **New Zealand** p.168

🍇 **Albariño** p.190, **Chenin Blanc** p.198, **Sauvignon Blanc** p.214, **Gewürztraminer** p.202

🍴 **Shellfish** p.257, **Pâtés** p.273, **Cream Sauces** p.284, **Chicken** p.265

For Gewürztraminer try

🍷 **Jurançon** p.69, **Rhône Valley** p.84, **Austria** p.96

🍇 **Grüner Veltliner** p.203, **Pinot Gris** p.205, **Marsanne** p.201, **Roussanne** p.212, **Viognier** p.222, **Muscat** p.206

🍴 **Shellfish** p.257, **Pâtés** p.273, **Cream Sauces** p.284, **Chicken** p.265

For Pinot Gris try

🍷 **Australia** p.156, **Italy** p.108, **Rhône Valley** p.84

🍇 **Gewürztraminer** p.202, **Marsanne** p.201, **Roussanne** p.212, **Chardonnay** p.196

🍴 **Shellfish** p.257, **Pâtés** p.273, **Cream Sauces** p.284, **Chicken** p.265

For the sweet varieties try

🍷 **Australia** p.156, **Jurançon** p.69, **Germany** p.98

🍇 **Gewürztraminer** p.18, **Riesling** p.206, **Chenin Blanc** p.194

🍴 **Foie Gras** p.272, **Pâté** p.273, **Runny Cheese** p.292, **Fruit-based Puddings** p.296

In the best years two sweeter styles of wine are made. Firstly *Vendanges Tardives*, or late-harvest wines. By harvesting the grapes later the wines contain a higher ratio of sugar. They are not out-and-out stickies, however, they are merely richer than usual. The next level up is *Sélection des Grains Nobles*, only made in truly exceptional years when the grapes are very **ripe** and have usually been affected by **botrytis**. The sensory overload offered by these wines can be overwhelming: a bottle of 1976 Gewürztraminer **Cuvée** Anne from Domaine Schlumberger is the greatest bottle of sweet wine I have ever drunk, causing me to need a recuperative lie-down afterwards.

With such a wide range of styles produced, the food and wine combinations of Alsatian wines are nearly endless. I prefer to drink Pinot Blanc and Muscat before a meal, although they both will help you wash down salads and simple fish dishes. Light Rieslings do the job of partnering shellfish and delicate fish wonderfully.

The big versions of Riesling, Gewürztraminer and Pinot Gris are just sensational food wines. Do as the Alsatians do and wolf them down with onion tarts, quiches, pâtés, chicken liver terrine, creamy fish dishes and chicken. Pinot Gris gets a special mention for its affinity with smoked salmon.

Riesling and Gewürztraminer are by far the best grapes to deal with fusion cooking, particularly loving Thai influences, provided the chilli count isn't too high.

White wine with cheese? You must do it, the richer wines love a good smelly number – try Münster or Stinking Bishop. *Vendange Tardive* wines pair well with fruit-based puddings, duck liver parfait, pan-fried foie gras and more ripe cheeses. I like to drink my halves of *Sélection des Grains Nobles* wines on their and my own (not enough to share), and without any food.

Bandol is a high-quality region situated in Provence, right on the coast to the east of Toulon. Producing mainly red, it's another of those areas that highlights what France does so well. The wines of Bandol are highly individual and as far away from marketed, bland, big-brand wine as you can get.

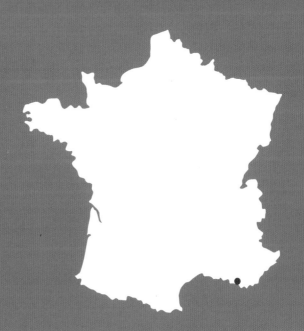

Tempier, Pibarnon, Gros
Noré, La Bégude, La
Suffrène, Lafran Veyrolles

Try

 **Northern Rhône** p.86,
Madiran p.80, **Cahors**
p.62, **North-west Italy**
p.112, **Puglia** p.128,
Spain p.142

Mourvèdre p.236, **Malbec**
p.232, **Syrah** p.243,
Grenache p.230

Stews p.275, **Sausages**
p.274, **Hard Cheese** p.291

Mourvèdre is the dominant grape, producing wines that are rich in spices, herbs and smoky, plummy fruits. Although some are made in an approachable style, most are uncompromising, tannic and seemingly unbalanced in their youth – most need five years in the bottle. Bandol ages superbly, developing **complex**, gamy aromas. The star producer is the astounding Domaine Tempier, whose wines are up there in my fantasy worldwide league. His single vineyard offerings like La Tourtine will happily last twenty years and are remarkable value.

You need to bring out the heavy artillery with a wine like this. Think cassoulet, oxtail, Lancashire hot pot and Toulouse sausages. It also suits good hard cheese.

The wines of Bergerac should be considered in the same light as those from Bordeaux, as they utilise the same grapes. They range from crisp, fresh Sauvignons and rich, creamy Sémillons to intense sweeties. Dry whites will often be indicated by the word 'sec' on the label. These generally appear under the Montravel (which can also include the prefixes 'Haut' or 'Côtes') or the Bergerac *appellation*. The Sauvignon grape dominates the crisp, dry versions. The richer and usually more expensive examples have a higher proportion of Sémillon and the best may be aged in oak barrels.

L'Ancienne Cure, Tirecul la Gravière, Tour des Gendres, Masburel, Château de la Jaubertie, Clos d'Yvigne, Domaine Touron

For whites, try
Loire Valley p.72, **Bordeaux** p.24, **New Zealand** p.168, **Australia** p.156

Sauvignon Blanc p.214, **Pinot Blanc** p.208, **Verdejo** p.219, **Vermentino** p.221, **Sémillon** p.216

Shellfish p.257, **Fish** p.252, **Chicken** p.265, **Veal** p.276, **Partridge** p.268

For reds, try
Right Bank Bordeaux p.33, **Loire** p.72

Cabernet Sauvignon p.228, **Merlot** p.234, **Cabernet Franc** p.227, **Dolcetto** p.228

Beef p.263, **Lamb** p.270, **Venison** p.269, **Cheddar** p.291, **Brie** p.292

For sweet versions, try
Bordeaux p.24, **Australia** p.156

Sémillon p.216

Foie Gras p.272, **Pâtés** p.273, **Fruit Puddings** p.296, **Steamed Puddings** p.297, **Tarte Tatin** p.297, **Crème Brûlée** p.295

Merlot and Cabernet Franc grapes dominate the red wines. Lighter in style than St Émilion and Pomerol, they offer uncomplicated, early-drinking pleasure. The reds will appear as Bergerac, and the better sites can use the prefix 'Côtes' and the rarely seen 'Pécharmant' appellation. A new wave of producers is starting to make more serious deeply coloured wines that will benefit from a few years in the cellar.

The highlights of this region are its undervalued sweet wines. The most famous are made in Monbazillac, which is often known, rather unfairly, as the 'poor man's Sauternes'. These are made from the same grapes as Sauternes (Sauvignon Blanc, Sémillon and Muscadelle) and in the right years they utilise the concentrating properties of *botrytis*.

These wines may not have the same ageing potential as great Sauternes and Barsac, but neither have they the same price tag attached. Recently, I tasted some wonderful sweet wines from the Saussignac area.

All these styles of wines represent superlative value when placed against a bottle of equivalent cost from Bordeaux.

Foodwise, the light Sauvignon-based whites need no more than shellfish and salads. Richer, creamy numbers all like fish and chicken.

Reds tend to be lighter than their Bordeaux counterparts, so stick to chicken, veal, and simple red-meat dishes.

The stickies range from mid-weight bottles that like fruit-based puddings to very sweet, orange-tinged versions that like all caramel-type puddings.

BORDEAUX

Where do you start with the most important fine-wine-producing region in the world? The bad news first: the most famous and finest Châteaux which were accessible fifteen years ago are now only within reach of the super-rich. Unless you know the wine, I would ignore all bottles that retail at under a tenner. 'Any good news?' I hear you cry. Yes. My top ten wine experiences would definitely contain at least four wines from this region. The complexity of great Bordeaux is rarely matched by wines from anywhere else in the world.

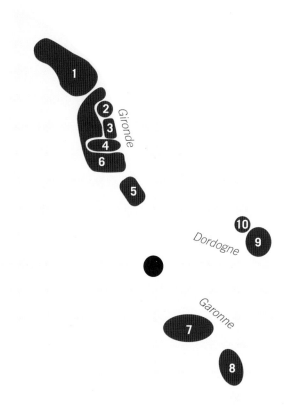

1 Médoc
2 St Estèphe
3 Pauillac
4 St Julien
5 Margaux
6 Haut Médoc
7 Graves
8 Sauternes/Barsac
9 St Émilion
10 Pomerol

The British consumer affectionately knows Red Bordeaux as 'claret'. This word is a bastardisation of the French '*clairet*' meaning light wine, used because in the Middle Ages we were accustomed to drinking the more robust Spanish and Portuguese wines. Despite this, the word '*claret*' conjures up images of big country houses and long lunches that finish with Port and Stilton, emphasising how this wine has always been synonymous with the upper classes.

The last fifteen years have seen a huge increase and democratisation in wine drinking. In my view Bordeaux has thoroughly missed the boat, a whole new generation of cosmopolitan drinkers are ignoring these wines. Many of my friends who drink wine regularly never touch red Bordeaux, the reason being that many of the entry level wines are so poor.

Great Bordeaux should not be a full-bodied blockbuster laden with flavours of **oak**, even though the same grapes grown in hotter regions do produce wines of this type. Thus for many of us who have been weaned on a diet of New World Cabernets and Merlots, trying a good wine from Bordeaux for the first time can be perplexing.

Many of us have forgotten or never tasted '**structure**' in a red wine; we are used to reds with low **acidity** and few **tannins**, and we are unaccustomed to dryness in a red wine. While these wines provide an instant fix of fruit and are universally appealing, Bordeaux is all about texture and complexity.

Good Bordeaux will have great **structure**, making it far more compatible with food than a big, juicy New World red. Many of my friends have an aversion to **tannin** and **acidity** in red wine. If you feel the same, next time you cook some roast lamb you should open two bottles of red (best to try this experiment with more than one other person). First try your favourite New World Cabernet/Merlot fruit bomb, then try a good bottle of Bordeaux. Have them without food first, then drink them together with your meal; you'll be surprised how much you prefer the Bordeaux by the end of the meal.

Bordeaux is also famous for its sweet wines. Considering the effort that goes into making these wines and their relatively low prices, in today's market they represent fabulous value. Sweet wine is deeply unfashionable among most people nowadays and consequently is great value all over the world. The dry white wines from the region are not nearly so well known in this country. This is odd as, together with sweet white, they make up nearly a quarter of all wine made in the area. They cover the full range of the taste spectrum, from refreshing good-value glugging to the serious full-bodied age-worthy stuff. The two important grapes are Sauvignon Blanc and Sémillon.

Five grape varieties are permitted in the production of Bordeaux red: Cabernet Sauvignon, Merlot, Cabernet Franc, Petit Verdot and Malbec, the first three being the most important. The reds of Bordeaux need to be divided into two distinct categories and the Gironde river that dominates the area does this rather neatly. Broadly speaking, vineyards on the left bank (as you look out to sea) are dominated by Cabernet Sauvignon. For those on the right Merlot holds sway. The latter is less full-bodied and lower in **tannin**, so the wines tend to be approachable at a younger age. I will start with the left side and an area collectively known as the Médoc, a strip of land a little over fifty miles long and ten miles deep that stretches from the mouth of the Gironde river to the outskirts of the town of Bordeaux.

The Médoc Label

The classification system used to grade the best properties was inaugurated in 1855. The highest grade was Premier (1er) **Cru** and the lowest Cinquième (5ème). The number will not appear on the wine label, merely the words '**Cru Classé**', literally meaning 'classed growth'. Rather misleadingly, descriptions in restaurants or wine shops do tend to make a play on the number.

Essentially this system was a good idea as it was very easy to

understand. However, a large pinch of salt must be taken when you find out that only one property has been regraded since then. Thus a second cru could happily make an inferior product, safe in the knowledge that its classification would not be threatened.

Beneath the classified estates are properties graded as *Cru Bourgeois*. There are three levels of *Cru Bourgeois* in descending order. *Cru Bourgeois Exceptionel*, *Cru Bourgeois Supérieur* and plain *Cru Bourgeois*. While I don't want to invoke the wrath of the wine lawmakers in France, these three gradings seem utterly pointless to me. They bear little resemblance to quality and only serve to make the whole issue more complicated. They are increasingly just lumped together under the one heading of *Cru Bourgeois*, which seems much more sensible and is how I will refer to them. Beneath this classification are Bordeaux Supérieur and straight Bordeaux.

Left Bank

MÉDOC OR BAS MÉDOC

Potensac, Les Ormes Sorbet, Patache d'Aux, La Tour de By, La Tour St-Bonnet, Loudenne, La Cardonne

Confusingly, the whole area from the mouth of the Gironde to the town of Bordeaux is known as the Médoc. However, when Médoc appears on a wine label it must come from the area north of St-Estèphe to the coast. It is hard to generalise about the style of wine from this region. Traditionally they were rustic and hard, needing some time in the bottle to soften – this was due to the high proportion of Cabernet Sauvignon in the blends. Now, though, many of the Châteaux have increased their plantings of Merlot, which is more suited to the heavy soils there.

In short, there is something for everyone in this region, from soft, fruity reds to be consumed at a young age to high-quality wines that are fit for the long haul.

The most important thing about wines from this region is their value. There are a good number of *Crus Bourgeois* making serious wines at affordable prices; this is the area to look at for wines that are affordable on a daily rather than a monthly basis.

Cissac, Sociando-Mallet,
Bel Orme Tronquoy de
Lalande, Chasse-Spleen,
Citran, Fourcas-Hosten,
Beaumont, La Lagune,
Cantemerle, Paloumey,
Poujeaux, Camensac,
Lamothe-Bergeron,
Caronne Ste-Gemme

HAUT MÉDOC, Listrac and Moulis

The Haut Médoc is a vast area that starts where the Médoc finishes just north of St-Estèphe and continues down to the outskirts of Bordeaux, and a huge range of wines are produced.

Listrac and Moulis are two underrated appellations. They sit between St-Julien and Margaux but further inland from the Gironde. Their production is small, with the total area under vine a little over 3000 acres (the Haut-Médoc region has over 10,000). Traditionally Listrac is seen as the more rustic of the two, but both can produce excellent wines that are accessible and characterful, representing great value.

It is in areas such as these that the Bordeaux virgin should be looking. These are wines of interest that won't break the bank. Many also will benefit from bottle age, debunking the myth that you need a fortune to set up a great cellar of Bordeaux.

Within the Haut-Médoc are the following four areas where the finest wines are produced. These are referred to as communes.

Calon-Ségur, Lafon-Rochet,
Haut-Marbuzet, Le Crock,
Phélan Ségur, Beau-Site,
Les Ormes de Pez, de Pez,
Meyney, Montrose, Cos
d'Estournel, Cos Labory

St-Estèphe

St-Estèphe is often, rather unfairly, regarded as being the ugly duckling of the big four Médoc communes. It is here that the famous gravel bank that runs alongside the Gironde finishes, giving way to heavier soils. This is mirrored in the style of the wines, which do not have the delicacy or finesse of the communes to the south.

In the past, these wines have contained a high proportion of Cabernet Sauvignon in the blend. These factors combined have tended to produce tough, burly wines that need plenty of time in the bottle. The market today, though, demands wine with more upfront fruit and early approachability. Better winemaking techniques, and the addition of Merlot to the blend, have achieved this; the wines have become more **commercial** without losing their authenticity. Having said this, St-Estèphe wines are still on the more butch side of Bordeaux.

Best of all for the drinker, the name St-Estèphe isn't seen to carry the same prestige as, say, Pauillac, so the wines are good value. There are some outstanding *Cru Bourgeois* and lower-level **cru classé** estates.

Pauillac

Pontet-Canet, Lynch-Bages, Pibran, Grand-Puy-Lacoste, Haut-Bages Monpelou, Pichon-Longueville (Baron), Pichon-Longueville Comtesse de Lalande, Les Forts de Latour, Mouton Rothschild, Latour, Lafite Rothschild, Haut-Batailley

Pauillac is the king of Bordeaux. Crammed into some 3000 acres of vineyards are some of the most illustrious and expensive wine estates in the world. Think of Château Latour – in my view the greatest red Bordeaux of all because of its longevity and consistency. Also Mouton Rothschild, who have commissioned an artist to adorn its label every year since 1945; the likes of Pablo Picasso and Francis Bacon have willingly obliged.

One needs to think big here: big wines, big buildings and above all big money. Three of the five first growths (Château Latour, Château Mouton Rothschild and Lafite Rothschild) are situated here, along with a bevvy of other world-class wines. The wines have great power and longevity, with the typical Cabernet flavour of blackcurrants. They possess the power and **structure** of St-Estèphe but are more restrained and delicate. Some of the greatest wines I have ever drunk come from this commune, but the downside is that none of this comes cheap.

St-Julien

Talbot, Léoville-las-Cases, Léoville-Barton, Langoa Barton, Ducru-Beaucaillou, Léoville-Poyferré, St-Pierre, Gloria, Gruaud-Larose, Beychevelle, Branaire, Lagrange

I don't think I'll be causing too much controversy by stating that, across the board, St-Julien produces the best quality-to-price-ratio wines of all the Médoc communes. It is sandwiched between Pauillac – with its first growths – to the north and the famous Margaux to the south.

This style of Cabernet is very friendly to the consumer. Going further south, the soils contain more gravel, which makes for lighter, more delicate wines. Although the style of each estate varies, in general I find these wines to be supple and softly fruity in their youth. They also age wonderfully, turning into round, smooth wines that, while not slapping you in the face like a Pauillac or a St-Estèphe, have great elegance allied with power.

Margaux

St-Estèphe, Pauillac and St-Julien are adjacent to one another, and then there is a short gap before you reach Margaux to the south. Not surprisingly, the style of wine produced here is very different. Even though the main grape is still Cabernet Sauvignon, it has the lightest soil of the four communes and consequently the wines are all about fragrance and finesse. When all these factors come together the results are sublime, with the wines often having the seductiveness of great red Burgundy.

Margaux has one first growth – Château Margaux – and the highest number of classified growths of all the communes, and thus you would think that it had the highest number of quality producers. Unfortunately, this is a long way from the truth, as this is the commune of underachievers and plain, poor wine. Two of the second crus here would be hard pushed to hold their own against some of the better *Crus Bourgeois*.

Too often Châteaux rely on an outdated classification and the name Margaux to sell their wine rather than the quality of the bottle. This is a shame, because this region has great potential to win over new converts to Bordeaux wines with its accessibility and charm. Things are starting to improve, however, as Châteaux with lamentable records have shown signs of progress in the last few years, but there is a long way to go.

GRAVES and Pessac-Léognan

This is a region that is on the up but still, to my mind, is perennially underachieving. This is a pity because, as with the other slouch Margaux, these wines have the necessary charm and elegance to win over new converts. The vineyards lie to the south of Bordeaux and, indeed some of the best are actually in the suburbs of the town. The wines from Pessac-Léognan clearly have the potential to be superior.

Not surprisingly, the name Graves is derived from the gravel soils of the area. This lends the best red wines an elegance and subtlety and, not unlike Margaux, they often have a Burgundian feel to them. Too often, though, elegance gives way to thin, unexciting wines.

As St-Julien et al are superior sub-regions of the Haut-Médoc, so Pessac-Léognan is the top plot of land within the larger Graves area. What makes the area interesting is how recent a phenomenon it is, created only in 1987. The Châteaux themselves were graded, for red and white, as late as 1959 with the simple rating 'classified growth' (this will appear on the label as '**Grand Cru Classé**' or simply '**Cru Classé**'). The sublime Haut-Brion was listed at the top, having already been listed as a first growth in the 1855 classification of Médoc; the rest were simply listed alphabetically. These rated estates, which produce red and white, all lie within the Pessac-Léognan region. Unfortunately there are many classified estates, especially ones making reds, that do not warrant their classification. Once again you need to use what is in the bottle rather than on the label to judge quality.

The whites of Graves are generally of a much more even standard than the reds and they account for 30 per cent of all cases made. Red Bordeaux has always been easy to sell whereas white hasn't, thus the whites need to work much harder.

The white wines fall into two distinct categories. Firstly there are those dominated by the Sauvignon Blanc grape: refreshing and designed to be consumed young, they are often great value, the best having mineral overtones that make them a good alternative to Loire Sauvignons such as Sancerre and Pouilly-Fumé. Secondly there are those that have a high proportion of Sémillon: these wines are unique to the region and are, to my mind, some of the best-value French whites being made.

The top three estates are very expensive but below that there are some bargains to be found. These wines are often approachable when young, revealing opulent tropical flavours; they then have a mid-life crisis, before emerging after ten or so years into **complex**, honeyed delights.

Sauternes, Barsac, Loupiac and Sainte-Croix-du-Mont

Loubens, de Ricaud, Domaine du Noble, Climens, Suduiraut, Coutet, La Tour Blanche, Filhot, Rayne Vigneau, Rabaud-Promis, Doisy-Daëne, Rieussec, de Fargues, Broustet, Liot, Bastor-Lamontagne, d'Yquem

Sauternes and Barsac were the only areas outside the Médoc to be included in the 1855 classification. D'Yquem was rightly seen to be in a class of its own and remains streets ahead of the competition. Beyond that the other estates were rated as first (Premier **Grand Cru Classé**) or second growths (**Grand Cru Classé**). Unlike the Médoc properties the grade of classification often appears on the label. However, as always, the track record of the estate should be your only guide to purchasing.

Barsac and Sauternes are the most famous patches of sweet-wine-producing vines in the world. They both fall within the larger region of Graves, along the banks of the Ciron river, a tributary of the Garonne. The river plays a major part in providing the necessary weather conditions for the formation of **noble rot**. However, producing truly great wine in this region is a nerve-racking and expensive affair. An estate can count itself lucky if it has four perfect years in a decade.

Barsac is a smaller sub-region within Sauternes and either name can appear on the label; indeed, some owners use both.

Sitting atop the pile is the fabled Château d'Yquem. This estate must stand above all others in Bordeaux for its fanatical dedication to quality. Loupiac and Sainte-Croix-du-Mont lie across the other side of the Garonne river. They do not produce as powerful or profound wines, but both are excellent sources of great-value sweet wine.

*The key to making good sweet wines is a mould called **Botrytis Cinerea** or '**noble rot**', whose growth is encouraged by misty nights and warm days. The effect of botyris is to concentrate the sugar and flavour levels in the grapes by reducing the amount of water in them. It is extraordinary to see heavily affected bunches for the first time; it seems impossible that anything palatable could be made from them. This is not an exact process, as even when conditions are perfect the pickers must go through the vineyards on numerous occasions to select only the affected grapes. This process might take six weeks. The **yields** per acre are typically one-fifth of what a top Médoc might expect. Poor weather conditions like heavy rain in October can ruin what crop there is left on the vines. You should be starting to get the picture now; this wine is an expensive labour of love to make.*

ENTRE-DEUX-MERS

Premières Côtes de Bordeaux, Côtes de Bordeaux

de Sours, Méaume, Haut-Rian, Plaisance, Tour de Mirambeau, Reignac, Balestard

Until fairly recently, this whole area produced little to excite the palate. This situation has changed drastically in the last few years, however, and clean, well-made whites and good-value fruity reds are now the norm. The reds are not the **structured**, **complex** style of the Médoc; they are rather soft, accessible wines that serve to introduce the consumer to the region. The area of land covered by these appellations is neatly tucked between the Dordogne and Garonne rivers, both tributaries of the Gironde, and therefore sandwiched between the Left and Right Banks.

Right Bank

Ausone, Figeac, Cheval
Blanc, Angélus, Canon,
Pavie, Canon-la-Gaffelière,
Magdelaine, Grand-Pontet,
Haut-Sarpe, La Tour
Figeac, Grand Mayne,
Faugères, La Dominique,
Clos de l'Oratoire

St Émilion

*On paper, this region has the most up-to-date and sensible
classification system in Bordeaux. It is a three-tiered system: Premier
Grand Cru Classé at the top, followed by **Grand Cru Classé** and, lastly,
Grand Cru. Most important, the system is reviewed every ten years
and estates are demoted and promoted. The last such change took
place in 1996 when some Châteaux were elevated to the top level.
These promotions were justified but, to my mind, there should have
been some highly warranted demotions. It will be interesting to see
what will happen at the next review; the validity of the system relies
on some of the underachievers being relegated.*

The first thing to understand about this region is its size. It is by far the
largest of the fine wine-producing areas, with over 13,000 acres under
vine, compared with Pauillac's 3000. The town itself is the most
picturesque of the region; it will restore your faith in the romanticism of
wine after the industrialisation of Bordeaux town.

St Émilion is well known for its fleshy, crowd-pleasing wines.
This is due to the high proportion of Merlot and Cabernet Franc in the
blend. Merlot is lower in **tannins** and **acidity** than the Cabernet
Sauvignon that is predominant over the river. Thus the wines are
approachable when young, but the best will also age well.

It is difficult to generalise about the style of these wines, as
there is an array of different soils. In addition, the proportions of the two
main grapes employed can vary greatly. Lastly, and really rather
strangely for an inherently conservative area, the Right Bank has
become a fashion victim.

Traditionally St Émilion is a medium-bodied wine, but the most
sought after of the new breed can be absolute monsters. The grapes are
now being left for longer both on the vine and also in the **oak** barrels
used to mature the wines after **vinification**. These wines have a creamy,
super-rich feel in the mouth and taste more like a Californian or
Australian Merlot than a French one.

Like with many things in life, I feel that the middle ground is the correct way forward. Undoubtedly riper, fruity wines appeal to the consumer; however, if they become over the top, the wine's sense of identity can get lost. The beauty of Bordeaux is that it should be unique. Generally, though, whatever the style of the wine, the overall quality in this region is high.

The satellites of St Émilion: Montagne, St-Georges, Lussac and Puisseguin

St-Georges, Rocher-Corbin, Bel-Air, Faizeau

All these villages are to the north of St Émilion and are allowed to attach their own name to that of their more prestigious southerly neighbour. They are a useful way to sample the delights of this region without breaking the bank, and they follow the same pattern, being dominated by Merlot and Cabernet Franc. The better examples do age but they lack the charm of the real thing, leaning towards a more rustic style.

Côtes de Francs and Côtes de Castillon

Cap de Faugères, Domaine de l'A, Clos l'Eglise, Puygueraud, Rocher Bellevue, de Pitray, Brisson

These two regions, lying further to the east of St Émilion than its satellites, are ones to watch. Castillon is the more well known of the two, but both are starting to produce chunky, Merlot-dominated wines.

These areas have benefited hugely from a relatively new trend whereby owners of the great vineyards in St Émilion and Pomerol have bought up properties and invested heavily. The financial clout and know-how brought by the big boys means that many of these estates are aiming high. Prices, while being high for the regions, are low compared with the quality and pedigree of these wines.

Plince, Gazin, Pétrus, La
Fleur-Pétrus, La Croix du
Casse, L'Enclos,
Beauregard, Lafleur,
L'Eglise-Clinet, Vieux
Château Certan, La
Conseillante, Clinet, Latour
à Pomerol, L'Evangile,
Petite Eglise

Pomerol

Pomerol is the smallest and most exclusive of all the communes in Bordeaux, with less than 2000 acres of vineyards. It is interesting to note that while people will beg, borrow and often do unspeakable things to get their hands on some of these wines today, this has not always been the case. Both St Émilion and Pomerol were ignored in the 1855 classification of the Médoc and it has only been in the latter half of this century that the wines have become highly prized. In general, I find the standard of winemaking to be very high – interestingly, this has been achieved without any classification system within the commune. Château Pétrus, for example, regularly fetches a higher price than the Médoc first growths, and the twenty most expensive wines from the region over the last ten years would arguably be the best. This would not be the case over the river – who ever said market forces don't work?

In Pomerol, Merlot is king. Cabernet Franc does play an important part in the blend, but less so than in St Émilion. While the great estates of the Médoc have their pretenders around the world, nowhere, in my opinion, is yet making Merlots in the same league as Pomerol. Stylistically the wines are more full-bodied than their neighbour but, similarly, are enjoyable when young. Pomerol wines do have the necessary guts to age well, but I find them the most difficult wines to judge in terms of how long they will last or when they should be drunk.

The Cabernet-dominated Médoc wines can be tannic and acidic when young; in short, they are for the masochist only. Pomerols, on the other hand, are generally delicious when young, yet they seem to remain on that plateau while developing levels of complexity.

Bel-Air, La Croix St-André,
Haut-Chaigneau, La Croix
de la Chenevelle

Lalande-de Pomerol

Pomerol has just one village that is permitted to use the name of its illustrious neighbour. These wines are similar in style to its big brother. The best are ripe plummy affairs that give instant gratification without having the ageing potential of the real thing. Again, this is an area to watch. Some of these estates are not content with playing second fiddle and are consequently producing some excellent wines at very good value.

Mazeris, La Dauphine,
Fontenil, Canon de Brem,
La Vieille Cure, Canon,
Canon-Moueix, La Grave

Fronsac and Canon-Fronsac

These two areas are to the west of Pomerol. With this close proximity one might think the wines would be very similar in style. This isn't the case: they have always had a reputation of being tough to get to grips with when young. Indeed, Fronsac wines have always been regarded as the most Médoc-like of the right bank wines, even though Merlot and Cabernet Franc dominate the blends. Fronsac is one of the last regions where Malbec, albeit in a diminishing role, plays any part in the blend. In the past the grape may well have contributed to the burly reputation of these wines, as it requires very good weather conditions to ripen sufficiently.

Recently, as in Côtes de Francs, large amounts of money and technical expertise have poured into some of these properties. The companies that own famous Pomerol and St Émilion estates have generally funded this. This is an exciting area as winemakers seek to carve out their own style and identity, rather than just trying to imitate their neighbours. The wines are still on the chunky side when young, but they offer great value. Their style is particularly good if you are looking to lay down some wine without making the bank manager cry.

Bel-Air la Royère, Falfas,
Roc de Cambes, Les
Jonqueyres, Grands
Maréchaux, Fougas,
Maldoror

Côtes de Bourg and Blaye

These regions lie opposite Margaux, just before the Gironde splits into the Dordogne and Garonne. They are large, consisting of roughly 18,000 acres of vines. Both produce red wines, dominated by Merlot, and

For reds, look to where the famous 'Bordeaux blend' is replicated around the world –

⚫ **Australia, California, South Africa, Chile and South Africa and, within Europe, Tuscany.**

If you like the chunky, Cabernet-dominated wines, try

⚫ **Ribera del Duero** p.145, **Cahors** p.62, **Madiran** p.80; **for the mid-weight wines, look to Bergerac** p.22, **and the Loire** p.72

⚫ **Cabernet Sauvignon** p.228, **Cabernet Franc** p.227, **Merlot** p.234, **Malbec** p.232

⚫ **Lamb** p.270, **Beef** p.263, **Venison** p.269, **Hard Cheese** p.291

For dry whites, try

⚫ **Bergerac** p.22, **Loire Valley**, p.72, **Australia** p.156, **New Zealand**, p.168

⚫ **Sauvignon Blanc** p.214, **Sémillon** p.216, **Pinot Blanc** p.208

⚫ **Shellfish** p.257, **Salads** p.288, **Fish** p.252, **Chicken** p.265, **Veal** p.276, **Light Game** p.267

For sweet whites, try

⚫ **Bergerac** p.22, **Australia** p.156

⚫ **Sémillon** p.216

⚫ **Foie Gras** p.272, **Pâté** p.273, **Fruit Puddings** p.296, **Steamed Puddings** p.297, **Tarte Tatin** p.297, **Crème Brûlée** p.295

whites made from Sauvignon, Sémillon and a smaller cast of less noble white varieties. Quality is patchy, especially in the Côtes de Bourg, with the main problem being the fertile soils and the large quantities of grapes produced by the vines. While this is good news for the producer, who can make more wine per acre, it is not so great for the consumer as the wines will be thin and diluted.

The best estates keep their **yields** down and make soft, approachable offerings that are designed for early consumption. The top châteaux in the Blaye region are entitled to the appellation *Premières Côtes de Blaye*. Again, these are areas to watch in the future. A handful of estates, most famously Roc de Cambes, have raised their game considerably and are competing with the big boys. These Châteaux are absolute bargains and well worth seeking out.

BORDEAUX AND FOOD

Contrary to popular belief, red Bordeaux is not the most versatile of food wines. The wines are **complex** in a restrained way, so avoid lots of herbs and spices otherwise the nuances of the wine will be lost. Bordeaux has always been a favourite with the British roast and for good reasons: rib of beef or leg of lamb with no herbal accompaniments will let the wine do the talking.

If you are drinking the wines young, be sure to have a good bit of gravy to counter the acid and **tannin** in the wines. The fleshier, Merlot-dominated wines love juicy rare meat: think fillet steak or venison. Cheese-wise, the older wines adore the hard stuff, while the lighter wines want something softer but not too smelly.

Among the whites, the light wines make good aperitifs and can help out with shellfish and, at a stretch, Salade Niçoise. The richer wines will take on all manner of creamy fish dishes and the best will happily deal with chicken, veal and even light game such as partridge.

For sweet wines, look for the lighter ones, less affected by **noble rot**, to partner fruit puddings, rich pâté and foie gras. The serious orange-tinged numbers work best with treacle sponge, tarte tatin and crème brûlée. If you have a really fine bottle, however, I would advise drinking it on its own.

Burgundy embodies all that is good and bad about French wine. Even for those who are clued up on this tricky-to-understand region, a tasting of ten bottles might reveal two crackers, six adequate wines, and two destined for cooking. Therein lies the essence of my favourite wine region.

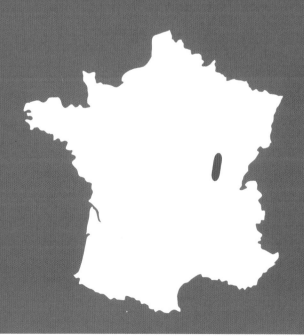

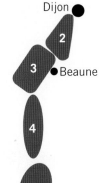

1 Chablis
2 Côte de Nuits
3 Côte de Beaune
4 Chalonnaise
5 Mâconnais

I undoubtedly drink more disappointing bottles from Burgundy than from any other region, and the wines are expensive, with little that retails at under a tenner worth drinking. The great bottles, though, send me into raptures, with their ability to ally power with subtlety and elegance. If I had the know-how, I'd probably write long, flowery poems about them.

Burgundy and Bordeaux are the undisputed top two regions in France. These wines consistently fetch the highest prices and are collected worldwide. However, not only are the wines completely different from each other, so is the feel of each region. Bordeaux has grand Châteaux, immaculate tasting rooms, wealthy international owners, and pomp and ceremony; at times it is possible to forget that they actually grow grapes. Burgundy, on the other hand, has small, family-owned estates whose forebears have often made wine from the same patch of vines for hundreds of years.

The owners of the most fabled **domaines** will greet you in dirty jeans with a pair of secateurs in hand. A tasting will involve washing out your own glass and going down to the cellar, where a few bottles will be opened on an upturned cask. Although this is a romanticised view of the region – there are now large companies with public relations teams in tow – one cannot escape the feeling that Burgundy is like a farming community compared with Bordeaux, which is more like a wine Disneyland.

A myth is perpetuated that Bordeaux is rare: it is not, it is simply expensive. If you sat on the Internet, provided you had just won the lottery, you could buy most major vintages of the five first growths of Bordeaux, going back to 1945, in an hour or so. Try to buy more than one or two wines from, say, the classic 1990 vintage in Burgundy and you'd struggle. Why? Many of Burgundy's finest wines are made in quantities measured in hundreds of cases; in Bordeaux it is thousands. Although we are talking about seriously expensive wine here, the same formula applies equally down the scale, and even modestly priced wines are often made in minuscule quantities. The reason behind this is historical.

Up until the French Revolution most of the vineyards were in the hands of the Church. Directly afterwards the land was divided up among the locals, and subsequent inheritance laws brought in by Napoleon ensured that every sibling was entitled to equal shares of the parents' lands. It is thus easy to see how a large plot could soon become only a few rows of vines. Being a tight community, many married within Burgundy, each bringing small parcels of land to the union. Hence we have the situation today where a family might own ten acres of land but in twenty different areas.

The absolute key to understanding Burgundy is to recognise the relevance of the producer. The single most important piece of information on a Burgundian label is in small print at the bottom, where it tells you who produced the wine. When confronted with a wine list or a selection of Burgundies in a shop, the first thing you should be looking for is the producer, not the region.

Equally, when a good bottle has been enjoyed, remember the name of the producer first and then the wine's actual name. I really can't go on about this enough. If you only had room in your memory bank for ten words associated with Burgundy, I would advise deleting every place name and replacing them with the top ten producers of the region.

Many people make the mistake of trying to draw comparisons with Bordeaux and the way in which a village name can be associated with a Bordelais Château. However, one person will run a Château in Bordeaux whereas a *village* in Burgundy will be owned by dozens of families all making wine of wildly varying quality levels. It is important to get away from the mindset of 'I like Burgundy' and think 'I love the Burgundy produced by . . .'

Ageing Burgundy is a tricky subject but one I have very passionate views on. If you are ever in doubt, err on the side of youth. The French are consistently amazed at how long we leave our wines in the cellar. I'll stick my neck right out now and say that there is only a minute proportion of either red or white Burgundy that needs to see the inside of your cellar for more than ten years, and this is the big, seriously expensive stuff.

Most are ready after five years and I've drunk some great Grands Crus from forward vintages after only three or four years in the bottle. Burgundy should be about decadence and must be enjoyed young. I have consumed many twenty-year-old Burgundies that are perfectly drinkable, but they'd have tasted even better ten years earlier.

All red Burgundy is made from Pinot Noir (apart from Beaujolais, which is discussed separately). All fine white, bar a minuscule quantity, is made from Chardonnay. The appellation laws in Burgundy can seem confusing. They are actually the most extraordinary achievement, being fastidiously precise and detailed. The best way to visualise them is as a ladder, with each rung indicating an area of land; the higher the rung, the more site-specific the indication becomes.

There are essentially four levels. The first is straight Bourgogne, literally red or white Burgundy. The grapes can be drawn from anywhere in the whole area and are thus classified as regional level. The next rung is a commune wine (this is often referred to as village level). All the grapes used to make the wine must come from inside the boundaries of that village; Puligny-Montrachet is an example of this. One more step up and you are in a Premier **Cru** vineyard. These are sites, identified within a village's boundaries, of superior quality. The name of the village must appear as a prefix, thus Puligny-Montrachet 1er Cru Champs Canet. It is possible to have a Premier **Cru** wine without a vineyard being specified, the grapes for these wines will have been drawn from a number of Premier Crus within the village. At the top of the ladder is **Grand Cru**. Reserved for the best sites, only the name of the vineyard need appear on the label.

At this level things can get quite confusing. Wily Burgundians realised many years ago that these **Grand Cru** names were great selling points for their wines, so villages that were near them adopted their names. Thus you have the village of Chassagne tagging on to the most famous white **Grand Cru** of all, Montrachet. A village Chassagne-Montrachet is of a very different quality level from a **Grand Cru** Montrachet.

It is very important to keep a perspective on this complex classification. If you find the whole thing a bit too much, fall back on your knowledge of the producer. Many wine bores will tell you very loudly that they were drinking some **Grand Cru** Burgundy last night. Your instant riposte should be, 'Which producer was it from?' You will be surprised how many blank looks you'll receive in reply.

Remember that the classification of a vineyard as Premier or **Grand Cru** is an indication of its potential, not its final quality. A sloppy producer's Premier **Cru** can easily be inferior to a great one's straight Bourgogne.

There are two types of producer in Burgundy and understanding the difference will help guide you towards a better bottle. First, there are those who make wine from grapes harvested in vineyards they own, which are indicated by the word **domaine** appearing on the label. Second come those who buy grapes from landowners and make wine. These are called **négociants**, but this fact will not generally be stated on the bottle.

In theory, **domaine**-bottled wines should be better as the producer has full control of the grapes, from day one in the vineyard right through to bottling stage. **Négociants**, on the other hand, don't have much say in what goes on in the vineyard. Until recently they didn't hugely care either. Traditionally they would often buy in the grapes by the tonne, thus the onus for the wine grower was on quantity rather than quality.

After years of entirely justified criticism, the **négociants** have started to get their act together. Long-term contracts with the growers have led to a shift of emphasis in the vineyard, and now houses such as Louis Jadot, Faiveley and, more recently, Antonin Rodet are turning out well-made, affordable wines.

The vineyards of Burgundy are not one continuous swathe and I'll divide the region into six areas. Chablis is the most northerly and lies only ninety miles to the south-east of Paris. Then there is a gap of some eighty miles before reaching the Côte de Nuits, immediately to the south of Dijon. The Côte de Beaune follows on immediately from this and collectively these two areas are known as the Côte d'Or (the golden slope). Next is a scattered collection of vineyards called the Côte Chalonnaise and then the sprawling Mâconnais. Lastly comes Beaujolais (dealt with separately in this book), which stops just short of Lyon, nearly 150 miles south of Chablis. It doesn't require a genius to work out that, over a scale this large, there is a plethora of different factors affecting the final taste of the wines.

CHABLIS AND PETIT CHABLIS

Raveneau, William Fèvre, René et Vincent Dauvissat, Jean-Paul Droin, Billaud-Simon, Laurent Tribut, Genèves, Verget

The old urban myth of the customer who states, 'I love Chablis but hate Chardonnay,' still causes much mirth among the wine hacks. The last laugh should really be on us, though, because Chablis really doesn't taste like other wines made from Chardonnay. It is a true expression of what the French call **terroir**, the notion that the geography of a region shapes the taste of its wines and not the grape or the winemaker.

I am somewhat suspicious of this region's success, as many of the wines that people seem to enjoy are rather poor. Yes, the wines are **fresh** and light – attributes much loved by our modern palates, which are conditioned to demand the driest white wines possible – but they should also taste of something; Chablis is too often low in flavour.

In a region that is increasingly becoming mechanised, look out for the traditional, quality-conscious producer, as at their best these wines can be beautifully focused. Forget about oaky, unbalanced New World Chardonnay; we are talking about taut, poised wines with underlying minerality. At their worst, though, the wines are thin and tasteless.

Forty sites are designated as *Premier Cru*, generally those situated up on the slopes around the commune where most sunlight reaches the grapes. In reality, only around a dozen or so of these are seen in the market place, and the best will develop in the bottle for up to seven years, gaining complexity.

At the top of the pile are the seven *Grands Crus* (one of which is the wonderfully named *Les Grenouilles* or 'The Frogs'). These are all grouped together on a prime site immediately around the village of Chablis. Unlike the *Grands Crus* of the Côte d'Or, these wines must have the prefix of the *village* (Chablis) on their label. In a good year these wines are a joy, combining clean mineral flavours with honey. The best will not get going for five years and will last for fifteen.

For me *Premier* and **Grand Cru** Chablis is what this region is all about, and compared with wines of a similar quality from the Côte d'Or they are not expensive.

The top producers have recently started to introduce some **oak** maturation into the wines, but most Chablis never gets within spitting distance of an **oak** barrel. One last note of warning: this is the most northerly region in Burgundy, hence vintages vary massively. Dilute or unripe grapes make thin, acidic wine, purely for the masochist.

Petit Chablis, as the name implies, is a region of inferior quality with vineyards around Chablis. I'll keep it simple: don't drink them. If much Chablis production is below par, these wines are far worse.

An oddity to look for, south-west of Chablis, is Sauvignon St Bris. As the name implies, these wines buck the Chardonnay trend and are made from Sauvignon Blanc. Look out for the wines of Goisot in particular.

CÔTE DE NUITS

Côte de Nuits is the spiritual home of Pinot Noir worldwide. Although many proud Pinot makers around the globe would not like to admit it, their wines are essentially trying to emulate those from this great region.

Pinot Noirs from here have more stuffing than those of the Côte de Beaune and this is reflected in the fact that all the **Grand Cru** reds, bar one, are found here. It is hard to comprehend how small the whole area is until you go there. After a hard tasting in the north at Gevrey-Chambertin there is barely time for ten minutes' recuperative shut-eye before arriving eight miles to the south where the area ends at Nuits-St-Georges. I will deal with the region from north to south.

Marsannay and Fixin

These two villages are frequently overlooked, being sandwiched as they
are between the illustrious Gevrey-Chambertin and the city of Dijon.
Marsannay was only given its own *Appellation Contrôlée* in 1987 and
there are no *Premiers Crus*; as a region it is still finding its feet.

The reds can offer you something of interest although it is
difficult to generalise on their style, as growers don't yet seem to know
whether they want to make light, fruit-driven Pinot or nod towards
Gevrey and try for something more robust. I prefer the wines made in
the former style, as the latter are often just hard work. This really is a
village to know and to pick your grower.

Fixin is also a tricky one. I am tempted to take the easy route
and tell you to move on as the wines lack charm when young. Being a
generally lazy person, I like an instant hit of Pinot fruit and Fixin doesn't
deliver. However, I am consistently surprised at how well these wines
turn out after a few years in the cellar: clumsy and rustic in their youth,
some bottle age brings the wine into balance. They are still not the most
charming wines of the region but they have the advantage of being
excellent value.

Gevrey-Chambertin

This is one of the most revered and idolised names in Burgundy – all the
wines are red. Eight *Grands Crus* reside here, more than in any other
village, but the quality of wine produced here is depressingly patchy. At
their best the wines are well **structured** with a deep colour and earthy
aromas of black fruits. I find the most irregular quality at **Grand Cru** and
village level.

Chambertin is one of the most fabled patches of vines in the
world. Napoleon was a big fan and I love the story, no doubt originated
by a Burgundian, of how his death was hastened by being forced to
drink Bordeaux and not his beloved Chambertin while in exile on St
Hélèna. Today the quality of wine made there is a disgrace. Only a few
of the producers, such as Rousseau and Leroy, make high-quality wines
and the rest seem content to push **yields** to the limit and produce for
wine tourists.

Basic Gevrey often suffers from being far too insipid and light

in colour truly to reflect the quality of the actual vineyard sites. The best buys are to be had at *Premier Cru* level.

Morey St-Denis

Ponsot, Armand Rousseau, Georges Roumier, Dujac, Hubert Lignier, Robert Groffier, Domaine des Lambrays
(Including **Grand Crus**: *Bonnes-Mares (only a small percentage, the rest lies within Chambolle-Musigny), Clos St Denis, Clos des Lambrays, Clos de la Roche and Clos de Tart*)

While Gevrey is a perennial underperformer, Morey is the opposite. Stylistically the wines straddle the fence between fragrant Chambolle to the south and butch Gevrey to the north. They are mostly red with tiny amounts of high-quality white made from Chardonnay and Pinot Blanc, and I love them, not only for their style, but the fact that there are so few duff producers here.

My theory is that because the name Morey St-Denis carries much less sales oomph than Gevrey or Chambolle, the producer is forced to make better wine. I am slightly biased, though, because my favourite producer in the whole of Burgundy lives in the tiny *village* of Morey. Domaine Dujac, run by the modest Jacques Seysses, makes sublime wine from *village* level right up to **Grand Cru**. Its wines are all about silky seductiveness and they have an uncanny ability to taste irresistible when young, yet age magnificently.

In the overall Burgundian picture, Morey has some great-value offerings. At all levels they are considerably cheaper than their northern and southern neighbours.

Chambolle-Musigny

Comte de Vogüé, Georges Roumier, Dujac, Christian Clerget, Ghislaine Barthod-Noëllat, Ponsot, Virgile Lignier
(Including the **Grand Crus**: *Musigny and Bonnes Mares*)

Nearly all the wine produced in this area is red. Buffs might like to know that a tiny plot of Chardonnay is planted in the **Grand Cru** of Musigny (this being the only **Grand Cru** white wine in the Côtes de Nuits). It is fearsomely expensive and, not having ever seen a bottle, let alone drunk one, I can't comment on whether it is worth the price.

At their best, the red wines are beautifully fragrant and floral with a red fruit character. They are lighter wines than both Morey and Gevrey, so drink them early. I adore these wines, they are instantly appealing and positively sexy.

Generally speaking, quality levels are not as patchy as Gevrey, but they are not up to Morey, so again choosing only the best producers is important (see the list in the margin on the previous page).

Of the **Grand Crus** Musigny, which I have tasted only a few times, is positively hedonistic in its fragrance. Bonnes Mares has a bigger, more tannic **structure** and is much more like Morey in style. Of the *Premiers Crus*, Les Amoureuses, Les Cras and Les Charmes are the pick of the bunch. If ever there were a place to introduce people to the joys of Burgundy this would be it.

Vougeot

Mongeard-Mugneret, René Engel, Château de La Tour, Jean Grivot, Domaine de La Vougeraie, Jean-Jacques Confuron, Jacques Prieur
(Including the **Grand Cru**: *Clos de Vougeot*)

The **Grand Cru** of Clos de Vougeot dominates this *village*, accounting for three-quarters of the acres under vine. This is by far the largest red **Grand Cru** area and it is justifiably highlighted by many wine writers as a perfect illustration of the vagaries of modern-day Burgundy.

The lower slopes of the vineyard are not generally deemed to be of **Grand Cru** status. Owned by nearly eighty different producers, they turn out wine that covers the full gamut of quality levels: thin, weedy wines for the unsuspecting consumer looking for a cheap **Grand Cru** (trust me, they don't exist), and sublime, velvety, dark-fruited numbers with good **structure**.

Vougeot has received much poor press; this is good news. If you pick the right producer these wines are conspicuously undervalued. Rarely seen are wines simply labelled as Vougeot. These are not of **Grand Cru** status, but there are a number of *Premier Cru* vineyards. If you can find them, they can be good value.

Vosne-Romanée

Jean Grivot, Henri Jayer, Jean Millot, René Engel, Emmanuel Rougeot, Leroy, Robert Arnoux, Méo-Camuzet
(Including the **Grand Crus**: *La Tâche, Romanée-Conti, La Romanée, Romanée-St-Vivant, Richebourg, Echézeaux and Grand-Echézeaux*)

To be strictly correct I should also include the *village* of Flagey-Echézeaux in this group, to which the last two *Grands Crus* belong. It is not a name you need to remember, though, as all the *village* and *Premier Cru* wines produced here label themselves Vosne-Romanée, for reasons that will soon become clear. At their best, these wines have an exquisite perfume, allied with serious power and **structure**, that make them the most long-lived of Burgundies.

The most expensive wines in the world are made in nineteen

acres of these vineyards. La Tâche and Romanée Conti are the stuff of wine legend; they are both **monopole** vineyards owned by the mythical Domaine de La Romanée Conti. First-growth **claret** is like a lunchtime quaffing wine compared with these – expect to pay £1500 per bottle for a great vintage of the latter. I have never tasted them (invitations are welcome), but by all accounts they come close to perfection.

The other *Grands Crus* are all excellent, with Echézeaux being the pick of the bunch for me, purely because it is produced in sufficient quantities to be within the reach of us mere mortals. Of the *Premier Crus*, Les Suchots, Les Beaux Monts and Les Brûlées are notable. *Village* level Vosne is improving but is still patchy: too much emphasis is placed on the word 'Romanée' and not enough on what is in the bottle when it comes to selling the wine. The producer, as ever, is vital.

Nuits-St-Georges

Robert Chevillon, Chopin-Groffier, Jean Chauvenet, Henri Gouges, Alain Michelot, Bertrand Ambroise, Daniel Rion

Again, to be 100 per cent accurate, the wines of Nuits-St-Georges also encompass those of Prémeaux-Prissy. As in Flagey-Echézeaux, all the village and Premier **Cru** wines choose to label themselves with the name of their more illustrious neighbour. Nearly all wine here is red with a tiny proportion of white being made from a mutant white Pinot Noir.

The village of Nuits splits the commune and also neatly divides the styles. Generally speaking, all the wines have more **structure** than their neighbour Vosne but they lack its Pinot fragrance. Nevertheless, they more than make up for this youthful austerity by ageing well, revealing an earthy **complex** character. The wines from the north of Nuits towards Vosne are the most delicate, while those to the south have more **tannin** and **structure**, reflecting their heavier soils. Of the former style, the Premier Crus Aux Chaignots, La Richemone and Aux Murgers are excellent. Les St-Georges and Les Vaucrains head up the big boys to the southern end. In the right hands they can make wines of **Grand Cru** quality.

While these are the least instantly beguiling of the Côte de Nuits wines, they are well worth seeking out. Value for money is high in this region and the wines show off a more masculine side of Pinot Noir. A word of warning, though: this is a commune to avoid in the poor vintages, as the grapes need to be fully ripened to overcome an innate toughness in them.

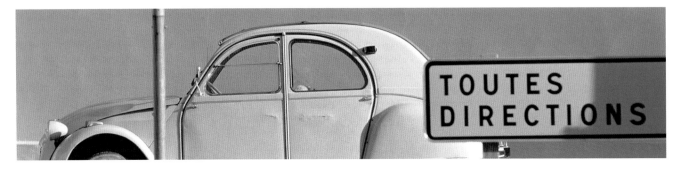

Nicolas Potel, Jean-Yves Devevey

Côte de Nuits-Villages and Hautes-Côte de Nuits

The *villages* wines come from the most northern and southern end of the Côte, while the 'Hautes-Côtes' vineyards surround many of the famous communes of the Côte proper. Both these *appellations* can be represented by excellent value wines, as many a famous producer in the Côte will own vineyards in them. Having said this, the wines are only half a step up from the bottom of the ladder, namely straight Bourgogne but not of the quality equivalent to a *village* wine.

CÔTE DE BEAUNE

All but one of the white *Grands Crus* are situated in the Côte de Beaune, so it might come as a bit of a surprise to find the whole of the north of this appellation being dominated by red wine. Generally the reds don't have the weight of the Côte de Nuits, but they often offer better value.

Really, though, Chardonnay is what it's all about down here. This grape has travelled well abroad – most notably in Australia – unlike its Burgundian partner, Pinot. However, if you asked me to name the ten greatest Chardonnays I have ever tasted, at least eight would be from here. One reason is perhaps that the success story of Chardonnay has spurred the Burgundian producers on to greater things; they have felt the increased competition at the lower end of the market and raised their quality significantly.

It is worth noting that a poor red wine vintage in this region does not necessarily mean a bad white. Chardonnay needs less sun to ripen and is altogether easier to grow than the fickle Pinot Noir.

Michel Juillot, Daniel Senard, Tollot-Beaut, Bonneau du Martray, Louis Jadot, Louis Latour, Dubrieul-Fontaine (Including the **Grand Crus**: *Corton for red (confusingly for a **Grand Cru** the wine may be labelled simply Corton, but there are*

Ladoix-Serrigny and Aloxe-Corton

In a confusing *appellation*, let's first dispense with the wines of Ladoix. I have tasted very few, but those that I have have been a mixed bag, some were thin and weedy, and none was spectacular, but what they are is cheap.

Stylistically the red wines of Aloxe-Corton nod towards the sturdy north rather than the pretty examples to be found further south.

Corton at its best is one of the finest value *Grands Crus*; they don't have the finesse of some, but they age well. Aloxe-Corton *village* and *Premier Cru* wines are generally good but they can be a little rustic.

Corton-Charlemagne is one of my favourite white *Grands Crus*; it has the power of something from further south and the **balance** and minerality of good Chablis. This is one of the few Burgundys that demands a good stretch in the cellar. Additionally, with nearly 180 acres under vine the wines are possible to find at an accessible price.

Pernand-Vergelesses

Jean-Marc Pavelot, Jean-Jacques Girard, Dubreuil-Fontaine, Louis Jadot, Maurice Rollin, Marius Delarche

This is a *village* that can offer great value, but the main problem is getting the grapes sufficiently ripe, so always avoid them in poor years. In the right hands the reds remain just the right side of austere. The best producers aim for fresh, lightweight wines with red fruits like raspberries.

Production of white is quite small, but in good vintages it offers some of the best bargains in the region. An unpronounceable and unfashionable *village* name often leads to good-quality wine in the bottle, as this is the only sales tool available to the producer. In style they are like a junior Corton-Charlemagne, the best needing a few years in the cellar before they reveal **complex**, mineral-laden flavours.

Savigny-lès-Beaune

Simon Bize, Jean-Marc Pavelot, Nicolas Potel, Tollot-Beaut, Jean-Jacques Girard, Catherine et Claude Maréchal

This is a Mecca for the thirsty Burgundy consumer whose wallet is feeling light after one too many forays into the more illustrious *villages*. While there is always room for a poor producer, quality is generally high. The majority of wine here is red but the tiny percentage of white is of excellent quality if you can find it. It is difficult to generalise about these wine styles. Due to the diverse geography of the *village* the reds vary from light, instantly appealing quaffers to big, masculine Pinots that will improve for ten years.

There are a number of *Premiers Crus*; ones to look out for are Les Lavières, Aux Guettes, La Dominode and Les Narbantons. At all levels they offer you a rarity in Burgundy, namely value.

Chorey-lès-Beaune

These wines are the little brothers of Savigny. Nearly all the wine is red.
They don't reach the heights of Savigny and the best aim to be early-
drinking, accessible, fruit-driven Pinot. Again, they can be stunning
value. There are no *Premier Cru* vineyards to complicate things, so just
stick to the best producers like Tollot-Beaut and Jacques Germain of
Château de Chorey for your instant Pinot fix.

Beaune

This town is the capital and the heartbeat of the region, containing a
large area of 1600 acres under vine, 95 per cent of which is red. It is
the third village in a row that offers excellent value.

The red wines don't have the stuffing of the Côte de Nuits or
the two villages directly to the south, but they are silky, fruity wines for
relatively early consumption.

The style of the whites owes more to the producer than the
area, but they are still great value. For some reason they have never
been that popular with the consumer, but nevertheless I urge you to take
advantage as a good *Premier Cru* can be the same price as a *village*
wine from the Côte de Nuits. Notable *Premiers Crus* are Clos des
Mouches (Drouhin's white from here can reach **Grand Cru** quality), Les
Grèves, Les Bressandes, Clos du Roi and Les Cents Vignes.

Pommard

These are the biggest red wines of the Côte de Beaune. Their style bears
little resemblance to Beaune in the north or Volnay in the south. The
best are **structured** wines that are, rather unfairly, often deemed to be
excessively coarse and rustic when young. They are, though, some of the
few reds from Burgundy that are unapproachable in their youth, needing
three or four years in the cellar to soften.

Pommard is a big *village* with over 1600 acres under vine, all
of which is red. I love these wines as they combine the delights of Pinot
fruit with a gamy, earthy character that gives wine of great complexity.
The quality of winemaking in the area is high, although *village* wines in

the poorer vintages can be a bit mean. The top *Premiers Crus* produce profound wines that, in my view, are the best reds of the Côte de Beaune, surpassing the one **Grand Cru** of the region, Corton. Those I would highlight are Clos des Epeneaux (a **monopole** vineyard owned by the outstanding Comte Armand), Les Rugiens, Les Pézerolles, Les Petits and Grands Epenots and Les Fremiers.

Volnay

Volnay is regarded as the Chambolle-Musigny of the Côte de Beaune. Many are silky, soft wines that are instantly pleasing, although some have a bigger tannic **structure** that echoes Pommard. They taste fabulous when young but I am constantly surprised at how well they age, so try to be patient and leave them for those extra couple of years.

The overall quality of winemaking is high and so is the price-to-taste ratio. Top producers from the right *Premier Cru* vineyards are responsible for some of Burgundy's most ethereal red wines. I am a big fan of them, and they do not receive as much acclaim as is due.

There is an abundance of good *Premiers Crus* to choose from: Clos des Chênes, en Champans, Taille Pieds, and Les Mitans. Producer-wise, I could write a very long list for this area but have restricted myself to those in the margin.

Monthélie

As these vineyards are adjacent to both Volnay and Meursault you would expect these wines to be widely known. You might hope for glimpses of both in the wines yet this rarely happens. The vast majority of wine is red, but I have trouble pinning down a style for the region.

Traditional wisdom tells us that the reds ought to be tannic and rustic, though my tasting tells me the opposite. Perhaps producers have realised more recently that consumers don't want a style of wine that requires bottle age from a region they have barely heard of. Whatever the reason, I like these light **fresh** reds and they represent fine value.

The whites have a tendency to be big and unbalanced, as if winemakers are striving to make Meursault but without the raw materials. I think this is an area to watch for good bottles on a budget. Producer, I suspect, is all important.

Dupont-Fahn, Louis Jadot,
Comte Armand, François
d'Allaines, Coche-Dury

Auxey-Duresses

These vineyards are situated to the west of Meursault and are split two-thirds in favour of red. The style of wines here is more clear-cut than in neighbouring Monthélie, and at their best the reds are chunky, less voluptuous versions of Volnay. There are some seriously grown-up producers who also make wine here. The wines from Coche-Dury (Meursault) and Comte Armand (Pommard) are a stunning way to sample some of Beaune's best growers without the credit card imploding.

The whites can offer you a taste of Meursault at half the price. Les Duressses is the one *Premier Cru* to watch out for, but avoid these wines in cool years when the exposure of the vines is less than perfect.

François d'Allaines,
Christophe Buisson,
Betrand Ambroise

St-Romain

Tucked away to the west of Auxey-Duresses, off the main drag, St-Romain is often bypassed by tourist and drinker alike. I urge you not to do the same. The reds can largely be ignored; the best are light and fruity but the grapes often taste underripe and better-tasting value red can be had elsewhere.

Chardonnay does much better here, producing crisp, **fresh** flavours, with creamy dimensions added in the hottest years. Like Chorey-Lès-Beaune, there are no *Premiers Crus* to worry about so just stick to the best producers.

Fichet, Michel Bouzereau,
Arnaud Ente, Patrick
Javillier, Guy Roulot, Marc
Rougeot, Coche-Dury,
Comtes Lafon

Meursault

We are now entering the heartland of white Burgundy production and it starts with a bang.

At their best, the whites are sensational: big, fat, unctuous Chardonnays which, while not having the finesse of their neighbours, more than make up for it in power. Don't tell any Burgundians I said this, otherwise I am unlikely to be allowed back into the region, but Meursault can be positively New World in its buttery fruit flavours. It is the perfect introduction to great white Burgundy. The wines are generally

lower in **acidity** than the other big two – Chassagne and Puligny-Montrachet – so drink them earlier.

Quality is generally high throughout the village. *Premier Crus* to note are Les Charmes, Les Genevrières and Les Perrières. There are also many single vineyard sites, or *lieu dit*, that offer bargains from good growers.

There are also a small number of reds produced here.

Puligny-Montrachet

Jean-Marc Boillot, Etienne Sauzet, Louis Carillon, Domaine Leflaive, Jean Chartron, Didier Larue, Jacques Prieur, Verget (Including the **Grand Crus**: *Le Montrachet, Bâtard-Montrachet (both these vineyards have some vines in the village of Chassagne-Montrachet), Chevalier-Montrachet and Bienvenues-Bâtard-Montrachet)*

There are nearly 600 acres of vines entitled to **Grand Cru**, *Premier Cru* and *village* status, in this most mythical of Chardonnay-producing areas. Puligny-Montrachet was enthroned as the king of the grape years ago. Rather unsportingly, no matter what the efforts of its neighbours to the north and south, and not taking into account its often lacklustre efforts, it has decided to keep the crown.

At the top of the pile is the **Grand Cru** of Le Montrachet, a nineteen-acre piece of real estate that purports to be more expensive than downtown Tokyo. Like its red equivalent, Chambertin, too many Montrachet producers are dedicated to making wines of great quantity, rather than quality.

The best bottles do reach the heights at which Dumas noted that they 'should be drunk kneeling with one's head bare', although I prefer a comfy sofa and a pint glass. Too many, however, are inexcusable rip-offs at £100 plus. The other *Grands Crus*, while still frighteningly expensive, offer more even quality.

Stylistically the wines are higher in **acidity** than Meursault, so they need longer in the cellar. They are not so flashy but ultimately are more stylish, allying minerals and citrus fruits with ripe, buttery flavours and appealing to the head as well as the heart. I find the quality of Puligny-Montrachet *village* wines, even from some renowned producers, depressingly patchy. This should not be the case when their price is often that of *Premier Cru* from either of the neighbours.

There are, however, a number of great *Premiers Crus* to choose from, some of which can reach **Grand Cru** quality for a fraction of the price. Look for Champ Canet, Les Folatières, Les Combettes, Le Cailleret, La Truffière and Les Pucelles.

Chassagne-Montrachet

Of the big three in the region, this is my favourite appellation for its consistently high-quality wines. Although Puligny certainly produces the more profound wines, one needs to wade through many disappointments to get there.

The style of the whites sits between Meursault and Puligny, having good levels of **acidity** but also managing to be plump and approachable in their youth. Roughly half the production here is red wine. The reds here are great value, overshadowed as they are by the more desirable whites. Characterised by bright, fresh, cherry fruit, these need to be enjoyed in their youth – strangely, this is a region where the whites outlast the reds.

The one **Grand Cru** is tiny at under four acres, and the only great wine I have tasted from there is made by Blain-Gagnard. This lack of glitz and glamour at the top end is good news for the consumer. Producers are forced to work hard to be able to sell them as effectively as Puligny and Meursault, and good *Premier Cru* Chassagne can often be had for the same price as *village* Puligny. *Village* Chassagne is cheaper and infinitely better than *village* Puligny.

There are a string of good *Premier Cru* sites for white: Les Chaumées, La Boudriotte, Les Grandes Ruchottes, Les Vergers, Les Chenevottes and Les Champs Gain all excel. To me the red seems less site-specific, especially as today's growers search for a more overtly fruity, early-drinking style.

St Aubin

After the bank-account-draining experiences in Puligny, Chassagne and Meursault, St Aubin comes as a welcome relief. The reds are good, but I find those in neighbouring Chassagne to be better and the prices are not wildly different. The whites, on the other hand, are outstanding; they are one of the bargains of Burgundy.

The best sites nestle next door to Puligny and Chassagne, and in the right hands they can make wine of equivalent quality. The *Premiers Crus* to watch are Les Murgers des Dents de Chien and En Remilly.

Girardin, Bernard Morey, Marc Colin, Jean Claude Belland

Santenay

Rather like Marsannay in the Côte d'Or, Santenay is often overlooked and suffers from a similar identity crisis. A minuscule amount of white is made, but this is an area dominated by Pinot. Traditionally the reds are regarded as tough, rustic wines that lack charm.

Improved winemaking techniques and a modern outlook have led producers in Santenay to strive for more fruit in their wines. That said, these are never going to be silky, voluptuous expressions of Pinot; fresh cherry flavours with an earthy edge are found here. There are a number of *Premier Cru* sites. The best, on account of their exposure, lie close to Chassagne: La Comme, Beauregard, Les Gravières and Clos de Tavannes.

Girardin

Maranges

This is the last village of the Côte d'Or, although the vineyards have now fallen off the 'golden hillside'. The wines are nearly all red and I can find little to recommend here. If you're after good value red it's better to look further south.

Jean-Yves Devevey, Nicolas Potel

Hautes-Côtes de Beaune and Côte de Beaune Villages

Like their northern equivalent in the Côte de Nuits, wines from these appellations can offer good-value drinking provided you choose only the quality-conscious producers. In theory the quality of the wines should sit in between a straight Bourgogne and a *village* wine.

Peculiarly for a region famous for Chardonnay, the wines here are predominantly red, although I find the whites to be of a more consistent quality. Those labelled '*villages*' come from a designated collection of villages. The vineyards of many might be in some of Burgundy's most famous communes. Those labelled straight 'Hautes-Côte' come from vineyards to the west of the Côte de Beaune.

CÔTE CHALONNAISE

Having dealt with the glamourous end of Burgundy, it's now time to look at the regions that we can actually afford to drink on a regular basis. These wines are considerably cheaper than those of the Côte d'Or. The top producers are turning out wines that are among the bargains of the region, and they serve to reinforce my ultimate Burgundy-buying tip: you should always buy the best wine you can afford from a great producer, rather than poor ones that have an illustrious name. The Côte Chalonnaise continues on almost directly from the bottom of the Côte de Beaune. There are three distinct areas of quality vineyards.

Bouzeron, Rully and Mercurey

Antonin Rodet, Jean-Marc Boillot, Chartron et Trébuchet, Vincent Dureuil-Janthial, Château de Chamirey, Château de Rully, Michel Juillot, Henri et Paul Jacqueson, Luc Brintet

The first of these villages is an oddity as it's the only *Appellation Contrôlée* for the Aligoté grape in France. I am not usually a fan of the grape unless it has a good slug of Cassis in the glass to counter its rasping **acidity**. Here, however, the grape makes a crisp white wine, which surprises with its depth. The village is tiny with less than one hundred acres of vines, and A. & P. de Villaine, the king of Aligoté worldwide, is the producer to look for.

Rully is split evenly between the production of red and white wines. I would ignore the reds, though, as they are very light and frequently taste acidic and unripe. The whites, on the other hand, must be on your shopping list. The cheaper versions remind me of good Chablis, with crisp apple fruit generally untouched by **oak**, while the top producers aim for an altogether different beast, utilising the best production methods usually reserved for the finest Beaune whites.

Mercurey is by far the biggest area under vine in the northern part of the Chalonnaise. Around 90 per cent of it is Pinot Noir; the rest is Chardonnay. The reds are some of the best value in Burgundy, although they can seem expensive for such a supposedly humble name. Don't be put off; the best are meaty, **complex** wines that are better than many of the Côte de Nuits *village* wines, whose style they resemble.

The lighter wines offer simple, pure fruit flavours for early drinking. The whites are potentially very good, having a rich minerality that reminds me of Puligny-Montrachet, but they come at a fraction of the price.

Givry

Joblet, Louis Latour, Michel Sarrazin

Givry is a largely forgotten village whose production is mostly red. Old wine books will dismiss the wines as being bitter and rustic, but I don't find this to be the case today. There are some excellent mid-weight reds being turned out. They don't have the body of Mercurey but are not thin like those from Rully.

The lowly standing of Givry does ensure that bargains are to be had. The whites are variable: too many are overly acidic and lacking in flavour. There are no *Premiers Crus* to confuse the issue.

Montagny

Antonin Rodet, François d'Allaines, Jean-Marc Boillot, Stéphen Aladame

This is a good area for those who like to with impress friends their knowledge of the oddities of French wine law. Firstly, it is the one village in the Chalonnaise where only Chardonnay may be grown. Secondly, any wine over 11° per cent alcohol may be labelled *Premier Cru*. This is rather extraordinary, as I would be very suspicious of the ripeness levels of any wine below this percentage.

The wines are not dissimilar to Rully in that the lighter versions have a Chablis-esque feel to them, while the best are creamy and ripe.

MÂCONNAIS

This is the engine room of wine production in Burgundy accounting for around three-quarters of it. About a quarter of the region is planted with the red grapes Gamay and Pinot Noir, but I find that these wines are generally poor. The whites range from insipid, overproduced **co-operative** wines to sublime beauties that are a steal.

Mâcon and Mâcon-Villages

Deux-Roches, Talmard, Cordier, André Bonhomme, Guffens-Heynen, Verget, Louis Jadot, Cave de Prissé, Louis Latour, Domaine Valette, Olivier Merlin, Les Héritiers du Comte Lafon

Straight Mâcon is rarely of reasonable quality so I stick to the superior Mâcon-Villages. There are forty-two *villages* that can use the prefix Mâcon, but in reality only a few choose to do so. The most common are

Clessé, Fuissé, Lugny, Davayé, Prissé and Viré (whose wines confusingly may now also be labelled just Viré-Clessé). The rest of the wines will simply be labelled *villages* indicating that the grapes have come from one or more of these villages.

Trying to categorise the style of these wines is impossible. They range from clean, well-made, but uninspiring quaffing wine to rich, age-worthy numbers. As ever, producer rather than location is paramount. Huge swathes of the Mâconnais is controlled by **co-operatives**, who should be avoided as they cater to those who want to drink white Burgundy rather than good wine.

A special mention must go to the sublime wines of Jean Thévenet, whom I believe – to borrow boxing parlance – to be the greatest producer in Burgundy, pound for pound. A bottle of his 1996 Mâcon-Clessé drunk at six years old could have been mistaken for a **Grand Cru** *from the Côte de Beaune. A sign of this quality is his continued irritation of the wine lawmakers in Burgundy: they have recently downgraded the classification of his wines from Mâcon-villages to Mâcon for not being typical of the region (i.e. too good?).*

Pouilly-Fuissé, Pouilly-Loché and Pouilly-Vinzelles

Michel Forest, Cordier, Ferret, Louis Jadot, Château Beauregard, Verget, Château Fuissé, Domaine Valette, Olivier Merlin, Guffens-Heynen

At its best, Pouilly-Fuissé produces the finest and longest-living white wines of the Mâconnais and Chalonnaise. They are marked by creamy citrus flavours, with the top ones revealing minerality after a few years in the bottle. They are also the most expensive, but a great producer's top wine is infinitely better value than one of the equivalent price point in the Côte de Beaune.

Unfortunately, these wines are in huge demand around the world and this has led to a disproportionate amount of them being low quality. I would advise you to not stray too far from my recommended producers.

The last two villages are rarely seen but are worth trying if you do as they represent good value.

St Véran

de la Croix Senaillet, Deux Roches

The junior sibling of Pouilly-Fuissé, the two feel close as so many of the same producers operate in both villages. Those made by the quality-conscious offer excellent, affordable wine.

I find that across the board the quality of winemaking is of a higher standard than that of Pouilly-Fuissé. The wines are lighter but much depends on producer; look out for the offerings from de la Croix Senaillet and Deux Roches and the producers listed by the Pouilly-Fuissé section (p.58).

BURGUNDY AND FOOD

Basic Chablis loves shellfish. As the wines move up through the gears, pair them up with progressively heavier fish. Start with cod or haddock and serve the best stuff with poached salmon and hollandaise. The **oak** on the expensive wines laps up a bit of cream in the sauce, but keep it simple with the herbs and spices. The serious stuff will happily stand up to chicken and guinea fowl. One of the finest and most hedonistic matches is fine, aged Burgundy and lobster, served with nothing more than a lump of brown bread and good-quality mayonnaise.

The lighter reds are perfect for those who want a drop of red with fish; stick them in the fridge for half an hour before serving. Roast chicken, cheese soufflé and cured ham are some of the other options. The best reds from the Côte d'Or demand serious food: beef stew is a local favourite. I start getting all misty-eyed when game is mentioned: old Burgundy and grouse, peasant or partridge is simply one of the best things ever invented. Squidgy cheeses like Camembert and the local favourites Mont d'Or and Epoisses are excellent matches.

For light wines try
Loire Valley p.72

Sauvignon Blanc p.214, **Pinot Grigio** p.209, **Chenin Blanc** p.198

Salads p.288, **Shellfish** p.257

For richer whites try
Australia p.156, **New Zealand** p.168, **South Africa** p.174, **California** p.180, **Rhône Valley** p.84,

Marsanne p.201, **Roussanne** p.212

Fish p.252, **Chicken** p.265

For reds try
New Zealand p.168, **Australia** p.156, **California** p.180, **Oregon** p.184, **Tuscany** p.120, **Côte Rôtie** p.86, **Beaujolais** p.60

Sangiovese p.242, **Tempranillo** p.245

Fish p.252, **Chicken** p.265, **Cured Meats** p.266, **Game** p.267, **Runny Cheese** p.292

This is a region verging on crisis. In 2002 a significant amount of its wine was sold off for distillation, which is nothing unusual for lowly table wines in France. Beaujolais, though, is an *Appellation Contrôlée* region, and therefore on the top rung of the ladder of the quality control system. The problems are largely of their own making: by putting all their eggs in the *nouveau* basket the region's growers have let the consumer forget about the serious side of the region. Now *nouveau*, along with much of the rest of the eighties, has been consigned to the dustbin labelled 'naff' and the Beaujolais consumer of old has moved on to other regions. This is a huge tragedy, not just for the region but also for your taste buds.

Beaujolais and Beaujolais-Villages

I would avoid all wine simply labelled 'Beaujolais'. Much of it is sold as *nouveau* and the rest is of a depressingly low standard. The attachment of the word '*villages*' indicates that the wine must be made from grapes grown in a selection of vineyards classified as being of superior quality. There are some competent wines made here, but what is the point of searching when you can drink the best stuff for so little more?

Georges Duboeuf, Marcel Lapiere, Henry Fessy, Paul Janin, Jean-Charles Pivot, Domaine Coudert, Calot, Louis Jadot
(Including the 10 Cru: Saint-Amour, Juliénas, Chénas, Moulin-à-Vent, Fleurie, Chiroubles, Morgon, Régnié, Brouilly, Côte de Brouilly)

Beaujolais Cru

These are the ten **cru** *villages* of Beaujolais that are entitled to use only their name on the label. I don't exaggerate when I say that the top producers of these wines are making some of the best-value bottles in France. In particular, look to the less well-known communes, where most wines can be had for under a tenner; these are gorgeous, raspberry-scented wines that demand to be drunk very quickly. An hour in the fridge before serving them only serves to heighten the freshness of the fruit.

The bigger, more **structured** crus still offer wonderful exuberant flavours but they veer towards more of a black fruit character, the best having a spicy, meaty complexity. They will also benefit from a few years in the cellar.

The lighter styles, after an hour in the fridge, make the perfect wine for those who like red as an aperitif, as well as solving the 'red wine and fish' conundrum. Try, though, to stick to the meatier fishes like monkfish or tuna. Heavier versions are very versatile as they have good **acidity** but are low in **tannins**. Try them with charcuterie, roasted vegetables, chicken, quail, or even spicy dishes, as they are one of the few reds to put up a decent performance against the challenge of strongly spiced food. Gooey, smelly cheeses are best.

Try

Loire Valley p.72, Valpolicella p.112, Burgundy p.38

Pinot Noir p.238, Cabernet Franc p.227, Sangiovese p.242, Dolcetto p.228

Fish p.252, Cured Meats p.266, Chicken p.265, Quail p.267, Asian Food p.281, Runny Cheese p.292

CAHORS

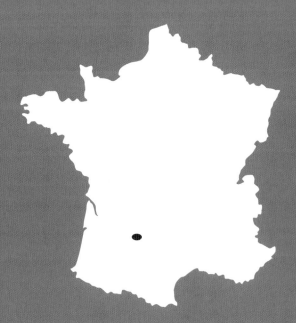
For many years the wines of Cahors were known as the 'black wine', famously rich in colour and tannin. The area is within Bordeaux's sphere of influence and its fearsome reputation comes from the use of one of that region's forgotten grapes, Malbec. Rarely used now in Bordeaux as it is very difficult to get sufficiently ripe, the hotter inland vineyards of Cahors suit Malbec well.

Very few producers now make this wine in the old style, as the demands of the modern drinker have forced a change in direction. New wine techniques have softened the wines, making a much more variable range of approachable styles, which are ready to drink after only a few years in the bottle. They are still gutsy, full-bodied affairs, full of plums and spices, and the old-fashioned producers, in the hot years, can turn out monsters of incredible value.

The fuller wines desperately need food to counter their **tannins** and **acidity**. Rich braised lamb shanks and oxtail are the kind of thing for this wine. The more **commercial** wines are better with simple red meat dishes.

The sparkling wines of Champagne hold a special place in our psyche. Champagne is associated with celebration and good times: birthdays, New Year and weddings are all good excuses for a drop of fizz. The odd thing, though, is that while we are generally fairly critical consumers of wine, our sense of value seems to fly out of the window when we purchase Champagne. There is no other wine region in the world where the cost of a bottle bears so little correlation to the quality.

The famous brands can produce great wine, but it often seems that image and 'brand loyalty' have become more important than the drink itself. In many ways these things matter, and purchasing a top brand is as much a fashion as a quality statement. Sponsoring a yacht race or a fashion show is not cheap, and we should remember that we are the ones paying for it – without the glitzy ad campaigns these bottles would be much cheaper.

Billecart-Salmon, Louis
Roederer, Bollinger, Gosset
Egly-Ouriet, Ruinart, Krug,
Larmandier-Bernier,
Jacquesson, Bruno
Paillard,
Vilmart, Salon, Veuve
Cliquot

**If you like light fruity
styles of champagne try
fizz from the Loire Valley**
p.72, **Northern Italy**
p.108, **Alsace** p.16

**For genuine Champagne
styles from around the
world, look out for the
words 'Traditional Method',
as this indicates utilisation
of Champagne's expensive
production methods. Try
New Zealand** p.168,
California p.180, **Australia**
p.156

The vineyards lying to the north-east of Paris encompass nearly 70,000 acres. They are planted with three grape varieties: Pinot Noir, Pinot Meunier and Chardonnay, the first two of which are red grapes. Pinot Noir and Chardonnay make the finest-quality wines.

The ownership of vines in Champagne is very similar to the system in Burgundy. There are a huge number of growers earning a living from grapes, which they sell to the larger companies who actually make the wines – these are referred to as Champagne houses. Many of the large houses actually own only a small percentage of the grapes used to make their products. This has allowed a recent trend whereby an increasing number of small growers are making and bottling their own wines. These represent the best buys of the region.

Most Champagnes fall into the following four categories:

Non-Vintage
This is the mainstay of most major houses. The base wine will be drawn from a number of different years, as unlike vintage Champagne, the aim here is to achieve a homogeneous style over the years. Each house aims for a unique taste. Most of these wines are drunk within hours of being purchased, but a good tip is to buy a few extra bottles of your favourite non-vintage Champagne and lay them down for a few years. You'll find that they take on extra layers of complexity and toastiness, not unlike a vintage wine but at a fraction of the price.

Vintage
These are wines that come from one single year. As Champagne is a northerly region, only the best years warrant a vintage. There are no laws governing the declaration of a vintage year. The best houses will limit themselves to four or five times a decade when the weather has been kind, but the less honest houses will extol the virtues of even the poorest years. Vintage wines will have more weight and complexity than non-vintage; many will last ten years or fifteen years and are often not ready to drink when they are released.

Prestige Cuvées
These are the best wines a house can offer and they are nearly always from a single vintage. They are mostly sublime wines but very expensive. Examples are Dom Pérignon from Möet et Chandon and Cristal from

Louis Roederer. As with vintage Champagne, these wines are mostly drunk too young; sadly by those who are usually more interested in the label than contents.

Rosé

These can be vintage, non-vintage or prestige **cuvée**. We have a rather dim view of these wines in the UK, perceiving them to be for frivolous summertime consumption, rather like fizzy rosé. This is a great shame as they can offer you lots more. The French take these wines very seriously, and the prestige **cuvée** of rosé is often more expensive than the equivalent white champagne. In particular, the bigger **structure** of rosé Champagne can be a good complement to food.

A seventeenth-century monk, Dom Perignon, is often credited with beginning the modern Champagne industry, supposedly having worked very hard to try to prevent bubbles from forming in the wine. The fizz today is created by adding a small amount of **yeast** and sugar to a still bottle of wine and then resealing it. Sugar and **yeast** together ferment, releasing carbon dioxide, and with the bottle closed the gas has nowhere to go, so it dissolves into the wine, waiting for the day when you pop the cork.

In Dom Perignon's time, wine would often still be in cask during the onset of winter. **Fermentation** ceases at low temperatures, so winemakers would be fooled into thinking the process had finished. They would bottle the wine and send it to their customers. The following spring, as the temperatures rose, the **yeast** would continue its unfinished work, causing many an explosion in an unsatisfied customer's cellar.

With the advent of better quality glass bottles and stronger stoppers, Dom Perignon was able to experiment with the positive aspects of fizzy wine. The bubbles became fashionable and the rest is history. The acidic still wines that this cool area naturally turns out are the ideal base for making Champagne.

Here are some other words to look out for on a Champagne bottle:

Brut and Ultra or Extra Brut

Most champagne drunk is **brut**, an indication that the wine is dry. A few houses have tried to satisfy our demand for dryness by releasing a blend that is even drier. They are usually labelled *ultra brut* – Laurent-Perrier is the most well-known example of this.

Demi-Sec

This is a style of semi-sweet Champagne that is greatly out of fashion now. These can be delicious wines, with flavours firmly in the fruity rather than the toasty camp, and for those who find **brut** champagne to be too acidic this is the answer. Lastly, these wines are a wonderful way to finish a meal.

Blanc de Blancs

These wines must be made from 100 per cent Chardonnay. Their style is rounded and full. Vintage versions with some bottle age can be a revelation, having a golden yellow colour and **complex** flavours of bread. This may sound like one of the stranger tasting notes, but it really is true. Stick your nose in a freshly baked loaf of white bread and then in a good glass of Blanc de Blancs.

Blanc de Noirs

These are made from red grapes only. This style is rarer than Blanc de Blancs and the wines seem tougher and not so instantly appealing, but they make up for this with an overtly fruity character.

Récemment dégorgé (usually shortened to RD)

The *lees* that are left after **fermentation** in the bottle impart flavour to the final wine. RD indicates that the wine has spent an extended amount of time on its *lees*. These wines are stored in cellars, with a date on the label that indicates when the **lees** were removed. This style is much loved by the English, and Bollinger are the leading exponents of it.

In the UK, we tend to view Champagne as an aperitif, a job it does admirably. Indeed the lighter wines are best drunk as an aperitif. In France, though, it is not uncommon to drink it throughout the meal, as the fizz and high **acidity** cleanse the palate; important attributes when pairing food and wine. Move up a gear to vintage, non-vintage Blanc de Blancs or rosé and a wealth of pairings arises. They will cut through, rapier-like, any cream-heavy dishes of fish, chicken and even fatty roast pork. Quaff **demi-sec** with light, fruit-based desserts, or strawberries and cream – decadent heaven (*see the recipe on page 305*) – or just as a perfect way to end a meal.

CORBIÈRES AND FITOU

Château de Lastours, Tardieu, Roquefort St Martin, Castelmaure, Bastide

Try

🍷 **Southern Rhône** p.90, **Languedoc and Roussillon** p.70, **Madiran** p.80, **Bandol** p.20, **Minervois** p.81, **Siciliy and Sardinia** p.128

🍇 **Carignan** p.226, **Grenache** p.230, **Syrah** p.243, **Mourvèdre** p.236

🍴 **Beef** p.263, **Pork** p.273, **Sausages** p.274, **Goat Cheese** p.293

These vineyards are deep in the south of France, sandwiched between Roussillon to the south and Minervois to the north. The reds have a Southern Rhône feel to them, so Grenache and Carignan dominate.

The more ambitious producers use higher proportions of Syrah and Mourvèdre. The full range of quality levels is represented here: overproduced bulk wines to full-bodied, deeply coloured, spicy reds. In theory, the best wines should come from the superior sub-region of Fitou. As ever, though, the producer should be your only guide to quality

There is no need for subtlety when dealing with Corbières: hearty stews and braised shin of beef are the kind of thing it needs. Also, try it with sausages, beef burgers and spare ribs off the barbecue, or with hard cheeses.

Cauhapé, Clos Uroulat,
Jolys, Clos Lapeyre

If you like the dry versions, try

Alsace p.16

Viognier p.218,
Gewürztraminer p.198

Cream Sauces p.284, **Fish**
p.252, **Brie** p.292, **Goats
Cheese** p.293

For the sweeter versions try

Loire Valley p.72

Chenin Blanc p.194,
Riesling p.206

Fruit Puddings p.296,
Blue Cheese p.292

The vineyards of Jurançon lie just to the south of Pau, close to the Pyrenees. Two types of white wine are made here: *sec* (dry) and *moelleux* (sweet), from the Petit and Gros Manseng grapes. The dry wines are delicious, packed with **fresh** citrus and floral flavours, and have an uncanny ability to seem heavier than they actually are. The sweet wines made in the best years can also be a revelation, full of tropical and candied fruits. Like other great sweet wines, such as those from Chenin Blanc or Riesling, they have great balancing **acidity**.

Considering their cost, these are some of the finest wines in France. They are all unique wines which, until recently, were rarely seen outside southern France; now, though, they adorn many wine lists and the shelves of good retailers. Being relatively unknown, they are conspicuously undervalued.

The good **acidity** of the dry wines and the weight of their fruit makes them diverse food wines. Drink them with rich, creamy fish dishes, Brie and full-bodied goat cheeses like Chaource. The sweet wines love blue cheeses, fruit puddings and, best of all, being drunk on their own.

Languedoc covers a huge swathe of land in southern France, encompassing the cities of Montpellier and Béziers. Ten years ago one would have found much to moan about here and little to recommend; now, though, it would not be rash to claim that some of France's finest-value wines are made here. The wines have a distinctly Rhône-like feel to them, so for red expect Grenache, Carignan, Mourvèdre and Syrah.

Mas de Morties, Grange des Pères, Estanilles, Mas Julien, Château Coujan, Les Roques, Mas Brugière, Château Grand Cassagne, Cazeneuve, L'Hortus, Mas de Daumas Gassac, Mas Blanc, Mas Amiel

For the lighter reds, try
Southern Rhône p.90, **Minervois** p.81, **Spain** p.142

Grenache p.230

Chicken p.265, **Pork** p.273

For the heavier reds, try
Madiran p.80, **Cahors** p.62, **Rhône** p.84, **Sicily and Sardinia** p.128

Malbec p.232, **Syrah** p.243, **Barbera** p.222, **Mourvèdre** p.236

Beef p.263

The best reds are meaty and full-bodied, and the rare whites tend to be fatter and more unctuous than those from the Rhône, which they resemble slightly. Within the district are a number of areas to note: St-Chinian, Faugères, Pic St Loup and l'Hérault.

Not strictly part of the Languedoc, but with the same slant, are the wines of Costières de Nîmes to the east. Vast amounts of wine are produced in the whole region under the vin de pays d'Oc guise, using internationally known varietals like Chardonnay and Merlot. It is a sad fact that these bland wines with no sense of identity are easier to sell than the true wines of the Languedoc. Do your bit and switch from the Cabernet Sauvignon described by the marketing team as having 'a bucketful of lip-smacking blackcurrants' to the proper stuff.

Roussillon's vineyards sit further to the south, centred on Perpignan. The reds are similar in style to the Languedoc, and the one superior area to note is Collioure. On the Spanish border, it produces earthy red wine. Banyuls and Maury are also worth seeking out. These are red **vin doux naturels**, i.e. **fortified** sweet wines, which make an interesting and cheaper alternative to Port.

It's difficult to generalise about Languedoc and Roussillon wines and food, as there is a huge range of styles. Treat them in a similar way to Southern Rhône reds: serve the lighter ones with some barbecued chicken or pork. The bigger versions require respect: slabs of proper steak, preferably with the bones still in it …

Try Maury and Banyuls with Stilton and hard cheeses, or even with that awkward customer, chocolate.

The Loire Valley is often talked of in one breath as if it is a compact, easily definable area. This is not the case. Not only is it geographically large, but also it has a huge variety of wine styles. For white wine lovers the area offers something for everyone – seafood-friendly Muscadets, great Sauvignons and idiosyncratic and dry Chenin Blancs. Lastly – and I'd be shouting now if it were possible in text – it offers some of the greatest-value sweeties in the world.

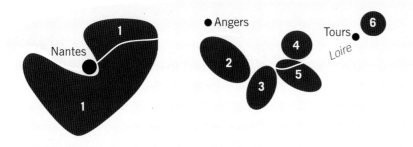

1 Muscadet
2 Coteaux de Layon and L'Aubance
3 Saumur and Saumur Champigny
4 Bourgueil
5 St-Nicolas de Bourgueil and Chinon
6 Vouvray
7 Sancerre and Pouilly-Fumé

I know, I know; not everyone likes sweet wines, but I defy you not to enjoy a great Coteaux du Layon or Vouvray. The secret is the Chenin Blanc grape responsible for these wines. It has the most wonderful natural **acidity**, so no matter how sweet the wine you are never left with a cloying taste in the mouth.

Reds make up a far smaller percentage of production. Delicate light Pinot Noirs from the end of the Loire can be a good alternative to cheaper red Burgundies. Gamay, the grape of Beaujolais, makes some great-value fruity reds. The most important red grape, however, is Cabernet Franc – also one of the components of red Bordeaux. People either love or hate this grape; there doesn't seem to be much middle ground. The best light examples have lovely **fresh** red fruit flavours that work well slightly chilled.

In great years some seriously **complex** bottles are made, which can offer excellent value when compared with red Bordeaux. However, too often I find the wines have a rustic green pepper character to them that I attribute to underripe grapes. I would put this down to the unsuitability of the region to ripen the Cabernet Franc grape fully every year, though, rather than to sloppy production methods.

The most important factor is that these wines are stupendous value. This is one of France's classic fine wine regions. Yet the top step of the ladder here can often cost the same as the bottom rung in regions such as Bordeaux or Burgundy.

The Loire has been blessed over the last decade with fabulous vintages. Whether this is because of global warming or luck, who knows? Be aware that, historically, this has not always been the case. The grapes here do not always get enough sunlight and warmth to ripen.

I'll deal with the regions starting on the coast at Nantes, where the Loire river ends its journey, and move inland ending – over 200 miles later – at Sancerre and Pouilly-Fumé.

Pierre Luneau-Lapin,
L'Ecu, Domaine de la
Quilla

Try

🍷 **North-east Italy** p.112,
Bordeaux p.24, **Chablis**
p.42

🍇 **Pinot Grigio** p.205, **Pinot
Bianco** p.204

🍴 **Fish** p.252, **Shellfish**
p.257

Muscadet

Muscadet is actually a grape. The region, south of Nantes, has taken its
name from it. It is also known as Melon de Bourgogne. The wine is a
relatively modern phenomenon and, as with many wines in Europe, its
success has come off the back of the local cuisine. It works fabulously
with fresh seafood. I am not talking about anything fancy. Don't start
drinking it with sea bass, lemongrass and sweet chilli sauce – instead
try the freshest Brittany oysters, lobster with a lake of home-made
mayonnaise and those vicious little langoustine that always manage to
lacerate your hands, along with a couple of hunks of brown bread and a
bottle or two of ice-cold Muscadet. The mere thought of it is enough to
get me off too book that Eurostar ticket.

Maybe I'm getting a bit overexcited, but if ever there was a
good example of a wine tasting better with, rather than just
complementing, food this is it. Always drink the youngest wine available
and look for the wines from the superior Sèvre-et-Maine sub-region.
Those with 'sur lie' on the label have spent additional time on their *lees*,
adding extra depth of flavour.

Jo Pithon, Baumard,
Ogereau, Pierre Bise,
Banchereau

Try

🍷 **Alsace** p.16, **Germany**
p.98, **Jurançon** p.69

🍇 **Riesling** p.206, **Chenin
Blanc** p.194

🍴 **Fruit Puddings** p.296,
Creamy Puddings p.295,
Blue Cheese p.292

Coteaux du Layon, Quarts-de-Chaume, Bonnezeaux, Coteaux de L'Aubance

These wines are some of the last great undiscovered wines of France.
The vineyards are situated to the south of Angers and fall into a sub-
region of the Loire known as Anjou. Coteaux du Layon is the largest area
and most widely available in this country. Quarts de Chaume and
Bonnezeaux are much smaller sub-regions within Coteaux du Layon that
over the years have been identified as producing better wines. They are
thus rare and more expensive.

The key to great sweet wine being made here is a tributary of
the Loire. The Layon river has over the years cut a deep gorge whose
steep sides provide great exposure but also sufficient shelter from wind.
This enables the grapes to become very **ripe** and high in sugar. In the
best years the valley walls provide shelter for foggy evenings and
mornings, ideal conditions for *botrytis* to form. A similar situation has
arisen along the Aubance river to the north.

I adore these wines. Even the most avowed hater of sweet wine is won over by them. The key is the high natural **acidity** of the Chenin Blanc grape, which leaves even the most intensely sweet wines with a refreshing zippy finish. The English have traditionally had a love affair with the sweet wines of Bordeaux, which I also love. Head to head in monetary terms, though, these wines win every time. I also find that the extra **acidity** makes them more compatible with desserts.

The lighter versions will take on fruit-based puddings while the big wines in the great years need something rich, yet simple, like crème brûlée. Creamy blue cheese is also great. This may sound a bit mad but it really does work: the saltiness of a blue cheese works as a foil to the sweetness of the wine – a bit like Chinese sweet-and-sour. Quite frankly, though, I think, like all great sweet wines, these are better drunk without food. My advice is to treat them as a liquid pudding.

Baumard, Joly

Try
Bordeaux p.24, **Alsace** p.16, **South Africa** p.174, **Loire Valley** p.72

Sémillon p.212, **Riesling** p.206, **Chenin Blanc** p.194

Cream Sauces p.284, **Oily Fish** p.254, **Chicken** p.265, **Veal** p.276

Try also
Provence p.83
Salads p.288, **Fish** p.252

Savennières

This small region produces distinctive, unusual and mostly dry wines. If you are used to quaffing soft, easy-to-drink Chardonnay from the South of France or Australia, these wines will come as a rude shock to the system. They have very high natural **acidity** and thus often need three or four years ageing in the bottle. Coupled with this is a wonderful minerality that makes these great food wines. If you want to start a cellar and buy some reasonably priced white wine with good ageing potential, this is a great place to start.

The high **acidity** of these wines is particularly good at cutting through creamy sauces. Try them also with oily fish like mackerel or salmon; in good **ripe** years they will equally take on chicken and veal.

Rosé d'Anjou

This is a delicate light rosé made from Cabernet Franc grapes. It is very different from the deeper, more powerful rosés from southern France and the New World, in that it tends to have subtle floral flavours rather than the red fruits one usually associates with these wines. I think they are best drunk on their own on a hot summer day.

This wine can also be drunk with light fish dishes and salads. It is particularly good with salmon.

Charles Joguet, Couly-
Dutheil, Pierre-Jacques
Druet, Jean-Paul Mabileau,
de L'Espy, Joël Taluau,
Bouvet-Ladubay, Langlois-
Château

For reds, try also

Bordeaux p.24, **Beaujolais**
p.60, **Bergerac** p.22,
Valpolicella p.115

Dolcetto p.228, **Pinotage**
p.240

Fish p.252, **Lamb** p.270,
Beef p.263, **Cream Sauces**
p.284, **Runny Cheese**
p.292

Saumur, Saumur Champigny, St-Nicolas de Bourgueil, Bourgueil, Chinon

This area is the heartland of red production in the Loire. All red here is
made from the Cabernet Franc grape. The wines can be light and fruity,
and are often chilled in the summer; however, in good vintages the best
can age for a decade and become serious and **complex** reds.

Saumur and Saumur Champigny follow almost directly to the
east of Coteaux du Layon and are still included in the sub-region of
Anjou. The lighter reds are made here; those with Champigny attached
to the name are in theory of a higher quality. A small amount of white is
also made using Chenin Blanc grapes. These and the wines from St-
Nicolas de Bourgueil are similar in style to Beaujolais, while Chinon and
Bourgueil make the most full-bodied wines of the region, having more in
common with Bordeaux than Beaujolais. It is difficult to generalise,
though, as the producer and vintage have a profound impact on each
wine's style.

When the weather has been kind these wines certainly warrant
a place in your rack, as they represent excellent value. The light, fruity
reds are crowd pleasers and the top **cuvées** offer mid-term wines for your
cellar at a reasonable price.

Look out also for the sparkling wines from Saumur and Saumur
Champigny. In the poorer years the acidic Chenin and Cabernet Franc
grapes make a perfect base for some of the Loire's most underrated
wines. These are made utilising the same production method as
Champagne but are considerably cheaper.

The chilled, lighter reds are perfect if you want to drink some
red with fish, but the top, age-worthy ones should be treated as
Bordeaux and drunk with simply cooked red meats. All these reds have
good **acidity** and so are useful for cream-based sauces. Cheese-wise, the
young light wines like a creamy number such as Vacherin or St Marcelin;
they also do a good job with the likes of Emmental.

Clos Naudin, Cray, Gaston
Huët, Aubuisières, Le
Taille aux Loups, Marc
Brédif

Vouvray, Mountlouis

Vouvray and Mountlouis lie east of the fabulous city of Tours. The
vineyards are respectively north and south of the Loire river. The wines
from Vouvray in particular are hugely underrated in this country. They

For dry wines, try
Germany p.98, **Loire Valley**
p.72, **Bordeaux** p.24,
South Africa p.174

Chenin Blanc p.194,
Riesling p.206

Oily Fish p.254, **Chicken**
p.265, **Cream Sauces**
p.284

For *demi-sec* wines, try
Loire p.72, **Alsace** p.16,
Germany p.98

Chenin Blanc p.194,
Riesling p.206

Fish p.252, **Chicken**
p.265, **Veal** p.276,
Partridge p.268, **Soft and**
Runny Cheeses p.292

For sparkling wines, try
Alsace p.16, **Champagne**
p.64

are all made from the Chenin Blanc grape and range from the bone dry to the intensely sweet. Wines are labelled as **sec** (dry), **demi-sec** (medium dry), and **moelleux** (sweet).

Unfortunately the words 'medium-dry' have the equivalent effect on most people as seeing 'anti-freeze' on a wine label. I sometimes wish producers wouldn't put it on as tasted blind you'll invariably prefer the slightly sweeter version. In my view, the **demi-sec** wines represent the region's wines in the best light. A little more sugar in the wine offsets the often searing **acidity** and the wines, like Savennières, age fabulously well, and they are widely available and still great value. These are the best-value age-worthy whites in the world. While Savennières is characterised by rich mineral flavours as it ages, Vouvray becomes honeyed and **complex**.

An important and often overlooked aspect of this region is the number of sparkling wines it produces. Due to the variable weather of the region growers are often left with unripe grapes, which are turned into generally high-quality sparkling wine made by the same method as Champagne. The word **mousseux** will appear on the label of these wines.

The dry wines are good food wines, working best with oily fish and chicken in creamy sauces. The **demi-secs** are great aperitifs and display amazing diversity with food. Rich fish dishes are obvious matches but have a go at a chicken casserole, veal in a creamy mushroom sauce, or partridge. Oozing full-fat cheese also combines well with these. The great sweet wines are best supped on their own, so you can marvel at the balancing act of acid, fruit and sweetness.

Alain Marcadet

For Sauvignon de Touraine, try

Loire p.72, **Chablis** p.42

Sauvignon p.210

Goats Cheese p.293, **Asparagus** p.286, **Asian Food** p.281

For Gamay de Touraine, try

Beaujolais p.60, **Loire** p.72

Cabernet Franc p.223, **Pinot Noir** p.238

Fish p.252, **Chicken** p.265, **Runny Cheese** p.292

Sauvignon and Gamay de Touraine

Regions such as Vouvray and Chinon hog the headlines by being so close to the riverside. These two less glamorous areas surround their more illustrious neighbours, but oddly enough they do not utilise the same grapes. The Sauvignons offer pure, simple, drinking pleasure (and I mean this in the best sense of the word), while the Gamays produced here are what we in the trade call 'fruit bombs'. No complexity, just juicy, fruity reds to drink rather than talk about.

Sauvignon de Touraine is delicious with *chèvre*, the local goat cheese of the region, as well as with asparagus. It also manages to hold its own pretty well against Asian food. The Gamays are useful if you want red on its own, just slightly chilled. If you wanted to combine them with food, I would suggest some fish or a chicken salad, or perhaps even a runny cheese, but nothing too smelly.

De Chatenoy, Jean-Jacques Teiller, Vincent Delaporte, Didier Dagueneau, Vacheron, Pascal et Nicolas Reverdy, Henry Pellé, Vincent Pinard, Jean-Max Roger, Cotat, Annick Tinel, Henri Bourgeois, Silice de Quincy

For the whites, try
🔵 **Bordeaux** p.24, **Burgundy** p.38, **New Zealand** p.168, **Australia** p.156, **South Africa** p.174, **Chablis** p.42, **Soave** p.115

⚫ **Sauvignon** p.210, **Verdejo** p.215, **Pinot Blanc** p.204, **Pinto Grigio** p.205, **Vermentino** p.217

🔴 **Shellfish** p.257, **Fish** p.252, **Goats Cheese** p.293, **Asian Food** p.281

For the reds, try
🔵 **Beaujolais** p.60, **Loire Valley** p.72, **Burgundy** p.38

⚫ **Gamay** p.229, **Cabernet Franc** p.223

🔴 **Fish** p.252, **Chicken** p.265

Sancerre, Pouilly-Fumé, Menetou-Salon, Reuilly, Quincy

The two most famous names in the whole of the Loire, Sancerre and Pouilly-Fumé, head up the last quintet of areas. All the white is made from Sauvignon Blanc, with the much smaller production of red utilising Pinot Noir.

Pouilly-Fumé and Sancerre are the two most widely available of these wines in this country. I urge you, though, to look at the wines from the lesser-known areas, in particular Menetou-Salon, whose vineyards lie to the west of Sancerre. Many producers own land in both areas and make wine of similar quality, yet the wines of Menetou are always cheaper. Further still to the west, the much smaller regions of Quincy and Reuilly are well worth searching out.

A small amount of red is made from the Pinot Noir grape, the most commonly seen being Sancerre. In good years these reds offer a reasonably cheap alternative to red Burgundy, but watch out, as too often they can taste thin and diluted. Some of these red grapes are also turned into rosé that is usually of high quality, but not cheap: my advice is to stick to the pink wines from Anjou.

The **fresh**, clean **acidity** and flinty flavours of the whites fire up the palate, so serve them as an aperitif to get the juices flowing. These wines love anything in a shell – mussels, oysters, that kind of thing. If you want to have actual fish instead of shellfish, it's best to stick to the simple dishes.

The French have been swigging these wines for years with goat cheese and I believe it is a wonderful pairing.

Be reassured that fusion cooking has not yet arrived in the Loire Valley. However, don't let this put you off using the richer versions of these wines to stand up to food with Thai flavourings like lemongrass or lime leaves. If the chilli count is too high, though, I'm afraid nothing can help.

The reds of this region are best off being lightly chilled and matched with some fish or a roast chicken salad, but anything heavier and they will be overwhelmed.

MADIRAN

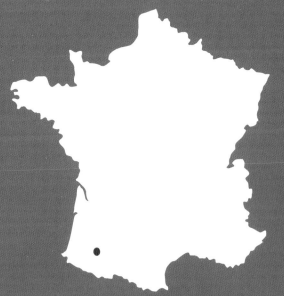
For the thirsty red wine drinker who likes big burly numbers on a budget, Madiran is an area to search for. The vineyards are north of Pau in south-west France, and the wines have a fearsome reputation for being tannic and downright difficult in their youth. The top examples do indeed need an extended stay in the cellar, but many of the cheaper wines are now delicious after two or three years.

The local grape that is responsible for Madiran's powerhouse style is Tannat. The best versions have dark, black fruits and are full of leathery, herbal flavours – they should be forgotten about in the cellar for at least seven years and they will happily last twenty. What is more, they can often be had for the price of cheap Bordeaux. The lighter examples are softened by the addition of Cabernet Franc and are characterised by more red fruits. The leading exponent of the region's wine is Alain Brumont. His top **cuvées** of Château Montus, if tasted young, are an exercise in masochism: ten years down the line they are a revelation.

These are rustic wines in the good sense of the word, so look to match them with good, hearty peasant food. There is not much that they can't handle but don't drink them with delicate meat dishes, as they'll jump all over the flavours of the food. Try rich beef stew with herb dumplings, roasted pork with sage and venison flavoured with juniper.

Borie de Maurel,
Gourgazaud

Try

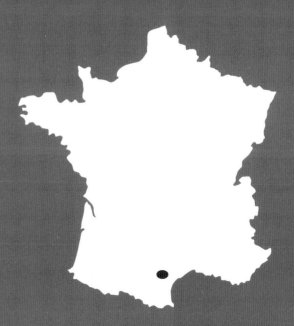 **Corbières** p.68, **Languedoc and Roussillon** p.70, **Southern Rhône** p.90, **Spain** p.142, **Sicily and Sardinia**, p.128

🍇 **Carignan** p.226, **Grenache** p.230, **Syrah/Shiraz** p.243

🍴 **Barbecued Meat** p.262, **Chicken** p.265, **Pork** p.273, **Lamb** p.270, **Beef** p.263, **Stews** p.275

These vines are situated north of Corbières in southern France. As with their neighbour and the wines of Roussillon further to the south, quality varies hugely. The best are big meaty wines with a decent slug of Syrah and Mourvèdre in the blend; the worst are diluted overproduced Carignan numbers.

A recently created superior **cru** of Minervois La Livinière indicates an effort to produce more serious wines. Rely on the individual producer as your guarantee, though.

As regards food, treat these wines as you would a Côtes du Rhône. The light wines want nothing more serious than some barbecued chicken or pork. The top producers make an altogether different beast, which will happily deal with any type of strongly flavoured stew or roasted red meat.

MINERVOIS

Gerard Bertrand, De Jau,
Des Chênes

Try

This is the most widely seen of the various Muscat *appellations* in the Languedoc and Roussillon region, and its vineyards are all contained within the Roussillon area.

There are a number of other similar appellations, such as Lunel (Languedoc) and St-Jean de Minervois. These white wines are all *vins doux naturels*, so **fortified**. They have floral, orange blossom flavours and the best are characterised by tones of marmalade. I do find many to be one-dimensional, though, and they can become tiresome after more than one small glass.

The alcohol levels of Muscat help to complement fruit-based desserts. Pair them with apple or apricot pastries and stewed rhubarb.

The whites are widely varied, so I won't recommend anywhere related.

As far as the reds are concerned, try

Bandol p.20, **Corbières** p.68, **Languedoc and Roussillon** p.70, **Minervois** p.81, **Rhône Valley** p.84, **Spain** p.142, **Sicily and Sardinia**, p.128

Grenache p.230, **Mourvèdre** p.236, **Syrah** p.243

Lamb p.270, **Venison** p.269, **Beef** p.263, **Cheddar** p.291, **Goats Cheese** p.293

Provence used to be more famous for its English tourists than for wine, but things are changing and this area is on the up. Gallons of fairly innocuous rosé are still produced but increasingly the spotlight is falling on the serious Rhône-like reds.

Provençal wines appear with three different prefixes: Coteaux d'Aix en-, Cotes de- and Les Baux de-Provence. Additionally, for those who like to get obscure French appellations under their belt there is a wealth of opportunity here. Try the minuscule Palette, of which Château Simone owns most, or Cassis (confusingly nothing to do with the blackcurrant liqueur) for peculiar whites. The Coteaux Varios is also turning out some very interesting wines. Provence is generally an innovative area and many estates experiment with grape varieties that do not conform to the local *appellation* laws. These wines (often some of the best) appear under various *vins de pays* guises.

Drink Provençal wines with well-flavoured meaty dishes – roast lamb with lots of garlic and rosemary, venison stew with juniper, steak and kidney and shepherd's pie. If you feel the yearning for cheese, look for real Cheddar and hard goat.

Let me get this off my chest now: I love the wines from this region and insist you try them. No excuses. Make it your mission this week to seek out a good bottle and drink it. The reason for this infatuation is that the region makes great wine at all prices. Most of all, though, the wines are interesting; commercial winemaking is balanced by a real sense of identity.

1 Côte Rôtie
2 Condrieu
3 Hermitage
4 Crozes-Hermitage
5 St Joseph
6 Cornas
7 Châteauneuf-du-Pape

Rhône

● Avignon

Remember that this is one of France's serious fine wine regions, on a par with Bordeaux and Burgundy. While prices for some of the really top stuff have started to rise, Rhône wines remain considerably cheaper than Burgundy or Bordeaux. Additionally, the quality of wine making across the board is better.

So, what's the catch? Well, this is not generally a region for the faint-hearted, as the earthy, almost rustic flavours of the reds can take some getting used to. These wines stand in complete contrast to the perfumed elegance of Burgundy and the cultured power of Bordeaux. The top-end wines are burly powerhouses, more a slap in the face than a gentle caress. Nearly all the wine produced here is red and the whites that are made are not often seen in this country. The whites are worth seeking out because their quality is high; in fact, if they only made a decent amount of great sweet wine, I'd probably go and live in the Rhône area.

Stretching along the Rhône river, this region starts to the south of Lyon and finishes at the coast near Marseilles. It is generally divided into two, referred to as the Northern and Southern Rhône. The Northern Rhône accounts for only about 5 per cent of total production, yet this small percentage encompasses most of the region's finest wine names, such as Hermitage and Côte Rôtie. The red grape Syrah is king of the north, producing big, gutsy wines that are full of fruits and spices.

The Southern Rhône's big claim to fame is Châteauneuf-du-Pape which, rather confusingly, is an area and not one estate. Its name derives from the fourteenth century, when the popes lived in a palace near Avignon at the time of the schism with Rome. Up to thirteen different grapes can be used in this *appellation*; this naturally leads to a plethora of different styles.

The bulk of production in the south, however, is made up from the ubiquitous Côtes du Rhône. This is an *appellation* that produces some of the world's most stunning-value wines, but it also makes its fair share of plonk that most self-respecting pieces of beef would be unhappy to find themselves marinated in.

NORTHERN RHÔNE

Guigal, René Rostaing, Daubrée, St-Cosme, Gallet, Clusel-Roche, Jasmin

Côte Rôtie

Whoever first decided to plant vines here was either mad or inspired, or, more likely, a bit of both. The stony, steep-sided valley makes it very difficult and expensive to manage the vines, while a wind known as the *mistral* constantly threatens damage. Despite these problems, the heady, individualistic wines of this area are a joy to consume.

One of the world's most sought-after and expensive wines comes from this region – expect to pay £100 plus for any one of Etienne Guigal's single vineyard offerings, and double that if you want one that you can actually drink within ten years. Although these prices are silly, what they have done is to raise the profile of the region sufficiently to halt its decline and encourage neighbouring vineyard owners to make the best product possible.

These wines are the most fragrant of the Northern Rhône. The best have a floral, herbal character that indicates that they are actually more delicate than they appear. The best will age for up to twenty years and take on a sweet, gamy character that is not unlike great red Burgundy.

Côte Rôtie loves all red meats, but keep it simple as these are not blockbuster wines. They are also **complex**, so don't let too many different flavours get in their way.

Try

Burgundy p.38, **all of Northern Rhône** p.86, **Australia** p.156, **Tuscany,** p.120

Syrah p.243, **Pinot Noir** p.238, **Sangiovese** p.242

Beef p.263, **Lamb** p.270

Clusel-Roche, François Villard, Georges Vernay, Pierre Gaillard, André Perret, Yves Cuilleron, Breze

Condrieu and Château Grillet

The recent interest in Viognier worldwide has sparked a resurgence in Condrieu. Thirty years ago, wines from this area were rarely seen in this country and the area itself, as a wine-growing region, was in danger of slowly dying. The wines are expensive, as Viognier is a tricky grape to grow and, as with Côte Rôtie, the best sites are difficult to manage. At best, Condrieu has pungent aromas of peaches, apricots and an oily rich texture; it is hedonistic, instantly approachable and 'in-your-face'.

I love a glass of good Condrieu as an aperitif but find that their flashy, slightly one-dimensional flavours tire a bit when drunk right the way through a meal. Don't fall into the trap of thinking that just because these wines are expensive they will benefit from ageing. The Viognier grape is all about showy primary flavours, which are best enjoyed two to three years after the wine is bottled.

Château Grillet is a unique appellation in that it is owned by a single producer and measures just less than ten acres. If you read old wine books it is always talked about as one of the world's great white wines. While this might once have been the case, it has become overpriced and overrated.

The richer versions go well with creamy fish dishes and can also stand up to simple chicken dishes. I am not usually one to dictate a perfect match because so much food and wine matching comes down to personal opinion. On this occasion, though, I'll stick my head on the block – I have always found good, rich Viognier to be an excellent match for anything with tarragon in it. This is useful because the strong aniseed flavours of tarragon don't work with many white wines.

Try
Alsace p.16, **Austria** p.96, **Jurançon** p.69

Gewürztraminer p.198, **Viognier** p.218, **Albariño** p.190, **Muscat** p.202

Cream Sauces p.284, **Chicken** p.265, **Fish** p.252

Pierre Gonon, Mortier, Pierre Gaillard, Bernard Gripa, Jean-Louis Grippat, Jean-Louis Chave, Chèze, Michel Desestret

For white wines, try
Rhône Valley p.84
Viognier p.218
Salads p.288, **Fish** p.252

St Joseph

At its best, St Joseph offers the chance to sample the delights of Rhône at a very affordable price. The vineyards hug the west side of the river and there is a large area under vine. The reds offer good honest fruit, the key grape being Syrah, but they never have the finesse or complexity of the wines to the north, or the power of Hermitage over the river to the east. They are approachable when young, with only the best benefiting from more than three years in the bottle.

For red wines, try

Australia p.156, **California** p.180, **Rhône Valley** p.84, **Minervois** p.81, **Bandol** p.20, **Languedoc and Roussillon** p.70, **Provence** p.83, **Corbières** p.68, **Italy** p.104, **Spain** p.142

Grenache p.230, **Mourvèdre** p.236, **Syrah** p.243, **Barbera** p.222

Beef p.263, **Lamb** p.270, **Pork** p.273

Paul Jaboulet Aîné, Jean-Louis Chave, Çhapoutier, Guigal, Henri Sorrel, Jean-Louis Grippat

From white Hermitage, try

All Rhône whites p.84

Sémillon p.212, **Chardonnay** p.192

Salmon p.254, **Mackerel** p.255, **Chicken** p.265, **Quail** p.267

Moving from the reds, try

California p.180, **Australia** p.156, **Bandol** p.20, **Languedoc and Roussillon** p.70, **Corbières** p.68, **Italy** p.104, **Spain** p.142

Zinfandel p.247, **Syrah** p.243

Lamb p.270, **Beef** p.263, **Game** p.267

As the regions are so close, many producers in Hermitage have vineyard holdings in St Joseph, and these wines are worth seeking out. Do beware, though: the region has expanded hugely in recent years, and many of the vineyards are planted on the valley floor and not on its granite sides. Wines produced here are no more interesting, but considerably more expensive, than the *vin de pays* Syrah made further to the south. The whites, made from Marsanne and Roussanne, are a junior version of white Hermitage, but the same problems occur. This really is an area from which to pick only the best producers.

The top age-worthy wines should be served with simply roasted red meats. The simpler wines are good with stews and barbecues in the summer.

Hermitage

Hermitage is the most famous, long-lived and expensive appellation in the Northern Rhône and some of my greatest wine moments have been provided by these wonderful vineyards. They make monstrous wines that are the benchmark by which all other wines made from Syrah are measured: Australia's greatest Syrah (or Shiraz, as they call it) is called Grange Hermitage in homage to this area.

These wines are packed with herbs and black fruits; while Côte Rôtie has finesse and fragrance, great Hermitage has a big, meaty, peppery **structure** that is unique. A word of warning here: although the appellation is small, there is still room for unscrupulous producers and good cheap Hermitage does not exist – £10 would be much better spent on a really top bottle of Crozes-Hermitage or St Joseph.

The white wines of this area are rarely seen, which is a shame because they are generally of very high quality and a good alternative to Chardonnay if you like rich wine. Made from Marsanne and Roussanne, they are **ripe** and peachy wines and are packed full of flavour. Unlike Condrieu, they do age, taking on a nutty, oily character after ten or so years. I find that these wines are best drunk when fairly young or quite old. Many seem to have a bit of a mid-life crisis, becoming very closed and seemingly over the hill – be patient, as they come good in the end. If you have enjoyed a red Hermitage the chances are the same producer will also make a good white, so seek it out.

White Hermitage suits rich, oily fish, such as salmon and mackerel. Due to its strong flavours, it will overpower more delicate fish.

Older stuff easily has the power to deal with roast chicken and light game like quail.

When young, good red Hermitage has a rustic feel to it and will stand up to most foods; rich winter stews etc. As it gets older and more **complex**, keep the food simple: roast lamb or beef is good but not with too many flavourings such as garlic. If you are lucky enough ever to drink the really old stuff then have it with game, as the wine takes on a Burgundian feel.

Crozes-Hermitage

Chosen carefully, Crozes-Hermitage can offer you a junior version of Hermitage. Unfortunately, though, this area is vast compared with Hermitage and there is also a huge range in terms of quality. Surrounding its more famous big brother on the eastern side of the Rhône river, the best producers in Crozes-Hermitage make great spicy Syrahs that can offer you a taste of Hermitage for a fraction of the price (nor do you have to wait so long). They also make a number of good fruity wines that are great for everyday drinking, but unfortunately the region is awash with insipid, diluted wines made by people who know their wine will sell because of the name on the bottle. Many of these large, **co-operative**-produced wines find their way to the supermarkets shelves, so be careful.

I find the whites from here are generally better in quality than the reds. I suspect this is because they are fairly unusual and so need to be sold on the quality of the wine alone. Although made from the same grapes as Hermitage, they are lighter in style and have less pronounced flavours: they should be drunk young. Look for the white wine of any of the red producers you have enjoyed.

White Crozes-Hermitage is a good aperitif wine. Try it also with simple, lightly grilled fish, shellfish and summer salads.

Treat the top red Crozes like Hermitage. The lesser, more fruit-driven wines are good on their own and can be drunk with a range of meats and chicken and are good barbecue wines.

Entrefaux, Cave des Clairmonts, Colombier, Alain Graillot, Paul Jaboulet Aîné, Albert Belle, Combier

For white wines, try
- Rhône Valley p.84
- Viognier p.218
- Salads p.288, **Fish** p.252

For red wines, try
- Australia p.156, **California** p.180, **Rhône Valley** p.84, **Minervois** p.81, **Bandol** p.20, **Languedoc and Roussillon** p.70, **Provence** p.83, **Corbières** p.68, **Italy** p.104, **Spain** 142
- Grenache p.230, **Syrah** p.243, **Mourvèdre** p.236, **Barbera** p.222
- Beef p.263, **Lamb** p.270, **Pork** p.273

Jean-Lionnet (Domaine
Rocherpertuis), Jean-Luc
Colombo, Auguste Clape,
Voge, Tardieu-Laurent,
Tunnel, Allemand

Try

- Bandol p.20, **Cahors** p.62, **Madiran** p.80, **Northern Rhône** p.86, **California** p.180, **Australia** p.156, **South Africa** p.174
- Zinfandel p.247, **Malbec** p.232
- Beef p.263, **Lamb** p.270, **Stews** p.275

Cornas

Cornas has a reputation even more fearsome than Hermitage for producing young wines from Syrah grapes which are big and tannic. These wines are a true expression of what the French call **terroir** – the notion that location is the major influence on a wine's taste, rather than the person producing it.

These wines are beasts. A young wine from a great vintage has a huge, earthy aroma of black fruits, tar and leather. They need four years in the cellar to pull together the slightly disjointed, youthful flavours and soften the often fearsome **tannins**. If this all sounds somewhat offputting, it shouldn't. These wines are full of character and the complete anthithesis of bulk production wines. If you crave big, strapping wines that are packed with flavour you are in the right place; if it's elegance you're after, move on.

Avoid delicate food flavours here, as you won't taste them once you've drunk the wine. You need big flavours – heavily stewed and flavoured red meats are good.

SOUTHERN RHÔNE

Beaucastel, La Nerthe,
Vieux Télégraphe, Rayas,
Marcoux, Tardieu-Laurent,
Vieille Julienne, Le Vieux
Donjon, Bosquet des
Papes, Les Cailloux, Clos
des Papes, La Janasse,
Pierre Usseglio, Pegaü

Châteauneuf-du-Pape

Châteauneuf-du-Pape is a large area encompassing over 8000 acres (Hermitage in the north has a mere 300), situated to the north of Avignon. Thirteen grape varieties are permitted in the blend, a number of which are white, but Grenache, Cinsault, Syrah and Mourvèdre usually dominate.

The good news first: I can't think of a region that has such a burgeoning collection of fine wine producers. Every year I taste wines from here that are better than previous efforts and a new generation of young winemakers are really upping the stakes, either rejuvenating under-performing estates or starting afresh. While lavish praise has been poured on these new-wave offerings, prices for many remain ridiculously low.

The bad news? There are some indescribably poor, overpriced wines made in this region. A poor £4 bottle of wine annoys me, but one for a tenner really gets my goat. It is the equivalent of buying a second-hand Mercedes but finding when you get it home that the engine has been replaced by a Skoda. As ever with French wine, avoid stuff from **co-operatives** and look for the word **domaine** on the label.

As you can imagine, with thirteen different ingredients all going into the pot, added in varying quantities by various producers, it is hard to generalise about the style of wine from Châteauneuf. Additionally, the new breed of winemakers are utilising much higher proportions of new **oak** than their forebears.

Those which are dominated by Grenache are lighter in colour and have sweet, plummy flavours; they also tend to drink the youngest. Add a bit more Mourvèdre and you get an earthy, wild, gamy wine with higher **tannins** that needs a few years in the cellar. Generally, though, the wines are not as full-bodied or tannic as their northern counterparts. The best will last fifteen years but can also be drunk young.

White Châteauneuf makes up a tiny proportion of total production but is well worth sniffing out. Only quality-conscious producers make it, as it's a labour of love to sell. The light, crisp versions are lovely wines to drink young. The top producers make an altogether different beast, however, that is dominated by the Roussanne grape. They are richly textured, age-worthy whites and, what's more, they are good value.

La Mordorée (Lirac), Maby (Lirac), Pesquier (Gigondas), Santa-Duc (Gigondas), Font Sane (Gigondas), St-Cosme (Gigondas), Château Trignon (Gigondas), Brusset (Gigondas), Château des Tours (Vacqueyras), La Monadière (Vacqueyras)

Gigondas, Vacqueyras and Lirac

These are three appellations well worth making the effort to find, as they are all superb value. They utilise the same mix of grapes as Châteauneuf but need to be drunk sooner. The majority of wines are red.

Gigondas and Vacqueyras lie to the east of their big brother and have been promoted from the ranks of Côtes du Rhône-Villages. Vacqueyras is generally the chunkier of the two, but much varies between producers. Many of the top wines can quite happily sit alongside and in many cases even overshadow Châteauneuf.

Lirac lies to the west of Châteauneuf over the Rhône river. Traditionally lots of rosé was made here. Thankfully, many producers are now starting to put their grapes to better use, making good-value fruity reds and whites. Generally speaking, the wines are designed for immediate consumption, not having the stuffing of Gigondas and Vacqueyras.

Tavel Rosé

I am not a big fan of rosé at the best of times and these wines are certainly not going to be the ones to convert me. I find them too high in alcohol and their **acidity** has usually been corrected, giving the wines an artificial taste. To me they miss the point of what rosé is about, namely to give you a refreshing slurp on a hot summer day.

Perrin, Rabasse-Charavin, Vieille Julienne, Fonsalette, Ferrand, Clos Val Seille, St-Anne, Jean Lionnet, Tardieu-Laurent, St-Cosme, Trapadais, La Soumade, Brusset, Hautes Cances, Grands Devers, Richaud, Paul Jaboulet Aîné

Côtes du Rhône and Côtes du Rhône-Villages

Côtes du Rhône is a vast appellation that covers the whole of the Rhône Valley, north and south, but the vast majority of its wines come from the south. The same key grapes that comprise Châteauneuf make up the blend, although the high-yielding, easy-to-grow Grenache plays an even stronger role.

It is impossible to generalise about these wines. The best junior ones taste like Châteauneuf. The worst are some of the poorest wines made in France; unfortunately, these confected abominations are the most widely available. The French appellation system has many merits but, by allowing producers to turn out such filth, it often bemuses the consumer and undermines itself.

'*Villages*' on the label indicates that the wine must come from one of sixteen *villages* in the Southern Rhône, which are deemed to produce higher-quality wine. The name of this *village* will usually appear on the label and there are some great buys here for the bargain-conscious. The best known are Cairanne, Rasteau and Sablet. Producers in the first two *villages* have really started to push the envelope in the last few years with some seriously gutsy reds. I don't think it will be too long before they are promoted to AC status in their own right.

Durban, Paul Jaboulet Aîné

Muscat de Beaumes-de-Venise

These vineyards border both Gigondas and Vacqueyras and are among the sixteen Côtes du Rhône villages. Peculiarly for such a small area, their sweet wines have become very popular in the UK. Muscat is strange in that it actually tastes like crushed grapes. It also has a floral, citrus nature that makes it very refreshing. Made by a method known as **vin doux naturel**, the wines are slightly **fortified**, but they should always be **fresh** and fragrant as they have neither the weight nor the complexity of sweeties from Bordeaux.

These are refreshing, zippy wines that don't like heavy desserts. Something light like a fruit tart is the best match.

Try other sweet Muscat from Southern France and Muscat de Rivesaltes p.82

Fruit Puddings p.296

La Vieille Ferme, Pesquié, Canorgue, Grangeneuve

Côtes du Ventoux, Côtes du Lubéron and Coteaux du Tricastin

At their best, these three regions make lighter versions of Côtes du Rhône. At their worst they suffer the same problems. Stylistically, the wines from Tricastin tend to have a bit more oomph; being the most northerly of the three, it still has one eye on the Syrah-dominated wines of the Northern Rhône. Again, look out for the good producers: the Perrin family who make Châteauneuf from Beaucastel have an excellent property in the Ventoux called La Vieille Ferme.

For whites try

Rhône Valley p.84, **Alsace** p.16

Viognier p.218, **Marsanne** p.201, **Roussanne** p.208

Fish p.252, **Chicken** p.265, **Veal** p.276, **Soft Cheese** p.292

For reds try

Rhône Valley p.84, **Minervois** p.81, **Languedoc and Roussillon** p.70, **Provence** p.83, **Bandol** p.20, **Cahors** p.62, **Corbières** p.68, **Priorat** p.147, **Sicily and Sardinia** p.128

Grenache p.230, **Syrah/Shiraz** p.243, **Mourvèdre** p.236

Stews p.275, **Liver** p.271, **Soft Cheese** p.292

SOUTHERN RHÔNE WINES AND FOOD

Lighter whites such as Côtes du Rhône need nothing more than delicate fish and salads with plenty of mixed herbs. Rich Châteauneuf will do a fine job with oily fish, chicken and veal, and creamy cheese is also a favourite. Only the best will age, but if you are lucky enough to have any old wines, dig up something special like partridge, goose and even foie gras, or anything containing truffles.

Looking at the reds, the lighter Grenache-based wines are deceptively high in alcohol and need stronger food than the colour of the wine would suggest. Try calf's liver, stew, ratatouille and other good, wholesome rustic food or even creamy cheeses. The deeper-coloured wines contain a higher proportion of Syrah or Mourvèdre, and need things like oxtail, lamb shanks, wild boar and harder cheeses. The best wines have strong, powerful flavours so don't be shy about adding herbs and spices into these dishes.

AUSTRIA

The vineyards of Austria are nearly all in its eastern half. At present the reds are good without being excellent: the finest come from blends utilising Cabernet Sauvignon, Merlot and Pinot Noir (known locally as Blauburgunder). Their quality seems to increase markedly every year, but that said, they are always going to be very difficult to sell in this country.

The whites, on the other hand, have what marketing teams love to bang on about and that's a 'unique selling point'. Grüner Veltliner is a delicious, spicy variety that is often compared with Gewürztraminer from Alsace. It has some of the same qualities, but is altogether better for **acidity** and **structure**. The best are rich and oily, and can take on a fiery, peppery taste. A few years' bottle age mellows them, as they become distinctly Burgundian in feel. The finest vineyards for dry whites are in the Wachau region.

The Rieslings lean towards Alsace rather than Germany, but tend to have more intense mineral flavours. Sauvignon Blanc and Chardonnay also play a role. If you like hugely concentrated sweet wine, Austria, and especially Burgenland, is the kind of place you might like to contemplate for retirement. Not only is the quality stunning, but they are far cheaper than the equivalent wines from Germany.

Like Alsatian wines, Austrian whites are a joy to match with food. They do tend to be heavier, though, so I am less likely to serve them as an aperitif. If you are thinking of fish, go for the oily, strong-tasting ones like mackerel, salmon, tuna or swordfish. The wines will cope with any kind of sauce you care to serve with them.

These wines come into their own when dealing with light meat and game dishes, as they have just the right **balance** of weight and **acidity**: roast chicken, veal, rabbit and partridge are good matches. Again, don't be shy with the herbs and flavours, some tarragon with chicken, mushrooms with veal or a few leaves of sage in some partridge will be no problem for these wines. Moving away from the traditional, Riesling's marriage with all things spicy and far eastern is well documented. The inherent spice of Veltliner is, if anything, even better.

ENGLAND & WALES

The wine business in this country deserves your support. There is something truly British in the fact that there are over 350 wineries fighting nature every year and trying to ripen grapes in our cold northerly climate – no other nation would be eccentric or bloody-minded enough. Most of the sites are concentrated in the warmer south, and while trying to make red wine is really a step too far in my view, the whites can be excellent. They utilise a collection of strange, Germanic-sounding grape varieties and stylistically they most resemble the crisp fresh whites from the Loire in France.

Where we can compete on an international level is with sparkling wine. The climate here is not dissimilar to Champagne and the south of England has many patches of the same chalky soil. Production in this country is in its infancy, as large amounts of investment are required. However, the quality-to-price ratio is high; when you need a cheaper bottle of fizz, buy British. Denbies, Chapel Down and Three Choirs are the most **commercial**, being widely distributed and of a high standard. Next time you have a wine bore round who won't drink anything but Champagne, track down some fizz from Nyetimber and see if they notice the difference.

The whites make good, crisp, palate-wakening aperitifs. These wines are extremely light, so I wouldn't serve anything more adventurous than salads and light fish dishes with them. Shellfish would be perfect.

GERMANY

German wine is a series of contradictions. On one side you have a stunning array of high-quality wines. Ranging from bone-dry to intensely sweet, there should be something for everyone. They are also very good value for money and, with an average alcohol content of around 9 per cent, you can drink more. The Riesling grape has been the darling of the wine press for many years now and wine merchants are forever extolling the joys of German wine. An advertising agency launching these wines on the market for the first time would imagine it to be the easiest job ever secured.

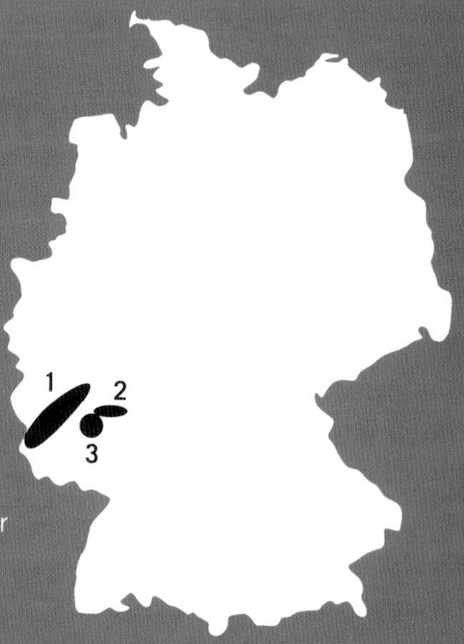

1 Mosel-Saar-Ruwer
2 Rheingau
3 Nahe

Things are rarely as they should seem within the wine world, though, and the flip side to German wine is that there are just as many negatives as positives. Quality is high now but this has not always been the case. The desire to make sweet wine every year led to a disastrous programme in the seventies and eighties of pulling up Riesling and replacing it with easy-to-grow, early-ripening varieties that were inferior in quality.

What can I do to make you change your mind about German wine? I have been known to force-feed it to my friends until they admit to liking it, but this is clearly not possible with a reading audience. You should make it a mission to track down a reputable bottle of German Riesling, clear your head of prejudices and enjoy it. Personally I believe Germany, when you take into consideration cost, makes the greatest white wines on the planet. Controversial? I hope it will cause you to stray from your lonely, Riesling-free world.

Riesling is the top dog in Germany, producing all the quality wines, with Müller-Thurgau, Gewürztraminer and Sylvaner among the supporting cast of white varieties. Some decent wines are made from these lesser grapes, but Germany is really all about the glories of Riesling, so I will be concentrating on the regions where this is the major variety. Red is also produced; avoid it.

The bit part players are generally the ones that turn out the big brand dross we associate with Germany, and poor old Riesling has been tarred with the same brush. I cannot emphasise enough the ridiculous value German wine has to offer between the £6 and £10 mark. Delicious when young, the wines mature wondrously as Riesling is one of the longest-ageing white grapes. Floral and delicate in their infancy, the best will easily outrun any Chardonnay, becoming honeyed, **complex** and often smelling of petrol. The wines are all about poise and balance. Your tongue treads a tightrope between sugar on one side and acid on the other, and there is never any influence of **oak** barrels to get in the way of the bright, clear flavours.

Don't be put off by the flowery Gothic labels. Germans know a thing or two about making good wine but designing labels is not their forte. Here are the things to look out for:

Tafelwein
The bottom rung of the quality ladder, avoid.

Landwein
A rarely used grading equivalent to France's *vin de pays*.

Qualitätswein bestimmter Anbaugebiete (Qba)
This is usually shortened to Qualitätswein on the label. Decent producers make good wine at this level but most of the sugary filth masquerading as German wine also qualifies for this quality grading, which really makes a mockery of the system.

Qualitatswein mit Prädikat (Qmp)
German wine proper begins at this level. There are a number of different levels of classification within this category which will appear on the label. Get to grips with these terms and you will have a greater understanding of the wines. The gradings are measured in levels of sweetness, the driest being first:
Kabinett
Spätlese
Auslese
Beerenauslese
Trockenbeerenauslese

Eiswein
Ultra-rare and expensive, these are sweet wines made from grapes that have been harvested while frozen, to concentrate the flavours.

Trocken or Halbtrocken
This indicates a wine that has been fermented to full or half dryness. Confusingly, you can get a *Trocken Spätlese,* a wine that is usually off dry, which in this case is bone-dry. From the hotter areas like Rheingau these wines can be good. Too often, though, by fermenting out all the sugar the wines become very austere.

Weingut
Very important, this literally means producer. As you may know by now, I'll reiterate this on every occasion possible: regions don't make great wine, producers do.
There may also be an indication of a vineyard site *(Einzellage)*

or *village* name *(Grosslage)*. In what has to be one of the most crass pieces of wine law, the label is forbidden to indicate whether the site mentioned is an *Einzellage* or a *Grosslage*. Thus, unless you are an expert on German vineyard sites the information is likely to be of limited use to you.

Mosel-Saar-Ruwer

Bischöpflicher Priesterseminar, von Schubert, Karthäuserhofberg, von Hövel, Reichsgraf von Kesselstatt, Fritz Haag, Willi Haag, Selbach-Oster, J. J. Prüm, Dr Thanisch, Dr Loosen, Egon Müller

These are three distinct regions. The vineyards of the Mosel are planted along the valley sides of the river bearing its name, which is a tributary of the Rhine river and runs from some eighty miles south-east of Bonn to the French border. The best sites are practically slate walls with vines clinging to them, and the labour that goes into working them is truly staggering. The Saar and the Ruwer are both tributaries of the Mosel and similarly the vines are planted on the valley sides of the corresponding rivers.

This is one of the coolest growing regions in Germany, but by using the steep sides that face south, the growers maximise the amount of heat and sunlight available to the grapes. The wines from this area are characterised by **balance** and elegance, with a distinct mineral character. They don't have in-your-face brash flavours and are more the aristocrat than the wide-boy. Those from the Saar are firmest, being from the coolest area; the Ruwer wines are more delicate and fragrant, and the Mosel wines sit between the two.

Recent vintages have been good in Germany, but these are not wines to buy in poor years, as they will be dilute and unripe. Buy every bottle you ever see from 2001 – it is already being talked of as the vintage of the century. My first tasting of the Mosel-Saar-Ruwer offerings was a semi-religious experience.

Rheingau

Johannishof, Georg Breuer, Langwerth von Simmern, Robert Weil, Vollrads

The Rheingau vineyards are situated along the banks of the Rhine river to the west of Frankfurt. The wines have all the flowery scent of good Riesling but are more powerful; they are fuller than those of the Mosel, due to the more reliable climate where the grapes get riper. Also, the river provides good misty conditions for the growth of **noble rot**, hence the production of great sweet wine.

A large proportion of wine from here is now made in the dry (trocken) style, so be sure to check the label to know what you are getting.

The second greatest sweet wine I have ever drunk comes from this region. Bought from a pub that had gone into liquidation, I didn't really know what I had until it was home: a bottle of 1971 Erbacher Marcobrunn Beerenauslese from Baron Langwerth von Simmern, the name alone sounded serious enough. The original importer had helpfully labelled it as 'light dry table wine', but it had the colour and consistency of engine oil and at thirty years old was still a baby.

Diel, Dönnhoff, Kruger-Rumpf

Nahe

These vineyards sit to the south-west of Rheingau along a tributary of the Rhine that is also called the Nahe. Stylistically they sit somewhere between the perfumed wines of the Mosel-Saar-Ruwer and the more powerful offerings of the Rheingau.

This really is a whistle-stop tour of German wine. Within the above three areas I believe all the greatest wines are made. Like great Burgundy, there are a huge number of nuances caused by climate and geography within each of these areas. I have also left out the wines from places such as Franken, Baden, Rheinhessen and the Pfalz, where Riesling is not dominant.

GERMANY AND FOOD

Where do I start? Germany can offer you a wine that will partner any dish you care to knock up. Basic wines and *Kabinetts* make ridiculously refreshing aperitifs – think of it as German lemonade in the summer (remember that low alcohol). These wines will also help you with all types of salads, shellfish and simply cooked fish.

Get into second gear and uncork some *Spätlese* or light *Auslese* and all things are possible; rich fish, creamy sauces, creamy cheese, quiche, chicken, pork and veal. I have been to Germany and fusion food is not exactly in vogue; however, it should be, because these fruity wines could have been created with it in mind.

Moving directly to fourth gear, try some rich *Auslese* with pâtés, foie gras or fruit tarts. If your wallet's feeling heavy and *Beerenauslese* or *Trockenbeerenauslese* is on the menu, knock up some crème brûlée or tarte tatin – better still, bin dessert and drink them on their own.

Try

Alsace p.16, **Austria** p.96, **North-east Italy** p.112

New World Riesling p.206, **Albariño** p.190

Almost anything apart from red meat.

HUNGARY

Hungary produces large amounts of wine and recently a little more confidence has seen greater emphasis placed on local grapes such as Furmint and Hárslevelű. These wines, both red and white, tend to be full-bodied, spicy and almost rustic, requiring food. You are unlikely to encounter them, but if you do, make sure you try them, as they are far preferable to a Hungarian Chardonnay with a ridiculous name. So why does Hungary warrant an entry in this book? Well, it is home to one of the greatest sweet wines on the planet.

Tokaji

Tokaji utilises a unique production method. Grapes that have been so heavily affected by *botrytis* that they are raisins (known as *Aszú*), are crushed into a paste. These are then added to a dry base wine and a second **fermentation** takes place. The amount of paste added, and hence how sweet the wine will be, is indicated by the number of *puttonyos* on the label. These are the traditional measures used and most wines today contain five or six.

The very rare and indescribably delicious Eszencia is made from the thick juice that runs from the raisined berries. It is so high in sugar content it will barely ferment and the wine is practically indestructible, lasting for decades – buy Michael Broadbent's wonderful book *Vintage Wine* and you can read tasting notes from the 1811 vintage. Usually bottled in the traditional dumpy, fifty-centilitre bottle, these wines have an orange tinge to them and are full of caramel and tropical fruits; some of the more traditional styles even have a nutty character to them. They usually drink well when young but have the substance to age beautifully.

These are very rich, sweet wines, so they will overpower any delicate puddings. Best with anything that has caramelised flavours in it, Tokaji likes crème brûlée, tarte tatin, steamed treacle pudding, banoffee pie and the like. Alternatively, strong blue cheese provides a heavenly contrast.

The Royal Tokaji Company, Oremus, Disnókő

Try

🍷 **Vin Santo** p.123, **Germany** p.98, **Austria** p.96

🍴 **Crème Brûlée** p.295, **Tarte Tatin** p.297, **Steamed Puddings** p.297, **Blue Cheese** p.292

ITALY

Italy vies with France in producing the most wine of any country every year; it usually prevails. As in France, wine is part of the fabric of society and the quality of Italian wine has never been higher. It is the most diverse red wine producing country in the world, and the range of grapes and styles available is breathtaking. When the quality is right these wines offer unparalleled value. Up-to-date production methods and investment have made their style more international, but generally the wines remain individual and authentically Italian. All in all, Italy can be a very exciting place for the drinker.

North East

North West

Central

Southern

There is, however, a darker side to this Utopian assessment of the country's wine. I'll discuss the actual wording on the labels in more detail below, but at best the classification system is a confusing jumble. At worst it is completely irrelevant. The most pertinent example is Chianti. Supposedly at the top rung of the classification ladder, many wines from here are fit only to be turned into vinegar.

The quality of winemaking is far more irregular than it should be. Italians seem to me to have an obsession with **yields** and, unfortunately for the consumer, the bulk of their energies is directed towards making them as high, rather than as low, as possible. High **yields** produce thin wines and when you factor in the naturally high **acidity** of many of the grape varieties used, this can add up to a truly unpleasant experience.

The producer is the only guarantee of quality. This is perhaps more true in Italy than in any other European country, as the wine laws protect the producer far more than the consumer. Don't let this gloomy picture of the country's wine put you off, though; Italy is on a roll and their fine wines have never been so sought-after in the market place. Each new vintage sees the emergence of yet another star and, most important, you can experience a huge range of different flavours without the wallet being hit too hard. Lastly, increased reliance on the export market has not, on the whole, led to a dumbing-down of the wines' styles; they remain distinct and true to their roots.

Italy's wine laws were initially modelled on the French Appellation Contrôlée system. While France's system is far from perfect, Italy's is a series of fudges and ducked issues. For the producers it was often just as important to know the right people as it was to make quality wine. Regulations that are already lax are rarely enforced, allowing growers to overproduce and sell an inferior product with a supposed seal of authority.

The lowest level, Vino da Tavola, does undoubtedly cover the worst wines, but you are unlikely to encounter any unless you are on holiday in Italy. The highest classification contains some of Italy's finest regions. However, there are many wines within the two categories below it which are of equal and often superior quality. As with the French system, the higher you move up the scale, the more stringent production methods and permitted grape varieties become.

The levels of classification are as follows:

Denominazione di Origine Controllata e Garantita (DOCG)

This is the supposed pinnacle of Italian wine production, and it does indeed include Italy's finest regions, such as Barolo and Chianti. However, a quick glance down the list of DOCGs causes a few eyebrows to be raised. What distinguishes the easily quaffable and simple Vernaccia di San Gimignano from other more interesting white regions languishing at DOC level, I am not sure. I suspect the answer is a few long lunches with well-placed officials in the wine bureau.

Denominazione di Origine Controllata (DOC)

These regions will often be of a similar size to a DOCG but are deemed to be of inferior potential. A translation of DOC and DOCG gives you an insight into the stringency of the application of the laws. DOCs have their production methods 'controlled' while DOCGs are 'controlled and guaranteed' – you would thus be correct in assuming that the letter of the law is not always rigorously observed.

Indicazione Geografica Tipica (IGT)

This new category was introduced in 1992, in response to a wave of new Italian wines that were operating outside the system altogether. Using non-native grape varieties such as Cabernet Sauvignon, some estates began to produce wines of very high quality, many of which became sought-after and very expensive (for example, the 'Super-Tuscans'). The problem was that these were only eligible for *Vino da Tavola* status. The problem still remains today: IGT is theoretically of a lower quality level than DOC, yet many of Italy's finest wines fall into this bracket. Additionally, wines that are produced within an obscure DOC will often label themselves by their lower IGT category, simply because they will then be more obviously recognised by the consumer.

Vino da Tavola

The bottom rung of the ladder, little of interest is now made here since the introduction of the IGT.

     If all this sounds a bit complicated and a mess you'd be right. When discussing the areas I will not be indicating which level the wines fall into as this will only serve to confuse. Focus your energies instead on finding the regions you enjoy and remembering the best producers.

I'll start in the relative cool of northern Italy and finish on the sun-drenched islands of the south. Without writing an entirely separate book it would be impossible to cover every region in Italy, so I have concentrated on the most famous and widely available wines in the UK. There are plenty of necessary omissions, for which I apologise.

The north-west of Italy is famed for the uncompromising reds of Piemonte. Barolo, Barbaresco and other powerhouse reds made from the Nebbiolo grape are individual and exciting wines. In addition to these, Piemonte produces Dolcetto (Italy's answer to Beaujolais), rich dark-fruited Barbera, and a host of lesser-known varieties like Freisa, offering fine value.

Milan

Barolo and Barbaresco

Angelo Gaja, Aldo
Conterno, Giacomo
Conterno, Luciano
Sandrone, Paolo Scavino,
Paitin, Bruno Giacosa,
Cigliuti, Robert Voerzio,
Bruno Rocca

These are two of the greatest and most traditional names in Italian wine, but sadly they do not get as much exposure as they deserve. The reason behind this is that, even with modern winemaking techniques, they remain stubbornly uncommercial. In this day and age when we demand immediacy from our wines, Barolo and Barbaresco remain nonconformists. Made from the Nebbiolo grape, they were traditionally tannic and acidic. These traits have been tamed slightly, but many still require an extended stay in the cellar. Thus the wines are rarely seen on shop shelves and those in restaurants are invariably too young.

Full of character and complexities, Barolo and Barbaresco are deceptively light in colour, with aromas of red fruits and spices when young. As they age they take on a gamy, earthy character and are not unlike great red Burgundy but with a tannic bite. However, poor producers and bad vintages turn out thin, acidic wines that are unpleasant, so beware. Of the two, Barolo is the larger area and produces the bolder wines, but each wine's success is all about its producer.

Drunk young, these wines demand food to counter their **tannin** and **acidity**, and there is little they can't take. They are particularly adept at dealing with fatty cuts of meat: pork belly, lamb shanks and that kind of thing. Once aged, Barolos and Barbarescos help you to food heaven. Any game is a treat, especially with some *funghi*, and all sorts of runny smelly cheese. Piemonte is also truffle country in Italy, so, if you are lucky enough to get hold of any, treat them with the respect they deserve and enjoy them with an aged example of either of these wines.

Try

Bandol p.20, **Madiran** p.80, **Northern Rhône** p.86, **Tuscany** p.120

Nebbiolo p.237

Pork p.273, **Lamb** p.270, **Game** p.267, **Mushrooms** p.287, **Runny Cheese** p.292

Barbera d'Alba or d'Asti

Elio Grasso, Braida,
Luciano Sandrone, Bruno
Rocca, Giacomo Ascheri,
La Spinetta, Principiano,
Renato Cigliuti

Barbera is the name of the grape that has attached itself to these two villages. Traditionally these wines have always been in the shadow of the grander offerings from Barolo and Barbaresco. They are deep in colour and full of ripe plums but have considerably less **tannin** than Nebbiolo, so they become approachable after only a couple of years in the bottle.

Try **Spain** p.142, **Tuscany** p.120, **Puglia** p.128

Syrah/Shiraz p.243, **Zinfandel** p.247, **Touriga Nacional** p.246

Stews and Casseroles p.275, **Hard Cheese** p.291

Recently the top producers have begun to branch out, maturing the wines in **oak** barrels, and the best examples are dense wines, full of black fruits and spices. The great Barolo and Barbaresco estates often produce this style of wine, thus offering you very grown-up winemaking at a fraction of its usual price.

Barbera is a good food wine as it has fine **acidity** but is generally low in **tannins**. Try it with all types of hearty red meat stews and casseroles, or drink it with some hard cheese.

Ca'Viola, Braida, Bruno Rocca, Roberto Voerzio, Luciano Sandrone, Giacomo Ascheri

Dolcetto d'Alba, d'Asti, di Diano d'Alba or di Dogliani

Like Barbera, Dolcetto is a grape that may attach its name to any of these regions, but the most commonly seen are Alba and Asti. These are the most forward reds of Piemonte, and they are characterised by fruits like red cherries and are low in **tannin**. The best take on a smoky, almost burnt character that doesn't get on with everyone – I prefer the straightforward quaffing style. As with Barbera, you will find many Barolo and Barbaresco estates turning out excellent Dolcettos.

Try **Valpolicella** p.112, **Chianti** p.121, **Beaujolais** p.60, **Loire Valley** p.72

Dolcetto p.228, **Gamay** p.229, **Cabernet Franc** p.223

Chicken p.265, **Quail** p.267, **Pasta** p.278, **Cured Meats** p.266, **Soft Cheese** p.292

Dolcetto is the Beaujolais of northern Italy and is equally as versatile with food. Think about roast chicken, light game such as quail, tomato-based pasta sauces and cured meats. The freshness of these wines also suits delicate soft cheeses.

La Spinetta, Conterno, Braida

Moscato d'Asti

This region was wise enough to dump the 'spumante' tag some time ago. However, it still struggles to be taken seriously. The wine is derided by wine bores for not being serious, but I say we should ignore them all; leave the wine anoraks to drink **claret** on a hot summer day while you get tucked into a glass of this refreshing, grapey fizz.

The whole point of Moscato is its frivolity. Additionally, it has the advantage of being low in alcohol, so your consumption can be measured in bottles rather than glasses.

Drink Moscato with strawberries or raspberries and a jug of cold single cream.

Try

Demi-sec **Champagne** p.67

Prosecco p.116

Strawberries p.296

Roberto Voerzio (Roero
Arneis), Asso di Fiori
(Langhe), Cigliuti
(Langhe), La Giustiniana
(Gavi), Braida

The Best of the Rest

Whites from Piemonte include Gavi di Gavi, which is produced from the
Cortese grape. Generally well made and fresh, these wines are held in
perplexingly high regard by the Italians. To my mind, they are far more
expensive than their taste warrants. Arneis is a floral, fragrant grape that
reminds me of a more restrained version of Viognier; the best from the
region of Roero are worth seeking out. Top estates have tried their hands
at international varieties like Chardonnay; many of the finest come from
Langhe and, while not cheap, can be superb.

Reds to note are those from the Grignolino grape. They are
lightweight, cherry-fruited numbers, which are usually adequate rather
than exciting. Freisa is another grape similar in style, but it can be more
fulfilling in the right hands. Regions like Langhe, Roero and Monferrato
are home to blends from these indigenous varieties. The region's more
famous producers are also using these DOCs for their exciting
experimental blends.

While the north-west is predominantly about red wine, the east is firmly in the white camp. Lots of red is made, but not much of it finds its way to these shores. There are a host of different wines to come from the region and the good news is that the majority are fiscally within reach of us all. Regional identity is important but much of the white wine relies on grape variety to do the selling; think of Pinot Grigio, Tocai or Chardonnay.

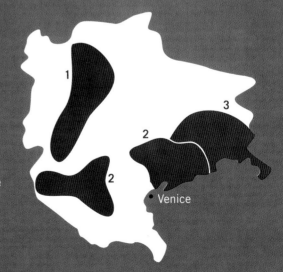

1 Trentino and Alto Adige
2 Veneto
3 Friuli-Venezia Giulia

Venice

Franz Haas, Hofstätter, San Michele, Paolo Cesconi, Ferrari, Enrico Spagnolli, San Leonardo, Colterenzio

Trentino and Alto Adige stretch from the northern end of Lake Garda to within a few miles of the Austrian border. They thus encompass some of Italy's most northerly and coolest vineyards. Grape varieties dominate the labels, so all you need to do is select a good producer and work your way through their range. White varieties include Pinot Grigio, Traminer, Pinot Bianco, Riesling, Grüner Veltliner, Sauvignon Blanc and Chardonnay.

Reds have an international feel to them: Cabernet Sauvignon, Cabernet Franc, Merlot and Pinot Nero (Noir) are used, with Teroldego being my favourite of the local varieties. In general all the wines, white or red, are designed to be drunk young. The cool climate of the region also provides ideal conditions in which to grow grapes suitable for the production of sparkling wine; rarely imported into this country due to their low profile, they can be tremendous value.

Above all, in a country where change is often only grudgingly accepted, this is one of Italy's most dynamic and forward-thinking regions. Many grapes end up in the hands of the **co-operatives** like Colterenzio, which buck another Italian trend and actually make decent wine, and I expect that the quality of wine from here will continue to rise.

For food recommendations and other wines related to this region I suggest that you be guided by the grape variety section beginning on page 186.

The Veneto encompasses all that is good and bad about Italian wine. There is a huge diversity of taste on offer: good cheap fizz from Prosecco, fine whites from Soave, fruity everyday reds from Valpolicella and huge unique monsters from Amarone that will effortlessly top 16% alcohol. The downside is that Italy's wine laws fail completely in regions such as Soave, where the wine authorities offer little protection to the consumer.

Leonildo Pieropan,
Tamellini, Gini, Inama,
Roberto Anselmi

Soave

If any region illustrates the ludicrous situation that exists with the
Italian wine law it is Soave, whose vineyards lie to the west of Venice. It
is to the lawmakers' shame that most of the wine produced under the
Soave label should struggle to make the grade as a *Vino da Tavola*.
Most of it really is that poor, and I can't for the life of me understand
how it has become Italy's most famous white wine. The trouble is that
most of it is produced by **co-operatives** who encourage the growers to
achieve monstrous levels of overproduction of Garganega, its component
grape.

Thankfully, a small, dedicated band of producers keep the flag
flying for 'real' Soave. These wines are ripe, with floral lemon notes and
the best, often from single vineyard sites, take on a nutty, oily character
after a few years in the bottle. While the low-end bilge is one of the
poorest wines produced on the planet, the best stuff has to be some of
the finest-value Italian white wine.

The terms *classico* and *superiore* will appear on the label to
indicate supposedly finer wines. Ignore them: the *classico* sub-region
undoubtedly has the best vineyards but they are just as abused as
standard Soave ones.

Fragrant, powerful, sweet wines made from dried grapes will
appear as Recioto di Soave.

Much Soave is light and innocuous, and will not cope with
anything much stronger than salads, simple fish and grilled vegetables.
Only the best will take on stronger flavours.

Try

🍇 **Loire Sauvignon** p.72, **San Gimignano** p.123

⚫ **Pinot Grigio** p.205, **Pinot Bianco** p.205, **Sauvignon Blanc** p.210, **Vermentino** p.217

🍴 **Salads** p.288, **Fish** p.252, **Antipasti** p.287

Allegrini, Dal Forno,
Cortegiara, Corteforte

Valpolicella (including Amarone and Recioto)

This is the red equivalent of Soave, although its production is not in
quite such a parlous state. The best wines should be Italy's other answer
to Beaujolais (besides Dolcetto); fruity, light reds to be drunk slightly
chilled in the summer. They should have fresh cherry fruits and a
slightly bitter (in the good sense of the word) **finish**.

Valpolicella is made for early consumption, but too many are
thin and overproduced. Try to stick to those from the *classico* region
whose vineyards are on the hillsides.

Two peculiar, ancient styles of Valpolicella are also produced: Recioto della Valpolicella and Amarone della Valpolicella. Both are made from dried red grapes and thus are potentially very sweet. Amarone is fermented to full dryness, to devastating effect. Recioto can be still or slightly sparkling. It is a bit lower in alcohol than Amarone and also sweeter. Both wines, however, are very high in alcohol and have flavours of bitter chocolate and black cherries. Both are uncompromisingly individual wines: Amarone is the one most commonly seen in the UK, and it needs a few years in the cellar and at best will last for twenty-five.

Valpolicella is very versatile, being light and fruity but with reasonable **acidity**. If you want red with fish while on holiday in Italy it is a good bet. It works wonderfully with all those salamis and cured meats that the Italians are masters at making – try it also with any pasta that has a cream sauce, especially Carbonara. Soft light cheeses will also go down a treat with a slug of Valpolicella.

Amarone can be a bit of a beast with food and it is traditionally served at the end of a meal in Italy. I am not one to disagree as it goes best with good hard cheeses; mature Pecorino (not strictly regional, but what the hell) is a favourite but Cheddar will be equally at home. Young Amarone is excellent at dealing with chocolate, which is useful as some wine and chocolate combinations should be avoided like the plague.

For Valpolicella try

Tuscany p.120, **Beaujolais** p.60, **Loire** p.72

Sangiovese p.242, **Dolcetto** p.228, **Gamay** p.229, **Cabernet Franc** p.223

Fish p.252, **Cured Meats** p.266, **Pasta** p.278, **Soft Cheese** p.292

Amarone is similar to super-ripe Californian Zinfandel, but that's about all.

Nino Franco, Ruggeri, Tonon

Prosecco

This is another of Italy's undervalued sparkling wines. The vineyards are to the north of Venice and take their name from the grape grown in them. The wines are bone-dry and refreshing, with those from the superior sub-region of Valdobbiadene being of a generally higher quality and the best having creamy citrus flavours. You will be able to pick up two good bottles of Prosecco for the price of an adequate Champagne, so this is an area worth remembering.

Drink as an aperitif, as they do not have the weight to take on food.

Try

Loire Valley p.72, **Alsace** p.16, **Champagne** p.64

Muscat p.202

FRIULI-VENEZIA GIULIA

Villa Russiz, Sergio and Mauro Drius, Jermann, Mario Schiopetto, Alvaro Pecorari, Le Vigne di Zamó, Giovanni Puiatti, Vie di Romans, Specogna, Lorenzon

This collection of vineyards follows the east of the Veneto and stretches to the border with Slovenia. They are situated in a cool region and subsequently I have a problem with most of the reds. To my taste most seem unripe and this, coupled with the usual overproduction, makes for an unpleasant glass of wine.

White wine drinkers, on the other hand, have a plethora of different flavours to choose from. Even better, this is an easy area to understand, as grape variety usually takes centre stage on the label. Find a good producer and you might have six or seven good wines to try.

Grave del Fruili is the largest area producing wines at all quality levels. To have a greater chance of striking the best wines, try to stick to the three smaller areas next to the Slovenian border of Colli Orientali del Fruili, Collio Goriziano o Collio (usually shortened to simply Collio) and Isonzo. It is here that all the region's top producers are concentrated.

Freshness and purity of fruit, rather than **oak** and richness, is the order of the day. Most will produce the full gamut of grape varieties, from international ones like Pinot Grigio, Chardonnay, Sauvignon Blanc, Pinot Bianco and Riesling, to interesting indigenous ones such as Malvasia and Ribolla Gialla.

For food recommendations and other wines related to this region I suggest that you be guided by the grape variety section beginning on page 186.

Ca dei Frati (Lugana),
Terre in Fiore 'Cantina di
Custoza', Venegazzù

**Bianca di Custoza and Bardolino are on the shores of Lake Garda. The
first utilises the Garganega grape (as used in Soave) and the second
Corvina, as in Valpolicella. Unfortunately, they also borrow the same
production methods, thus turning out large volumes of low quality wine.**

Lugana makes the best of the wines produced on the lake's
shore, somehow managing to turn out interesting white from the
terminally dull Trebbiano grape. To the east of Venice, in places such as
Treviso, some decent reds are produced from a classic Bordeaux blend
of Cabernet Sauvignon, Cabernet Franc and Merlot. Too many sit the
wrong side of austere, though, being bitter and thin.

The small area on the north-west coast of Tuscany has had a profound impact on Italian wine over the last twenty years. Estates such as Sassicaia began to produce wines that used Bordeaux grape varieties like Cabernet Sauvignon rather than the indigenous grape, Sangiovese, that could only be classified as a table wine. The market, though, couldn't get enough of them and they soon became the most expensive wines from Italy, spawning the phrase 'super-Tuscan'.

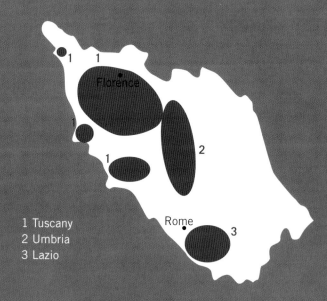

1 Tuscany
2 Umbria
3 Lazio

For lighter styles, try

Valpolicella p.112,
Beaujolais p.60, **Burgundy**
p.38, **Loire** p.72

Sangiovese p.242,
Dolcetto p.228, **Cabernet
Franc** p.223, **Pinot Noir**
p.238

Pasta p.278, **Pizza** p.279,
Cured Meats p.266,
Chicken p.265, **Fish**
p.252, **Soft Cheese** p.292

For full-bodied styles, try

Piemonte p.108, **Puglia**
p.128, **Rioja** p.146,
Ribera del Duero p.145

Sangiovese p.242, **Barbera**
p.222, **Merlot** p.234,
Tempranillo p.245

Pork p.273, **Lamb** p.270,
Beef p.263

Chianti

Chianti is a huge area, on the one hand producing millions of litres of unspeakable wine, yet on the other representing all that is best about Italy. Its predominantly Sangiovese vineyards are enriched (both metaphorically and literally by droves of tourists) by being so close to two of Italy's most spectacular cities, Florence and Siena.

The wicker flagon is now thankfully all but extinct. Unfortunately, the terrible wine that went in them is still very much with us, just bottled in a different guise. These industrial wines pumped out by the local **co-operatives** will continue to make the region's wine laws obsolete to the consumer, unless their quality dramatically improves.

At its best Chianti should offer you two differing drinking pleasures: first, an uncomplicated, medium-bodied, cherry-fruited red that shouldn't cost you much more than a fiver; its second guise is a richer wine, redolent with ripe red fruits and spices. This latter wine is designed for medium-term cellaring and, while being more expensive, it still represents great value in the scheme of things. Like all Italian reds, these wines have good **acidity** but are not overly tannic.

A number of sub-regions in Chianti have vineyards which hog the premium sites: Chianti Classico, Colli Senesi and Rufina are the best. The word 'Riserva' on the label indicates one of the estate's finest offerings that usually requires a few years' bottle age.

The 'super-Tuscan' phenomenon has firmly taken hold in Chianti. Every self-respecting estate makes a wine that might contain Merlot, Cabernet Sauvignon or Chardonnay and be labelled under the IGT Toscana. How to distinguish the wheat from the chaff? It is all down to the producer.

Good, simple Chianti is just that, a wine designed to be drunk without fuss every day, so match it to similar foods. All types of pasta sauces based on tomatoes, pizza, cured meats and roast chicken. The lightest examples can easily spend half an hour in the fridge and accompany some fish. The best wines require simple meat dishes, roast pork with fennel is a classic regional match or try some lamb with rosemary. A few years' bottle age and some game will go down a treat. Cheese-wise, think of soft light Pecorino Fresco for the light wines and the same cheese, but mature, for the serious stuff.

Try

 North-west Italy p.108, **Burgundy** p.38, **Rhône Valley** p.84, **Ribera del Duero** p.145

 Sangiovese p.242, **Tempranillo** p.245

 Fatty and Rich Meats p.271, **Venison** p.269

Try

 North-west Italy p.108, **Rhône Valley** p.84, **Burgundy** p.38

 Sangiovese p.242, **Tempranillo** p.245

 Fatty and Rich Meats p.271, **Venison** p.269

Montalcino

The vineyards that produce Brunello di Montalcino lie within the southern extremes of Chianti and are centred on the picturesque town of Montalcino. Brunello is a local term for the Sangiovese grape of which these wines, unlike Chianti, must contain 100 per cent.

The wines are rich in black fruits, spice and leather, and are more full-bodied than Chianti. Traditionally they require a good few years in the cellar to soften. Modern winemaking techniques have tamed them slightly but many still need five years to get going, while the best will keep for twenty. Brunellos are not cheap, so be sure to buy only the best producers.

A soft, early-drinking style, made from the same vineyard area, is bottled under the name Rosso di Montalcino. Treat Rosso di Montalcino as a Chianti and drink it with tomato-based pastas and simple roast meats. Brunello has more weight, so can cope with most rich meat dishes. As well as the roasts try stew, pot-roast belly of pork with lentils and any other fatty cuts of meat. As the wines develop pair them up with some well-hung game or venison. At the end of a meal hard cheeses are the order of the day.

Montepulciano

The Vino Nobile vineyards of Montepulciano lie to the east of Montalcino and the style of their wine sits neatly between Chianti and Brunello. Sangiovese is again the order of the day, although producers are supposed to use other grapes in the blend. Most wines need a couple of years to be approachable but they will then last ten years.

As the name does not carry the cachet of Brunello, these wines can be much better value, with Rosso di Montepulciano being the more accessible early-drinking version.

The wines of Montepulciano suit similar foods to those of Montalcino and so are best drunk with good tomato pastas and rich roasted or stewed meats.

Isole e Olena, Leonardo, Capezzana, Brolio

Vin Santo

One of Tuscany's most exciting wines is the decadent Vin Santo. This is a heavenly sweet wine, produced by drying Malvasia and Trebbiano grapes before fermenting them. The resulting wine is then matured in barrels and allowed to oxidise slightly, producing a cross between sherry and great sweet wine. Many a good Chianti producer will make Vin Santo; if you ever get to try those from Isole e Olena grab the biggest glass available, take a seat and prepare to be transported to vinous Nirvana.

The Italians traditionally dunk Cantuccini biscuits in their Vin Santo. This is fine for the cheaper versions but sacrilege for the top stuff; instead, try it with tarte tatin or crème brûlée, or bin the food altogether.

For Vin Santo, try

🍷 **Tokaji** p.103, **German or Austrian Beerenauslese/ Trockenbeerenauslese** p.96/98

🍴 **Tarte Tatin** p.297, **Crème Brûlée** p.295

Teruzi e Puthod, Panizzi, Leonardo

San Gimignano

San Gimignano produces the best white wine made from Tuscany's predominant local grape variety, Vernaccia. These wines are **fresh** and floral, but the best producers, such as Teruzzi e Puthod, manage to add nutty, creamy flavours to the wines. I like these wines in a simple refreshing way, but do not think they deserve to be a DOCG. I suspect that the ridiculously pretty town of San Gimignano has done more than anything else to elevate their status.

These wines make worthy aperitifs to liven up the palate for more serious things to follow. Otherwise, I wouldn't get much more adventurous than light salads, grilled vegetables and simple seafood.

Try also

🍷 **Soave** p.113

🍷 **Muscat** p.202, **Viognier** p.218, **Vermentino** p.217

🍴 **Salads** p.288, **Antipasti** p.287, **Shellfish** p.257

This is an area ready to explode with good wine, but the traditional regions do not inspire. Orvieto is one region known internationally for its whites, but a dull grape variety (Trebbiano) and overproduction often result in a tedious product.

Traditional wines from Umbira that excite are those from the Montefalco area and the region's most famous wine, Rubesco, made by the Lungarotti estate south of Perugia. This wine is tannic and steeped in black fruits. It shows Italy at its best, uncompromisingly making unique wine that reflects the land it is produced on.

Lamborghini, Lungarotti, Antinori, Arnaldo Caprai, Falseco, Salviano, Spoletoducale

Try

🍷 **Montalcino** p.122, **Piemonte** p.108, **Rhône Valley** p.84

🍇 **Sangiovese** p.242, **Shiraz/Syrah** p.243, **Zinfandel** p.247

The action happens in this region under the IGT tag. There are some real stunners being made using international grape varieties like Chardonnay, Merlot and Cabernet Sauvignon. A large amount of investment is being poured into the area and I expect the trickle of quality wine soon to turn into a flood. Even the elite of Italian society is attracted to the area: Lamborghini started a winery in 1997. Its top wine is designed for millionaires, but the second wine, Trescone, is amazing and can be had for a song.

For the international varietal use the grape variety section to get some food and wine recommendations. Rubesco and Montefalco are uncompromising wines and like hearty, rustic meat dishes – think of fatty cuts of pork and all types of slow-cooked stew.

Frascati

The vineyards are just to the south of Lazio, and along with Soave, Frascati is probably Italy's most internationally recognised white wine. Similarly, I do not have a clue as to how we have arrived at this point. Even good old-style Frascati made by the likes of Fontana Candida offers little more than a refreshing, zippy glass of white that is useful to wash down some seafood. If it is possible, overproduction is more rife and the standard of winemaking even lower than in Soave. Please discourage the producers of these wines and don't buy from them.

Salvation for the region may be coming. Recently estates have been adding interesting varietals like Viognier to the blend. This style of wines is still in its infancy and not widely available yet, but it may show the way forward.

These wines cannot offer much help to food as they lack body. Stick to using them as a warm-up or with light salad and seafood dishes.

Try

🍷 **San Gimignano** p.123, **Soave** p.113

🍇 **Pinot Bianco** p.205, **Pinot Grigio** p.205

🍽 **Salads** p.288, **Shellfish** p.257

The Best of the Rest

Umani Ronchi, Eduardo Valentini, Di Mato, Norante

The eastern coast of central Italy is the engine room of production for the region and there is much adequate rather than exciting wine made here. Emilia-Romagna's most famous liquid export is Lambrusco, the fizzy red. Personally I would steer clear of this and stick to Sangiovese di Romagna, the one red of the region that can be acceptable. White-wise, I can find little to recommend as Trebbiano is the main grape.

Head south along the coast and you'll enter the Marche. Here the white grape Verdicchio makes some worthy wines that are crisp, refreshing and excellent for washing down the local seafood; it is Italy's answer to Muscadet.

Further south still you get to Abruzzo, where Montepulciano (Sangiovese) and Trebbiano (white) are the main players. The Trebbiano wines are dull with one notable exception, the extraordinary wines of Eduardo Valentini. Don't confuse the reds with the more full-bodied and finer wines from Vino Nobile di Montepulciano. A couple of producers try to think outside the box but most, at their best, will offer good everyday fruity drinking. This is a large area, though, and it also churns out a lake of mediocre, overproduced red.

Molise is the last noteworthy area you reach before entering Puglia – here a couple of estates get a special mention for persevering with the unusual red grape, Aglianico.

PUGLIA

Candido, A Mano,
Tormaresca, Aliante,
Botromagno

If you like Primitivo, look at

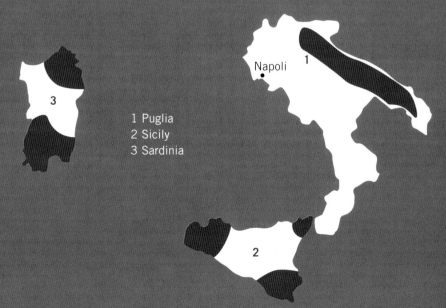 **Tuscany** p.120, **California** p.180

Primitivo p.241, **Zinfandel** p.247, **Sangiovese** p.242

Beef p.263, **Lamb** p.270, **Spices** p.280

For Negroamaro try

North-west Italy p.108, **Cahors** p.62, **Madiran** p.80, **Bandol** p.20

Barbera p.222

This large area encompasses the heel of Italy and another hundred miles of coastline up the main part of the boot. It is a very hot area, so all grapes ripen every year without a problem and consequently a vast amount of wine is made here. Until a few years ago most of this wine was destined for local consumption, but recently the large bulk producers have moved into the area in force.

The exciting stuff is no more expensive than the one-dimensional, but is infinitely more rewarding. Start by exploring the region's native grapes. Primitivo produces spicy, juicy red wine and might be seen on its own as a Puglia IGT or blended in one of the host of small DOCs. Negroamaro produces big, bruising reds that are full of black fruits, leather and chocolate, and can even be Port-like in consistency.

The reds often have a ripe, New World feel to them and, by Italian standards, are low in **acidity** and **tannins**. Avoid the whites as the region is too hot to produce quality white wine.

These are ripe, juicy wines that like to be paired with good, juicy meat dishes. Think of rare steaks and pink lamb. They also have the guts to cope with a range of spices and, being relatively inexpensive, make great barbecue wines. They can, however, lack the **acidity** to deal with really rich sauces and stews, so try to keep it simple.

Napoli

1 Puglia
2 Sicily
3 Sardinia

Montevetrano, Librandi, Colli di Lapio, Cantine del Taburno

For Fiano and Greco, try

 **Viognier** p.222, **Marsanne** p.201, **Roussanne** p.208, **Gewürztraminer** p.198, **Pinot Gris** p.205

After having dealt with most of Italy in a reasonable amount of detail it seems odd to be writing off this vast area in a short paragraph. The heat of the south makes it difficult to produce quality wine and so the best sites tend to be concentrated in the cooler coastal regions. Traditional white wine of interest in this area is Greco di Tilfo, from the east of Napoli in Campania, and also that made from the same grape right down in the south of Calabria – practically on the toes of the boot – Greco di Bianco.

I highlight these wines because they have such a unique flavour; they are fragrant and honeyed. The Fiano grape can also make some interesting floral wines in Campania.

Traditional red regions from Ciro in the south and Taurasi near Napoli can be of interest, but the most exciting wines currently being produced are from previously unknown areas. Estates such as Montevetrano on the coast in Campania are showing the possible potential of the region.

CAMPANIA, BASILICATA AND CALABRIA

The wine industry of both these islands is going through a period of rapid change. Traditionally the islands have always produced vast quantities of wine that was sold off in bulk to the mainland. Now, though, there is a growing interest in making quality wine.

Cantina Satadi, Argiolas, Planeta, Villa Tonino, Mandarossa, Salvatore Murana

For the whites, try

Soave p.113, **San Gimignano** p.123

Albariño p.190, **Vermentino** p.217

Antipasti p.287

For the reds, try

Provence p.83, **Languedoc and Roussillon** p.70, **Minervois** p.81, **Corbières** p.68, **Rhône Valley** p.84

Grenache p.230, **Syrah/Shiraz** p.243, **Carignan** p.226

Lamb p.270, **Pork** p.273, **Sausages** p.274

For the sweet wines, try

Portugal (Madeira) p.138, **Spain (Sweet Sherry)** p.148

Rich Puddings p.295-7

As with the less heralded regions on the mainland, the best way forward was initially deemed to be with international grape varieties like Chardonnay and Cabernet Sauvignon. Excellent estates such as Planeta in Sicily produced profound wines with these grapes that were rightly regarded as some of the best new-wave offerings in Italy. More recently, these international offerings have been tempered with a rediscovery of the island's indigenous grapes. In Sicily watch out for whites made from Grecanico and Inzolia, as well as succulent reds from the Nero d'Avola. Sardinia lags behind somewhat; excessive **yields** are the main culprit.

Excellent producers such as the Cantina Satadi and Argiolas have proved, though, that all the raw materials are present. They utilise white grapes like the lemon-scented Vermentino and Vernaccia. Reds are likely to have a spicy Rhône feel to them, coming from Cannonau (Grenache) and Carignano (Carignan).

These islands used to be famous for sweet wine production. Marsala is the most renowned; similar in style to Madeira, it has now truly fallen from grace and sadly the wine is all but extinct. What is still produced is usually used for culinary purposes. The other more traditional styles are made from the Muscat grape; Moscato di Pantelleria is the best and most decadent, coming from a small island off the south coast of Sicily. Marco de Bartoli, one of the lone flag bearers for Marsala, makes a stunning example. It is like liquidised Christmas pudding with some orange peel thrown in for good measure.

The traditional whites all make good aperitifs and are fine for washing down antipasti. Only top-notch, lemony Vermentino likes anything richer. Serve the reds with hearty fare, such as roast lamb with rosemary, pork and Italian sausages.

Moscato and Marsala taste like Chrismas pudding, so I see no reason not to drink them with that and mince pies.

PORTUGAL

Portuguese wine is famous for two things: first, the outstanding fortified wines of Port and Madeira; second, its rather sickly rosé, which is designed solely for export (the Portuguese quite rightly won't touch the stuff). However, to limit yourself to Port and Madeira would be to miss out on a collection of interesting and ever improving bottles.

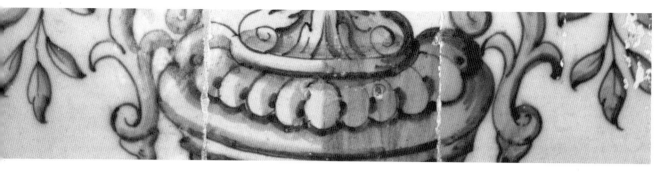

The country has always produced a huge quantity of red and white that was consumed by the thirsty locals, and the methods used to make them were very traditional, resulting in wines that, at best, would have been described as rustic. Modern international palates desire a different type of wine, though, and Portugal's producers have started to respond by embracing the usual band of varietals (Chardonnay, Merlot et al).

Portugal's climate could be perfect for turning out lakes of rootless, bland wine. Hopefully, though, its producers realise that in today's ever more cluttered wine market offering a unique product, rather than conforming to stereotype, is the way forward. Portugal's wines may not yet have a large presence on our shelves, but those made from indigenous grapes are full of character and will satisfy those who like a bargain.

Like most European countries, Portugal has used France's wine regulations as a blueprint and it has four quality levels, starting with the highest:

Denominação de Origem Controlada (DOC)
Indicação de Proveniência Regulamentada (IPR)
Vinho Regional
Vinho de Mesa

Many of the demarcated regions have as yet unproven track records. Additionally the system suffers from all the usual flaws, such as regulations being too lax and producers who just ignore them altogether. Thus, as ever, your purchasing decisions should be made on taste and producer alone.

Over the centuries Portugal has been an invaluable source of wine, in particular during times when we were at war with France. Problems arose, though, as the red wines spoiled during the long and hot crossing from Portugal. Winemakers soon learned that a good slug of brandy in the barrels preserved the wine. These red wines with an extra kick not surprisingly became very popular and the rest, as they say, is history.

Taylor's, Graham's,
Fonseca, Smith
Woodhouse, Niepoort,
Warre, Ramos-Pinto, Gould
Campbell, Quinta do
Noval, Quinta de la Rosa,
Quinta do Crasto, Dow's

Port is essentially a red wine that has been partially fermented and then **fortified**, bringing it up to around 20 per cent alcohol. It is made from a number of grapes, but Touriga Nacional and Tinta Roriz (Tempranillo) are the most important. By stopping the natural **fermentation** halfway through, sugar is preserved in the wine, making it sweeter than normal wine. Port has always been very popular in the UK and many of the leading brands carry the names of their British owners.

Port vineyards are situated in northern Portugal along the Douro Valley. Along with the Mosel Valley in Germany and the Northern Rhône in France, this has to be one of the most difficult and inhospitable areas on the planet to grow grapes. Stories abound of having to blow dynamite holes in which to plant vines in some of the finest areas; there is literally no soil, just hard rock. The amount of work it must have taken to build the terraces that many of the vineyards are planted on is mind-boggling.

The estates that make Port are referred to as houses. Rather like their counterparts in Champagne, these houses will buy many of their grapes from small farms known as *quintas*. Exciting changes are afoot in the region, though, as an increasing number of these *quintas* choose to make wines of their own.

There are many styles of Port, all of which fall into two distinct camps: those that are aged in wood and those that will age in the bottle. The former style is usually ready for consumption on release while the latter will require patience and a cellar.

White Port

Rarely seen in this country, it is made in the same way as other Ports but utilises white grapes. The Portuguese swear by it as an aperitif but I have never been particularly convinced.

Ruby Port

This makes up the bulk of Port production and ranges from the diabolical to the fabulous. It is aged in wood barrels for the shortest amount of time and is designed for consumption on release. The wines tend to be mid-weight and have red fruit characters but it is hard to generalise. They are certainly the most rough and ready of the styles and you are likely to have drunk them if you have ever asked for a glass of house Port in a restaurant. Expressions like 'vintage character' might appear on the label in an attempt to add gravitas.

Tawny Port

This is my favourite style of Port to drink on a regular basis. Its name derives from the brown-tinged colour the wine acquires after an extended stay in a barrel, and the wines will be labelled as ten, twenty, thirty or over forty years. I prefer the twenty-year-old wines, as they seem to have just the right **balance** between fruit and complexity. The wines get paler the more time they spend in the barrel, taking on nutty characteristics not unlike a good Oloroso Sherry, and their flavours are heightened and freshened by chilling the bottle. A bottle labelled as Colheita will have a vintage year but will have spent the intervening years maturing in a barrel.

Late-Bottled Vintage (often shortened to LBV)

This is a halfway house between a tawny Port and a vintage one. The wine will have been aged for four to six years in a barrel and then bottled. The time in the barrel will have advanced the wine far more quickly than if it had been in a bottle. It is thus ready to drink on release and will have shed its deposit in the barrel, so there is no need to decant it.

From the good houses these wines will offer you a glimpse of a vintage Port without having to wait for years and shell out all your savings. Beware, though: too many estates' offerings are not up to scratch.

Vintage Port

This is what all the fuss is over. Good vintage Port is one of the world's greatest wine experiences – it is a **complex** powerful drink that demands attention. Only four or five years out of ten will be deemed of sufficient quality to be declared as a vintage year. All the wine's maturation takes place in the bottle and this happens at snail's pace compared with in a barrel. With all the above styles the house has in effect done the maturation for you, with vintage Port the onus is on you. The best years are not approachable for ten years and will last for fifty; remember that patience is a virtue.

Port and cheese is an age-old British tradition. One, though, that was founded when the number of cheeses available in this country was small and they were generally hard. So stick to what our ancestors knew – good hard English cheeses like Cheddar and Double Gloucester. Stilton also works a treat as the sweetness of the wine counters the saltiness of the cheese. Creamy and light cheeses, though, can easily be overwhelmed.

Young vintage Port or ruby is particularly good with rich chocolate puddings – a useful match as not much else will stand up to them. Chilled tawny Port is a grand aperitif and loves a good bowl of nuts.

Try

Banyuls and Maury p.71

Chocolate p.294, **Hard Cheese** p.291

MADEIRA

Madeira, like Sherry, is deeply unfashionable. Most people in Britain are only likely to have come across it as an ingredient used for cooking; indeed, after being championed on television as a good cake ingredient by the *grand dame* of cooking, Delia Smith, sales soared. It does indeed make very fine cake but is just as good drunk out of a glass. Like Sherry, fine Madeira is ridiculously good value, especially if you like to drink old wine. These wines are indestructible – you could go and buy a young bottle that will outlast you, your children and your grandchildren.

Blandy's, Henriques &
Henriques, Cossart Gordon,
D'Oliveiras

Madeira is a volcanic island, owned by Portugal, that lies off the east coast of Africa. Its wine is steeped in history and, rather like Port, it came into existence more or less by accident. Sweet wines had always been made there, but in an unfortified guise. During the seventeenth century the island was one of the last places to take supplies on board before making the crossing to America or the Indies. Sailors soon learned that a flagon or two of brandy in a barrel preserved the wine for the long journey. These barrels were lashed to the decks and fulfilled the dual function of keeping the crew happy and providing important ballast. Being exposed to high temperatures in the sun, the wine was effectively slow-baked, producing Madeira's typical nutty, caramel flavours.

This process is re-created on the island today, as wine is **fortified** and heated up. For the cheapest wines this is done quickly in what is really a large kettle; better wines are kept in warm rooms in large barrels and the finest are often kept for twenty years or more in the Madeira lodges, relying only on the sun's heat. This heating process is referred to as *estufagem*. The best wines will have a vintage date on the label. Most, though, will appear like a tawny Port with an indication of how long the wine has matured – five, ten or fifteen years.

The best Madeira wines are made from four grape varieties, which all turn out different styles. These are still very good value, so cook with the inferior stuff that won't have a grape specified and drink only the best. I prefer to serve all styles slightly chilled. They are:

Malmsey (or Malvasia)

This is the sweetest style. They have a deep brown colour, are full-bodied and taste of brown sugar and raisins.

Bual

These still have a dark colour and, while being a notch down in sweetness, are definitely in the dessert wine camp. They are fragrant and rich with a distinct smoky character. This style is rare today.

Verdelho

These wines have a golden rather than a brown colour and are medium-dry. They have a refreshing citrus tang to them.

Sercial

Strangely this, the driest style, is the most long-lived of Madeira wines, seemingly defying age. It is light in colour and has a fragrant, almost floral character. As it ages a nutty character becomes evident. These wines require extended bottle age, so again they are rare.

The sweet styles are a godsend for tricky desserts. Malmsey is great for Christmas Day, not only warming you up but also happily dealing with Christmas pudding and mince pies. For those who want to skip dessert these wines make the perfect substitute. Better still, drink some Bual at tea with gingerbread or Delia's delicious Madeira cake.

The drier styles are best as aperitifs and have the advantage of marrying with the requisite pre-meal nibbles like nuts. Don't be shy about opening a bottle, Madeira is one of the few wines that will not deteriorate when opened; a couple of weeks in the fridge for an open bottle is fine.

If you like the sweet styles, try

Sherry (sweet) p.148, Sicily p.128

Steamed Puddings p.297

The drier styles are fairly unique, although they do have some of the traits of Amontillado Sherry.

Quinta de la Rosa, Quinta
dos Roques, Cortes de
Cima, Quinto de Pancas

The Best of the Rest

Excluding rosé, Vinho Verde is probably Portugal's most internationally
recognisable unfortified wine. It is a crisp white that is produced in vast
quantities in the Minho region that borders Spain. **Fresh** and light might
be a positive description of it, while dull and tasteless would suffice if
you were feeling less generous.

If you like full-on sweet wine that slaps you in the face,
Moscatel Roxo from Setúbal will hit the spot. All the excitement at the
moment, though, really revolves around red wine.

Leading the pack is the red grape, Touriga Nacional; one of
Port's components. It makes spicy, full-bodied reds. Try those from the
home of Port, the Douro Valle. Further south in Dão and Bairrada where
the uncompromising local grape Baga takes centre stage. Success is
also being had with the other Port grapes like Tinta Roriz, more
commonly known in Spain as Tempranillo.

Go further south still and you'll get to Alentejo, which is
quickly becoming Portugal's most fashionable and hip region. Grand
estates from Bordeaux, such as Lafite Rothschild, own wineries here,
making wine from international varieties and local ones like Periquita
and Alicante Bouschet. As long as the temptation to make 'cult' wines is
avoided, the future for this innovative region looks rosy.

SPAIN

Spain is beginning to live up to its huge potential. It is, of course, famous for two wines: the much-reviled Sherry (resistance is futile, I will convert you) and the ever-dependable Rioja. Both these areas are solidly back on form, but there is now a wealth of other riches to choose from. Don't get me wrong – as with every wine country poor wines will always be made. However, the equilibrium between innovation, bringing new ideas, equipment and grapes to Spain has been maintained, with just the right amount of respect for tradition.

1 Rías Baixas
2 Ribera del Duero
3 Rioja
4 Priorato
5 Sherry
6 Aragon
7 Catalonia
8 La Mancha
9 Jumilla

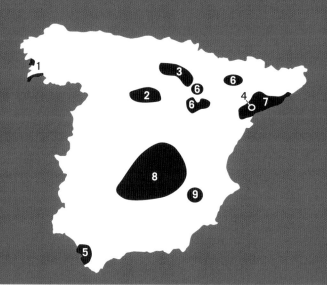

Until recently, Spanish whites have left me underwhelmed. They used to be so heavily oaked that any flavours of the actual grape or region were obliterated. Now, though, a greater awareness of what the export market wants has led to the production of some fresh, fruity whites, the best of which utilise indigenous grapes.

Things are forever changing within the laws I am about to highlight: many regions are at an embryonic stage, and politics plays its part as ever. Rioja is as yet the only region entitled to Spain's top classification. This is despite much of its production still being only adequate and the market price for regions like Ribera del Duero being higher. Spanish estates are also notorious for only following the regulations that suit them. In their defence, though, many ignore rules in the process of striving for higher-quality wine.

There are five levels of classification. You are unlikely to encounter the bottom two unless on holiday, and even then I'd make an effort to avoid them.

The importance of these terms is starting to diminish. Don't be fooled into thinking all Gran Reserva will be fantastic as the base wine needs to be mighty fine to stand up to the ageing treatment. Too many old-style producers hang on to wine for far too long so as to create a Grand Reserva; many of these would be better off drunk earlier. To confuse the issue further, some of the best new-wave producers don't use these expressions even if their wine qualifies for them.

Denominación de Origen e Calificada (DOCa) – only Rioja belongs to this category
Denominación de Origen (DOC)
Vino de la Tierra
Vino Comarcal
Vino de Mesa

You also need to be aware of three terms that relate to how long a wine has been aged:

Crianza
This is a wine that has been aged for two years before release. At least six months of this (twelve in Rioja and Ribera del Duero) must be in **oak** barrels.

Reserva
This is a wine that has been aged for three years before release; one of these years must be spent in the barrel.

Gran Reserva
These wines will be a minimum of five years old before release; at least two of these must be in the barrel.

RÍAS BAIXAS

Terras Gauda, Valmiñor,
Lusco do Miño, Adegas,
Galegas

Try

Alsace p.16, **Germany**
p.98, **Austria** p.96

Viognier p.218, **Riesling**
p.206, **Muscat** p.202

Shellfish p.257, **Asian**
Food p.281

This region lies in Galicia, north-west Spain, in one of the country's coolest regions. Until very recently these white wines were rarely seen outside Spain, although they have always been held in high regard there. They are fresh, floral and the best have a peachy, oily character that is reminiscent of another crowd pleaser, Viognier. Most of those exported are made from 100 per cent Albariño, which will then appear on the label.

There are a host of good wines now being made, all of which should be drunk young. Recently there seems to have been some experimentation with **oak** maturation. These wines are more expensive and I would avoid them, as the **oak** masks the flavours of the grape.

The wines' good **acidity** and floral flavours make for a delicious wake-up call for the palate before a meal. Traditionally, as this is a coastal area, they should be paired with the freshest shellfish and seafood – keep it simple, these are not wines to be serving with rich sauces. If you are feeling more adventurous in the kitchen and feel a fusion meal coming on the wines work well, but as always, try to keep the chillies in check.

This region for me produces one of the most profound wines on the planet, Vega Sicilia. For many years it was an oddity, as it alone flew the flag for the region, but now a new player emerges on the scene every year. Don't get put off by the ludicrous prices that many of the top wines now command as there is plenty at the lower end that is within reach.

The vineyards of Ribera del Duero lie in the centre of northern Spain. Rioja is not far away to the north, and the same grape, Tempranillo, dominates, yet these wines couldn't be more different. They have the **structure** of great Bordeaux but with more sweet black fruit flavours. It is difficult to be too specific as every producer utilises different degrees of varieties, but they are all united in trying to make serious, grown-up wine. These are wines that require a few years in the bottle and the best will go on for twenty and beyond.

Try

Regardless of the grape mix these are big, full-blooded affairs. The young wines will take on any chunky meat dish – the Spanish love a leg of lamb and they don't mind strong spices or herbs. Like any old wine, you should treat it with respect and let it do the talking. With the older wines, strong flavours like garlic should be kept to a minimum. The sweet fruit contained in these wines loves strong, hard cheese; if you want to stay in Spain, Manchego will do the trick, otherwise enjoy them with the plethora of good stuff available from our shores.

Marqués de Murrieta, Viña Tondonia, La Rioja Alta, Allende, Palacios Remondo, Roda, Muga, Contino, Artadi

Rioja is a region in the throws of a massive identity crisis. Traditionally Rioja is medium-bodied, doesn't have the deepest of colours and derives much of its character from the American oak barrels it is matured in. Modern Rioja is deeper in colour, altogether fruitier in style and its producers prefer to age their wines in smaller French oak barrels. Both sides accuse each other of the ultimate winemaking heresy – producing bland wine that does not reflect its origins. Who is right? Well, as ever, the correct path seems to be somewhere in the middle. Too often those in the old school put overproduced red wine into oak barrels for far too long, and the result is a sweet, toasty red that lacks roots and excitement. The modernists also have to admit, though, that initially their wines were fruity to the point of blandness.

Rioja's vineyards are in the north-east of the country, and the primary red grape is Tempranillo, backed up by Garnacha (Grenache). Traditionally, like most of Spain, many of the old estates own vineyards but they also have to buy in significant proportions of their grape requirements. This enables them to draw from the three separate sub-regions of Alta, Alavesa and Baja, each with their own characteristics. Over the coming years I expect these regional identities to become more apparent as more grape growers start to bottle their own wines.

White Rioja leaves me mystified: why do the growers bother? Traditionally, the wines were very heavily oaked, to the point of being **oxidised**. Now crisp, light white is made in deference to the international market. These are competent wines, but they are invariably too expensive.

Try

🍷 **Ribero del Duero** p.145, **Tuscany** p.120

🍇 **Tempranillo** p.245, **Grenache** p.230, **Sangiovese** p.242

🍴 **Veal** p.276, **Chicken** p.265, **Lamb** p.270, **Soft Cheese** p.292

With a host of different styles now being produced it is difficult to be specific. Old-school Rioja is a medium-bodied red so don't overpower it. Meat dishes like veal and roast chicken are good and as they take on some age, game of all sorts. Soft cow's or sheep's milk cheese works well, nothing too strong, though.

The modern, fruitier style prefers meats with a red slant, but they often lack the **structure** to deal with rich sauces, so keep the meat simply grilled. The best new-wave offerings should be treated like the finest wines from Ribera del Duero.

PRIORATO

Alvaro Palacios, Clos Mogador, Cellars de Scala Dei, Mas Martinet, Mas d'en Compte

Try

Ribera del Duero p.145, **Southern Rhône** p.90

Grenache p.230, **Tempranillo** p.245, **Syrah** p.243

Beef p.263, **Lamb** p.270, **Hard Cheese** p.291

This region has literally come from nowhere in ten years, but in that short period it has influenced winemakers throughout the country. It has convinced them that if you produce superb individual wines the market will pay top dollar for them, no matter what the name on the label says.

It is perhaps a surprise to find Grenache producing such concentrated, deeply coloured wines which are full of herbs, spices and black fruits; they also have great balancing **structure** resulting from the vineyards' high elevation. This grape is much abused throughout Spain and southern France, but Priorato just goes to show what can be achieved when **yields** are kept down.

Most of the wines have the requisite sweet fruit to be approachable when fairly young, but they also have the guts for a long stay in the cellar.

These are big, chunky affairs. While the wines are powerfully fruity, the high altitude of the vineyards gives them good **acidity**. This enables them to take on pretty much anything you can throw at them – all roasted red meats and any kind of powerful stews. Don't be afraid to use strong herbs and flavours, especially any like paprika, as the inherent spices in the wine will easily deal with them. Keep cheeses hard and strong.

I am impressed you are even reading this section, such is the low regard with which Sherry is held by those under sixty. I absolutely adore the stuff. There are two reasons you don't like Sherry. Firstly, it's deeply unfashionable, but this shouldn't be a problem. I am sure you would prefer to be a trendsetter rather than follow the crowd. Secondly, I doubt you have ever tasted real Sherry.

Before we continue with your conversion, two vital rules. One: Sherry is a wine, not a spirit. You wouldn't leave the former open for three weeks before drinking it, so afford the same respect to Sherry and put a wine saver in it or buy half-bottles. Two: the light dry wines must be chilled properly. The other styles are more open to debate, but I prefer them when they have been in the fridge for an hour or so.

Sherry vineyards lie on the southern tip of Spain, to the west of Gibraltar. A white wine is made and then **fortified** to around 15 per cent alcohol. The resulting wine is then placed in barrels (or *butts*, as the Spanish call them). The lighter wines are earmarked and in their *butts* a film of **yeast** forms on the surface known as *flor*. These sherries become those known as *fino*. The heavier wines are put to one side and **fortified** to 18 per cent alcohol. They become known as Olorosos, and will take on a deep brown colour as they have no protecting layer of *flor* to stop them oxidising.

Rather like Champagne houses, a Sherry estate's reputation is built on a non-vintage product. They have thus developed an intricate blending system to guarantee a uniform product year in, year out. This is known as a solera. *It is a series of* butts *stacked on top of each other. Every time an estate needs to bottle some Sherry it does so from the bottom row of* butts. *This row is then replenished from the one above and so on until one reaches the top level, usually about five rows later. The empty space left in the top* butts *is filled with young, recently **fortified** Sherry. Thus very old soleras, some of which were started in the nineteenth century, still contain a small amount of the original wine used to create them. It is important to note that I am only referring to dry Sherry. Truly sweet Sherry is made only from very ripe, dried grapes, **fortified** and then put through the* solera *system. The semi-sweet cream Sherry, created for us in the UK, is made by drawing off dry Sherry and blending it with this super-concentrated stuff.*

Fino

This is the style the Spanish drink like water. The colour is the same as a normal white wine. It is delicate, fragrant and refreshing yet at the same time powerful, with a lingering aftertaste. It absolutely must be drunk cold and within a few days (hours is better) of opening.

Manzanilla

This is one of the most refreshing drinks on this earth and one of my top five white wines. Famous for having a salty, mineral tang to them, supposedly on account of the wine being matured so close to the sea, they are more delicate and refined than a normal fino, so ditto for chilling and drinking times.

Amontillado

This is wine that started life as a fino, but within the *butt* the *flor* has failed to develop properly. Once the film has disappeared oxygen gets to the wine, accounting for the amber colour and their wines have a nutty, **complex** character. True Amontillado should be bottled unadulterated from the cask and thus be dry, but unfortunately many estates add some sweet wine, making a medium Sherry. Wine laws crassly allow them to do this, creating a very confusing situation for the consumer.

Oloroso

No flor has ever developed in these *butts*, so they are the darkest in colour and the most **oxidised** in taste. They have a burnt, dried fruit character and, being higher in alcohol, should be sipped. They suffer the same problem as Amontillado in that when the wine is drawn from the *solera* it is dry, and then is sweetened. There are very fine sweet Olorosos, but unless otherwise labelled it should be a dry style.

Pedro Ximénez and Moscatel

Sweet hardly does justice to these wines; they are so concentrated as to defy belief. The wines are black in colour and have the consistency of Castrol GTX. They are full of the most decadent sweet flavours you could imagine; raisins, brown sugar and black treacle.

SHERRY AND FOOD

I don't think it would be possible to create a more perfect aperitif, especially on a hot day, than Fino or Manzanilla Sherry, but don't stop there. The tapas that the region is famous for involves a bewildering range of flavours for any wine to cope with. These two styles somehow manage to come up trumps against all the odds, though, happily taking squid, marinated peppers, chorizo and – the death knell to most wine – anchovies in their stride.

Amontillado is also a great aperitif; more a sipper than a glugger and perhaps suited more to the evening and the colder weather. It also has the advantage of working beautifully with nuts, especially toasted almonds. In Spain they are content to drink Amontillado all the way through a meal, and it will happily take on veal, quail, chicken, rabbit and pork, having all the necessary **acidity** to deal with rich sauces.

Oloroso is very powerful and I find it best drunk on its own after a meal. The sweet stuff is practically a meal in its own right and will overwhelm most dessert. Try it with Christmas pudding or gingerbread, or in the summer pour it neat over vanilla ice cream.

If you like oxidised styles of Amontillado and Oloroso try Madeira. The others are unique.

Ochoa (Navarra), Torres (Penedès), Enate (Somontano), Jean León (Penedès), Casa Castillo (Jumilla), Casa de la Ermita (Jumilla), Palacide Bornos (Rueda), Valduero (Toro)

The Best of the Rest

Toro, to the west of Ribera del Duero, is rapidly becoming a source of very fine value red wine. Produced from the same grape mix as Ribera, its wines are more rustic but considerably cheaper. Between the two lies the white only area of Rueda. Modern winemaking has had a huge influence as it now enables the region's winemakers to capture the fruity freshness of the local Verdejo grape. Along with Albariño, in Rías Baixas, it is making Spain's finest whites. Sauvignon Blanc is also making an impact here.

Navarra, to the east of Rioja, makes a wide variety of wines that range from dull, overproduced **co-operative** numbers to good-value, Rioja-like reds. It is also increasingly turning out adequate international varieties like Chardonnay and Cabernet Sauvignon. Further east still in Aragón you come to Somontano. A relative newcomer, it has little historical baggage and concentrates on making good-value red and white from international and native varietals.

Enter Catalonia and you come to Penedès, the area that is first and foremost responsible for producing most of Spain's Cava. I have never been hugely enamoured with Cava, preferring to look elsewhere for cheap fizz. The market is so dominated in this country by a couple of large but only adequate brands that I find it difficult to see how the few really good ones I have tried will ever find a presence over here.

The real reason to look out for Penedès is to taste the offerings of two men who have shaped modern Spanish wine. Jean León makes spectacular wine and is credited as being the first to plant Chardonnay and Cabernet Sauvignon in Spain. Miguel Torres runs a far larger operation and proves that big doesn't have to be bland and bad; his whole range is excellent and widely available.

As you move south the temperature rises and it becomes harder to make quality wine. La Mancha is a vast area in central Spain that is responsible for much of the country's bulk requirements, although some interesting wines come from the Valdepeñas.

Lastly the hot, arid region of Jumilla in the south-east has started to attract some attention. Here Tempranillo is allied with Monastrell (France's Mourvèdre) to produce big wines with lots of character. Some of its producers aim for New World-like levels of ripeness.

NEW WORLD

This section is laid out differently from the rest of the book. The reason for this is that New World wine is nearly always led by the grape variety rather than by the region.

Use the grape variety section to find food matches and other similar-tasting wines. My intention is not to devalue the importance of the region within each country, as taking note of their individual characteristics will help you to select the right bottle. For example, if you have enjoyed a full-bodied Australian Chardonnay from the Hunter Valley, you'll learn that it is a hot area and so look for Chardonnays grown in the hotter New World zones around the world. Equally, a cool-climate Chardonnay from the Adelaide Hills might lead you to other countries with a similar climate, say, Burgundy in France.

I don't disguise the fact that my preference when matching wine with food is for European styles. By this I mean white wines with fine acidity and reds with acidity and tannin. In the New World these restrained types of wine are generally found in the coolish areas. So it follows that if in the food section I recommend lamb with Cabernet Sauvignon, I am thinking of one from a cool area like Coonawarra in Australia rather than a commercial fruity example from Chile.

ARGENTINA

Colomé, Alta Vista, Anubis,
Norton, Weinert, Finca El
Retiro, La Agrícola,
Catena, Viña Amalia,
Prelatura de Cafayate,
Achaval Ferrer

Try

🎯 **Malbec** p.232, **Tempranillo** p.245, **Sangiovese** p.242, **Syrah** p.243, **Barbera** p.222, **Cabernet Sauvignon** p.224

Argentina has been the latest of the New World gang to burst on to the scene. As little as ten years ago it didn't feature at all on our shelves, but today an exciting range of fine-value wine pours out of the country. One of the keys to the country's success is the altitude at which the vines are grown. Many are over the 1000-metre mark, an elevation at which we would be more comfortable skiing in Europe. Even at these altitudes the grapes have no problem getting ripe, yet the cool evenings provide the required structure.

The bulk of the vineyards are situated just over the border from the Chilean city of Santiago. The most famous region for fine wine is Mendoza, although I am sure it won't be long before other areas come to prominence. Within Mendoza there has been a push lately to mark out the best sites such as the Maipú; these new areas will soon start appearing on the front labels.

The real excitement of Argentinian wine comes from the diversity of the flavours on offer. Fine examples of the usual suspects – Chardonnay and Cabernet Sauvignon – are made there, but they are unlikely to make you rush to discover the region as similar flavours are on offer from elsewhere around the world. For whites, the floral, lemon-scented Torrontés is unique to the country. It is one of the most delicious of summer quaffing wines. Sémillon and Chardonnay are the pick of the other whites.

Malbec is the red grape to put the country on the map. Along with Cahors in France it can justly claim to be making the best examples of this long-forgotten grape. As you would expect the wine has more upfront and is softer than its French counterpart but it does retain an earthy, leathery complexity. Tempranillo, the grape of Rioja in Spain, is grown with particular success, as is Syrah, Bonarda and Cabernet Sauvignon.

AUSTRALIA

Imports of Australian wine to the UK are at an all-time high; we now drink more of it than French wine. This is quite an extraordinary fact, as France has dominated our wine consumption for hundreds of years while Australian wine has only been seriously imported from the eighties onwards. This success is founded on fruity accessible flavours that have democratised wine drinking – you don't need a cellar, as the wines are all ready for immediate consumption.

European styles of wine are intricately linked to food: our modern palates find them difficult to appreciate without it. Australian wine, on the other hand, is perfect to drink at any time. All this makes the Aussies very bullish at the moment. The amount of wine set to come out of the country is also increasing sharply as newly planted vineyards come on stream. World domination beckons.

I suspect, though, that storm clouds are on the horizon. The main problem is the polarisation of the producers. In one camp you have an unhealthily small number of very large companies controlling the majority of wine production, and in the other there is an incredibly diverse range of small-niche wineries turning out stunning products. The problem is that they do not necessarily have the marketing budgets or clout to get on to our shelves.

The good news, though, is that as the industry in Australia matures, there has been an increasing emphasis on regional identity. This has yet to be really passed down to the consumer, but it stands to reason that some grapes will be more suited than others to certain areas. To get more out of the country than just a good, dependable, but ultimately forgettable bottle, it is worthwhile getting to grips with these regions. Don't worry – they are a walk in the park to understand compared with their European counterparts.

Many bottles seen on the shelves will simply be labelled with the state name, i.e. Western Australia. This gives you very little indication of what is in the bottle as every state contains very different styles of fruit. There is nothing wrong per se with casting a wide net to make a blend; for example, very ripe Shiraz grapes from a hot region will often benefit from a slug of some grown in a cooler region to add **acidity** and **structure**. Indeed, Australia's most sought-after and acclaimed red, Penfolds Grange Hermitage, is made in this way using grapes drawn from the entire Southern Australian region. On the other hand, this blending often leads to bland, fruity, one-dimensional wines. Vigorously marketed, they press all the right buttons for those who have conducted the consumer research, but ultimately they excite no one.

New South Wales's most famous area is the Hunter Valley – one of the longest-established wine-growing regions in the country. The upper half of the valley does have some cooler areas but generally Hunter equals hot. This produces big, bold styles of wine.

Hunter Valley

Brokenwood, Tulloch, Rosemount Estate, Rothbury, Tyrrell's

For whites, Chardonnay and Sémillon are the main players. The former produces full-bodied, tropical-fruited wines that usually have a good helping of spicy oak. The latter should, in my view, be far more widely appreciated as it is one of the country's unique wines. They can be tricky when young, seemingly grassy and vegetal. However, after a few years in the bottles they blossom, taking on a deep golden colour and bursting with honeyed fruit flavours. They are one of the few Australian wines that improve with age.

Shiraz is the chief red grape; making typically leathery wines that age surprisingly well.

Try
🍇 **Chardonnay** p.192, **Sémillon** p.212

🍇 **Shiraz/Syrah** p.243

The Rest

Clonakilla, Lark Hill, De Bortoli

Producers in New South Wales over the last few years have been seeking out cooler sites. Firstly, this lets the wineries experiment with grapes such as Pinot Noir and Sauvignon Blanc, which don't enjoy the heat. Secondly, the cooler climate produces a very different, more controlled style of wine from the usual varieties like Chardonnay and Shiraz. This development is still very much in its early stages, but regions such as Canberra, Orange, Hilltops and Mudgee show lots of promise.

Try
🍇 **Sauvignon Blanc** p.210, **Chardonnay** p.192

🍇 **Pinot Noir** p.238, **Shiraz/Syrah** p.243

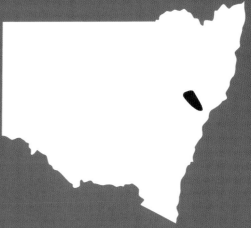

TASMANIA

Pipers Brook

Try

Riesling p.206,
Chardonnay p.192

Pinot Noir p.238

Tasmania lies off the coast of New South Wales. Here the wine industry is really in its youth. Being the most southerly point of the country it is by far the coolest, so Pinot Noir, Riesling and Chardonnay, to a lesser extent, are the key grapes. The climate also allows for the production of excellent sparkling wine. This is one of the few areas in Australia that is cold enough for vintage variations to be obvious; something I find reassuring in an increasingly homogenised wine world.

Most estates currently produce on a microscopic scale and so the wines are rarely seen outside Australia, but this will soon change. The one exception is the fabulous Pipers Brook who make an exceptional fizz called Pirie, a fine age-worthy Riesling and a great Pinot Noir. Their widely available second label Ninth Island is also excellent.

North of Melbourne lies the Yarra Valley – Victoria's most famous wine-growing area. Its complex geography allows for the full range of grapes to be grown, and the quality of winemaking in the Valley is extremely high – James Halliday, the country's most influential wine critic, was so enamoured with the region that he started a winery here, Coldstream Hills.

Yarra Valley

The cool areas of the Yarra are home to some of Australia's finest Pinot Noir, while in the hotter parts Cabernet Sauvignon and Shiraz dominate. These are beautifully balanced versions of the grapes, having all the upfront fruit you'd expect but also the fine **structure** that allows them to be stuck away in the cellar for a few years.

Chardonnay dominates among the whites. The best from the cool sites lean toward the **complex** and finely **structured**, rather than the round and buttery camp. The coolness of the valley produces fine grapes for the production of sparkling wine. The champagne house Moët et Chandon leads the way with its excellent Domaine Chandon and indeed, for many years I would be so bold as to say it made better wine here than back home in France.

Yarra Yering, Coldstream Hills, Domaine Chandon, Diamond Valley Vineyards

Try
Chardonnay p.192

Pinot Noir p.238, **Cabernet Sauvignon** p.224, **Shiraz/Syrah** p.243

The Rest

This is the most diverse of Australia's wine-growing states. In the north, for example, a relic from the pioneer days still flourishes: Liqueur Muscats from Rutherglen are sweet, raisined delights that usually make me think indecent, unprintable thoughts when drunk. Farther south, Beechworth is home to some of the country's top producers of Chardonnay and all things Rhône/Roussanne-like, and Viognier for white and Shiraz for red.

South of Melbourne on the coast is the Mornington Peninsula. This is a truly cool area and produces **fresh** Chardonnays, Riesling and some of Australia's finest Pinot Gris. Reds can be more variable, but there is some excellent Pinot Noir around.

Across the bay and to the north-west of the city are two other cool coastal areas, Geelong and Sunbury. Both make great Pinot Noir, Sauvignon Blanc and Chardonnay. Further inland Shiraz and Chardonnay play a more prominent role in areas like Heathcote, Pyrenees (not a high mountain range as the name might imply) and the Grampians. The style of wine here is big without being blockbuster.

Campbells, Chambers Rosewood Vineyards, Mount Langhi Giran, Dalwhinnie, Redbank, Jasper Hill, Heathcote, T'Gallant, Bannockburn, Scotchmans Hill, Craiglee, Stonier, Delatite, Giaconda, De Bortoli, Taltarni, Seppelt

Try
Sauvignon Blanc p.210, **Chardonnay** p.192, **Pinot Gris** p.205

Pinot Noir p.238, **Shiraz** p.243

The Barossa Valley is probably Australia's most internationally recognised fine wine region. It lies to the north-east of Adelaide and is famous for its inky, purple, intense Shiraz. Gorgeous glasses of wine they can be, but subtle and restrained they are not. The heat plus an unusually high proportion of old vines helps to fashion them. These are some of the most concentrated wines on this planet, and international recognition and demand has pushed the prices right up, in some cases into the stratosphere.

Elderton, Coriole, St Hallett, Torbreck,
Rockford, Greenock Creek, Charles Melton, Peter Lehmann

Try

🍇 Sémillon p.212, **Chardonnay** p.192, **Riesling** p.206

🍇 **Shiraz/Syrah** p.243, **Grenache** p.230, **Mourvèdre** p.236

Barossa Valley

Leaving aside its famous Shiraz, full throttle Grenache can be a good-value bet in the Barossa. Like Shiraz the wines often benefit by coming from ancient vines. Provided producers are vigilant and keep down **yields** of this naturally high-cropping grape, results can be spectacular: juicy, strawberry-fruited reds that develop spicy, gamey flavours after a few years in the bottle. Blends of Grenache and Shiraz, along with other Rhône stalwarts like Mourvèdre, are also making good wines.

Sémillon, Chardonnay and to a lesser extent Riesling head up the white grapes and they follow a similar style to the reds, namely full-bodied and ripe. Dessert wines made in a tawny Port style (aged ten, twenty, thirty years in the barrel) are a rarely seen delight. The reds age well but the whites' low **acidity** generally demands immediate consumption.

Hollick, Katnook, Petaluma, Geoff Weaver, Lenswood, Barrat, Fox Creek, Shottesbrooke, Shaw and Smith, D'Arenberg, Noon, Nepenthe, Tim Adams, Grosset, Jim Barry, Knappstein, Henschke

The Rest

Eden Valley borders the Barossa but has a distinctly cool feel to it. It is most famous for its floral elegant Riesling. Chardonnay and Cabernet Sauvignon also flourish but are less in-your-face and more **structured** than the Barossa versions. The world-famous Hill of Grace vineyard, also in the valley, is responsible for one of Australia's greatest and most long-lived versions of Shiraz.

Clare Valley to the north turns out some of Australia's finest Rieslings. These are classy affairs, having not just upfront floral fruit but also intensely steely, mineral flavours that really speak of where the grapes are grown. They age magnificently. The reds from Cabernet Sauvignon and Shiraz tend to have more natural **tannin** and **acidity** than those from the Barossa and also age well.

To the south of Adelaide city lie McLaren Vale and the Adelaide Hills. The former makes great Shiraz, Cabernet Sauvignon and outstanding Merlot, all with a silky feel to them. The latter is one of the finest cool sites in the country. It produces world-class whites from Chardonnay, Sauvignon Blanc and Riesling. While being distinctly Australian, many of these wines have a European feel about them as well.

The Piccadilly Valley and Lenswood are two superb sites within the hills. Both excel at well-structured Chardonnay, Pinot Noir and lime-scented Riesling. In the far south of the state lies the Coonawarra region, which is famous for its Cabernet Sauvignons; these are top-notch wines full of blackcurrants and mint. It is also a cool region, while the famous red soil no doubt leaves its mark.

Try

🍇 **Riesling** p.206, **Chardonnay** p.192, **Sauvignon Blanc** p.210

🍇 **Shiraz/Syrah** p.243, **Merlot** p.234, **Pinot Noir** p.238, **Cabernet Sauvignon** p.224

Western Australian wine is widely seen in this country. From the amount of its wine available on our shelves, you would imagine it was one of the major players in terms of volume. In fact, though, the state produces only a tiny proportion of the country's total output; what it does turn out, however, is a large proportion of the quality bottles.

Amberley, Moss Wood, Brookland Valley, Cullen, Cape Mentelle, Leeuwin Estate, Devil's Lair, Vasse Felix

Try

🍷 Chardonnay p.192, **Sauvignon Blanc** p.210, **Sémillon** p.212

🍷 Cabernet Sauvignon p.224, **Shiraz/Syrah** p.243, **Zinfandel** p.247

Margaret River

The quality in Australia really intensifies when you get to Margaret River, 150 miles south of Perth. This coolish region has the greatest concentration of fine wine producers in Australia and can easily lay a claim to being one of the great wine regions of the world. It is stuffed full of the great and the good of Australian wine.

Cabernet Sauvignon dominates the reds. These are serious **structured** affairs full of typical Cabernet fruits, such as blackcurrants, but also with **complex** earthy flavours that give the wines a real sense of identity. Smaller amounts of controlled spicy Shiraz and Zinfandel are also produced.

Chardonnay garners all the plaudits for white. It is responsible for some of the country's most **complex** and long-lived examples. Sauvignon Blanc and Sémillon are rather unfairly in the shadow of Chardonnay in this region. They both turn out some fine wines in their own right, but also mimic white Bordeaux by producing excellent, creamy, fruity bottles when blended together.

Baldivis, Capel Vale, Howard Park, Madfish (the second label of Howard Park), Frankland Estate, Lost Lake, Plantagenet, Lillian

Try

🍷 Chardonnay p.192, **Sauvignon Blanc** p.210, **Riesling** p.206

🍷 Pinot Noir p.238, **Cabernet Sauvignon** p.224, **Shiraz/Syrah** p.243, **Merlot** p.234

The Rest

Margaret River is firmly established in the country's winemaking culture, but the cooler regions further to the south are just starting to find their feet, and a large amount of money has recently poured into these regions. Pemberton is producing some fine Chardonnay and Pinot Noir, while Frankland River and Mount Barker have excelled with spicy Shiraz and some good Bordeaux blends of Cabernet Sauvignon and Merlot. Zippy Sauvignon Blancs and steely **fresh** Riesling seem to be the way forward for whites. Subtlety and restraint, rather than in-your-face fruit flavours, is the mark of these wines.

The areas around Perth such as the Swan Valley are the hottest of the region, producing reliable but middle-of-the-road wine.

CANADA

Blossom Winery,
Inniskillin, Magnotta

This may seem a rather peculiar entry, as most people's image of Canada is one of a land covered in snow and therefore wholly unsuitable for growing grapes. However, it does have a rapidly expanding wine industry.

British Columbia – on the West Coast – produces **fresh** whites from varieties like Riesling and Sauvignon Blanc, but you are unlikely to encounter them unless on holiday there. However, it's on the East Coast that most of the action happens. Here again, it is the cool-loving varietals like the above and Pinot Gris that hold sway.

The quality of red wines is patchy as producers struggle to ripen varieties such as Cabernet Sauvignon. What is all the fuss about, then? Ice wine.

The spiritual home of ice wine is Germany and, unless you are very wealthy or have hugely generous friends, you are unlikely ever to taste any. It is only produced in certain years when ripe, frozen grapes can be harvested in the cold nights of November and December. These berries are pressed immediately and the juice that emerges from them is highly concentrated, as any water is left behind in the form of ice.

The resulting wines in Germany are delicious but frighteningly expensive (top producers' bottles regularly fetch prices in excess of £1000 a bottle). All a bit silly, but with conditions for making this type of wine occurring every year in Ontario, ice wine can be produced economically.

The wines are unctuous and very sweet but they have a fine, balancing **acidity**. They can be drunk on their own after a meal, or their **acidity** makes them a fine match for sweet, fruity desserts or a hunk of salty blue cheese. The best are made from Riesling and require a few years' bottle age. The other important grape is Vidal, which produces luscious wines with a slight pink hue.

Try
 German Eiswein p.100

CHILE

Montgras, Errázuriz, Casablanca, Concha y Toro, Almaviva, Carmen, Casa Silva, Los Vascos, Miguel Torres, Casa Lapostolle, Valdivieso, Montes

Chilean wine burst on to our shelves in the mid-nineties, providing fruity, accessible wines from grape varieties that we had all heard of. A hefty dollop of foreign investment backed rapid expansion and as a result Chilean wines are made in hi-tech wineries reminiscent of their cousins in North America.

High **yields** and young vines, however, led to diluted and uninspiring wine. Thankfully, inspired by a few 'cult' wines, the producers now realise there is more to the market than producing £3.99 Chardonnay. Indeed, the way to our loyalty lies in better quality at the low end and more diversity in the mid-price bracket. That said, I still find too much Chilean wine falls into the two polarised camps: well-made but ultimately formulaic, forgettable bottles, and excellent but expensive, difficult-to-get-hold-of ones.

Chile's one unique selling point is the red grape Carmenère. This is one of Bordeaux's forgotten grapes and is very similar to Merlot. Until recently many Carmenère vines in Chile were thought to be Merlot. The more honest producers are now rather grudgingly labelling their wines as Carmenère, though I suspect that many stick to the more bankable name of Merlot.

Production is centred on Santiago, with most of the action happening to the south of the capital. To the north of the city lie the Aconcagua and Casablanca Valleys. The first has only a small area under vine but is responsible for some of the country's best and most finely **structured** Cabernet Sauvignon. The Casablanca Valley is a cooler area and is dominated by white wine. Chardonnay was initially the grape of choice as that's what the world demanded. It still plays an important role but increasingly fine Sauvignon Blancs are emerging and point the way forward.

The Maipo Valley is south of Santiago. This is essentially red wine country and is dominated by the Bordeaux varieties Cabernet Sauvignon and Merlot. Next stop is the region known as the Rapel Valley. This is a large and varied area, with the full range of varieties. Indeed, superior sub-regions like that of Colchagua for Merlot are starting to be identified on labels. The last two regions are the Curícó and Maule Valleys. The usual grapes dominate although the climate is wetter and cooler, making for more restrained styles.

Try
🍷 **Sauvignon Blanc** p.210, **Chardonnay** p.192

🍷 **Merlot** p.234, **Cabernet Sauvignon** p.224

NEW ZEALAND

The amount of wine that New Zealand produces globally is insignificant, the equivalent of spitting in a large lake. However, our shelves are stacked with it and those who try them are usually smitten. The country's producers are heavily reliant on the export market. Not only are there very few people who live there, but those who do consume little wine. The growers realised that the vagaries of their climate does not allow them to turn out lakes of fruity, undemanding wine, thus they have concentrated only on the quality end of the market.

We are prepared to spend more on a bottle of New Zealand wine than on any other country's wines. This has a beneficial effect on the producers; they can concentrate uncompromisingly on making fine wine, safe in the knowledge that we will pay for it. This is an enviable position to be in and one their neighbours, Australia, would do well to take note of. This is not to imply the wines are expensive, they are not.

The history of New Zealand wine really starts with one wine, Cloudy Bay. It was as if a collective hand grenade had dropped on our palates. We had only ever known Sauvignon Blanc in the very variable guise of Sancerre and Pouilly-Fumé. Suddenly you could drink one that reeked of gooseberries and tropical fruits. Wine had never tasted so damn good and we couldn't get enough of it. People jealously guarded their bottles and every vintage was soon sold out within weeks of arriving on our shores. It was extraordinary; a country's reputation and market presence was founded on the back of one wine. Every New Zealander with a few spare dollars to invest suddenly discovered a new passion, wine.

New vineyard plantings continue unabated today. Since the early days an array of other tastes has been added to the range. Profound Chardonnay, crisp Riesling, Pinot Gris and Gewürztraminer – it's the reds, though, that have been the real revelation. Pinot Noir leads the pack of new grapes and the country could well lay claim to producing the finest examples of this grape outside Burgundy. More surprising, given the climate, has been the emergence of some outstanding wines from a classic Bordeaux blend of Cabernet Sauvignon, Merlot and Cabernet Franc.

As these newly planted red vineyards start to mature, truly profound wines could well be on the way and there are a number of areas that have their own distinct characteristics. Many wineries, though, draw fruit from various different sub-regions, so a specific region will not appear on the label.

Auckland, not surprisingly, is the hottest of the country's regions, being the northern tip of the North Island. Only a few of the region's wineries solely use local fruit and Chardonnay seems to be their main success. Waiheke Island off the coast of Auckland is the exception to the rule. Here a host of tiny wineries are turning out exceptional Bordeaux blends from grapes cooled by the maritime air. The only danger is that some of them seem to want a 'cult' status and are pushing up prices. Gisbourne has a fine reputation for Chardonnay, but again most of its fruit ends up in larger blends.

Auckland

Wellington

1 Gisbourne
2 Hawkes Bay
3 Wairapa

Kumeu River, Collards, Selaks, Matua Valley, Villa Maria, Kim Crawford, Stonyridge, Esk Valley, Craggy Range, Church Road, Trinity Hill, Palliser Estate, Ata Rangi, Martinborough Vineyards, Dry River

Try

⬤ **Chardonnay** p.192, **Sauvignon Blanc** p.210

⬤ **Merlot** p.234, **Cabernet Franc** p.223, **Pinot Noir** p.238

Hawkes Bay has firmly established itself as a source of fine wine in its own right. The area is positively ancient in New Zealand winemaking terms, red wine has been firmly established here since the 1980s. Initially Cabernet Sauvignon was thought to be the way forward, but this being a cooler region than Bordeaux, only the best years saw the fruit ripen properly. Merlot and Cabernet Franc now dominate.

Though New Zealand is lumped in with the New World, with which fruity forward wines are associated, those from Hawkes Bay have far more in common with Bordeaux. Finely balanced Chardonnay and rich Sauvignon Blanc are the most important whites made. A recent innovation has been to label wines grown on a strip of land known as the Gimblett Gravels. Whether this fledgling attempt to mimic the French appellation system is just a marketing tool or a serious attempt to make better wine, only time will tell.

The southernmost region on the North Island is situated around Wellington. Officially called Wairarapa, most wine labels will refer to it as Martinborough. A couple of wineries here started the country's addiction to the trickiest of all red varieties, Pinot Noir; excellent meaty examples are made. Fine Chardonnay with good **acidity** is also a hallmark of the area.

Just over the Cook Strait lies Marlborough, the region where our love affair with Sauvignon Blanc started. The intensity the grape achieves here is unrivalled around the world. The hot days ripen the grapes while the cool nights leave Sauvignon trademark acidity intact. Some critics point out that many of the wines are one-dimensional and somehow not worthy of serious attention. Don't listen to them; easy to understand and accessible they are, but this does not detract from them being utterly delicious to drink. The naturally high acidity of the grapes also means that some fine sparkling \wine is made.

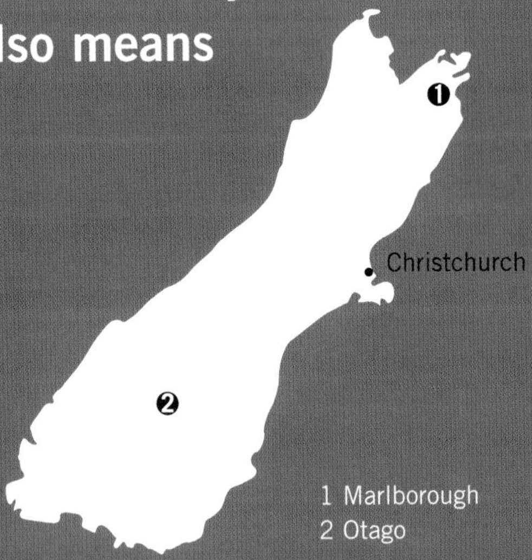

Christchurch

1 Marlborough
2 Otago

Villa Maria, Isabel Estate,
Kim Crawford, Cloudy Bay,
Cainbrae, Fromm Winery,
Seresin, Koura Bay, Felton
Road, Akarua, Peregrine,
Mud House, Huia

Try

🍇 **Sauvignon Blanc** p.210,
Chardonnay p.192,
Riesling p.206, **Pinot Gris**
p.205

🍇 **Pinot Noir** p.238

Chardonnay and Pinot Noir are now also making an impact. The number
of wineries is expanding daily; many who used to be content to sell fruit
to the big players now bottle their own wines. The one black mark
against the region is the number of young vineyards rushed into
production. Young vines and overproduction dilutes the intense
Sauvignon flavour, surely the whole selling point of the wines in the first
place.

Languishing in the shadow of Marlborough to the west is
Nelson. A similar style of wine is made although the emphasis is more
evenly spread between Sauvignon, Chardonnay and Pinot Noir.

The further south you go the more marginal the climate
becomes for ripening grapes successfully year in, year out. Much of
Canterbury remains undeveloped. Otago, though, as well as being the
world's most southernmost wine-producing region, gets the Pinot lovers'
hearts racing.

Otago is hotly tipped to take on the mantle of the greatest
Pinot-producing region outside Burgundy. For a grape that travels so
poorly this is high praise indeed. Many of the vineyards are in their
youth and vintages vary. However a number of the wines being
produced, especially those from hillside sites, are some of the silkiest,
sublime expressions of this grape. Great Germanic-style Riesling, Pinot
Gris and, in the hot years, Chardonnay are also being made.

SOUTH AFRICA

South Africa's wine industry is still suffering from its years of international isolation. Two factors combine to lower quality: a desperate attempt to play catch-up with its New World competitors and the state of the economy, which means that producers are keen to make a quick buck. Land and labour are inexpensive, making it an ideal place to churn out bucketloads of cheap wine designed to be sold at the lowest prices.

In the short term these wines might assure the country a chunk of the market share, but they do no favours in the long run as the consumer comes to associate South Africa with cheap, bland wine, making it very hard for the quality producers to sell their wares.

The second problem for South Africa has been the parlous state of many of the vineyards. Generally, the predominant grape varieties that have been planted – such as Chenin Blanc – are not those that the international market desires. Even when grapes like Chardonnay and Cabernet Sauvignon appeared they were more often than not planted in the wrong areas.

A final, more serious problem that is only just starting to be addressed is the amounts of disease and virus carried by these vines, the effect of which is to inhibit the grapes from reaching full ripeness. This is a particular problem for red grapes and, I believe, accounts for the excessively green, vegetal flavours that so often dominate their red wines.

On the upside, progress is now happening at an astonishing rate. Producers are going through an amazing period of innovation, with new sites being planted every year, along with the appearance of exciting growers. South Africa has much going for it: climate-wise, it straddles the Old and the New World in style.

Like California with Zinfandel, it has a unique grape in the form of Pinotage, which is capable of making either easy-drinking fruity red or more serious, spicy wine. If you have read my entry on Pinotage in the grape variety section you will realise I am not a fan. This is my personal palate, though, and you should go and make up your own mind.

Lastly, as I have already pointed out, this is a cheap country in which to make wine and the best offerings give outstanding value. Provided the country keeps its eye on making specifically South African wine rather than generic New World wine the future looks rosy.

The wine-growing regions are in the southern tip of the country centred on Cape Town, and the association of certain varieties with specific sites is still very much in its infancy. As for the New World in general, it is not uncommon for wineries to own land across a number of different areas, so don't be surprised to find a winery based in Stellenbosch making wines from all over the Cape province.

Vergelegen, Meerlust, Grangehurst, Rust en Verde, Louisvale, Jordan, Thelema, Kakonkop, Rustenberg, Warwick, Simonsig, Mulderbosch

Try

🍷 **Chardonnay** p.192, **Chenin Blanc** p.194

🍷 **Syrah/Shiraz** p.243, **Merlot** p.234, **Cabernet Sauvignon** p.224, **Pinotage** p.240

Stellenbosch has overtaken Paarl as the unofficial centre of the South African wine industry. It is a diverse area, with the cool sea air influencing the southern end, while the north is distinctly hotter. Recently there has been an effort to try to distinguish between these differing geographical areas. A system of 'wards' has been set up but producers rarely have the confidence to put them on the label; Stellenbosch has more sales clout than, say, Simonsberg.

Among the whites, Chardonnay flourishes. When **yields** are kept down and the vines are old some exceptional Chenin Blanc can be made. Only in the coolest areas, however, does Sauvignon Blanc make good wine.

Red, though, is what the region is known for. Pinotage always crops up and a recent wave of Syrah (confusingly, South Africans label this grape both as Shiraz and Syrah) planting shows promise. The Bordeaux grapes – Cabernet Sauvignon, Merlot and Cabernet Franc – are the ones that are now taking centre stage. Thankfully, in a day and age when wineries are often obsessed with making wine from a single variety, many of the Cape's producers still make a traditional blend. In this case check the back label to be sure of what you are getting.

The style of the reds in particular definitely sits on the fence between Europe and the hotter climes of somewhere like Australia. They have that appealing, upfront fruit, while retaining good **acidity** and **tannins**, making them food-friendly and also candidates for a few years in the bottle.

Steenberg,
Buitenverwachting, Neil
Ellis, Bouchard Finlayson,
Hamilton Russell, Glen
Carlou, La Motte, Plaisir
de Merle, Jean Daneel

Try
🍇 **Sauvignon Blanc** p.210,
Chardonnay p.192

🍇 **Cabernet Sauvignon**
p.224, **Merlot** p.234,
Syrah/Shiraz p.243, **Pinot
Noir** p.238, **Pinotage**
p.240

**The fertile and hot interior of Paarl is perfect for bulk production, much
of which is still destined to end up going into the vast distillation
industry. Unfortunately, many of these bland products end up on our
shelves and, unless you know the estate, I would treat these wines with
deep suspicion.**

A ward within Paarl that is worth looking at is the cool zone of
Franschhoek. Producers here make great Sauvignon Blanc and
Bordeaux-like reds, and are experimenting with Pinot Noir. Unlike the
wineries in Stellenbosch, these wineries are keen to distance themselves
from the name Paarl and so are likely to use their ward name on the
label.

To the north-west of Cape Town lies Groenekloof, where Neil Ellis makes
an outstanding Sauvignon Blanc, surely a precursor of more emerging
fine wines from here. Directly south of Cape Town lies Constantia,
containing some of the country's most historic vineyards – Sauvignon
Blanc in particular flourishes here. Follow the coast further south and
you arrive at Walker Bay. Here, around the town of Hermanus, two
wineries – Hamilton Russell and Bouchard Finlayson – have gained an
international following for their Chardonnay and Pinot Noir.

Inland, as the temperatures rise, bulk production again is the order of
the day. However, some fine sites are being developed in Robertson.
Once you get to the baking region of Little Karoo, **fortified** stickies are
the only thing that is seriously produced. Very rarely seen in this country,
they can be delicious.

USA

The United States produces vast quantities of wine from the East and West Coasts, and a not insignificant amount in between. The success of the industry is a fairly recent phenomenon, having been achieved in the last thirty years. It may seem a long time ago, but alcohol was banned altogether between 1920 and 1933. Abolition not only killed off the fledgling wine industry but it also created a situation where alcohol is still viewed with deep suspicion by one teetotal third of the population. Buy a bottle of wine in the States and the health warnings on the back might lead you to conclude that it is laced with arsenic. Of those who do drink, beer and spirits are the preferred choice. That said, those who consume wine love the stuff.

Americans have taken over the British mantle as the most fanatical wine buffs and obsessive collectors. American wines reflect this; take aside the usual no-brainer brands and the quality of US wine is startlingly high. Wineries in the States are often reminiscent of science laboratories and in the vineyards the growers pay astounding attention to detail. Naturally, the home market is predisposed to its own product.

There's nothing wrong with this – the major European countries barely acknowledge each other's wine, patriotically consuming only their own – but America is unique among the countries lumped into the New World category. Australia, New Zealand, Chile etc. are all heavy exporters.

The problem for the British consumer, who wants to get some of these delectable wines in his or her glass, is that the best American wineries can sell most of their product to their own kinsfolk. Unfortunately for us, the American drinking public are prepared to pay top dollar for their wine. Additionally, it is still very much perceived as a luxury, rather than an everyday product. Thus the average spend on a bottle is way higher than here.

Until recently producers have been in the enviable position of being able to sell all their wine internally, if we wanted any we had to pay the same amount. Good as the wines are, the price-to-pound ratio just does not add up when you consider what else is available to us in the UK.

Trouble, if not crisis, is just around the corner, though. Americans have recently discovered Australia (much to the chagrin of the UK importers who are now forced to pay more for their wines), whose wine style is similar, but at a lower price. Areas such as California have been so rapidly developed that there is now a glut of grapes. This, painfully for the estates, has coincided with an implosion in the regional economy and $40 bottles are suddenly much harder to sell. Unfortunate as these problems are, hopefully they will lead to a more realistic pricing structure for the export market.

In such a small space it is impossible to do justice to the various states, so I have concentrated on the ones that have a presence in the UK.

CALIFORNIA

Californian wine is often criticised for homogenous, super-ripe fruit flavours and no substance. This is not the case today, as there has been a real search to identify the best and most distinctive areas for each grape variety. This notion of *terroir* has taken the French hundreds of years to perfect. Why wait 200 years, though? California has taken advantage of technology and recently commissioned Nasa to produce shots of its vineyards from space to help...

Viader, Staglin, Stag's Leap Wine Cellars, Napanook, Shafer, Frog's Leap, Château Montelena, Beringer, Duckhorn, Clos du Val

Try

🍷 Chardonnay p.192

🍷 Pinot Noir p.238, **Cabernet Sauvignon** p.224, **Merlot** p.234

Saintsbury, Etude, Acacia, Havens, Domaine Carneros, Château St Jean, Matanzas Creek, La Crema, Sonoma-Cutrer, Kistler, Ramey, Clos du Bois, Peter Michael, Doug Nalle, Gallo Sonoma

Napa Valley

I can think of few other regions whose wines I love to drink so much, but never buy. This may sound paradoxical, so I'll explain. Taken on their own, Napa Valley wines are of extremely high quality and diversity; add price into the equation and very few are worth it. Too many wineries believe that charging more than their next-door neighbours somehow makes their wine better. Unfortunately, this policy has met with much success in the hugely wealthy local market. Take the same wine and put it on the shelf or in a restaurant in the UK and the sums just don't add up.

Only when you visit the Napa wineries and vineyards is it possible to comprehend the seemingly bottomless pit of money that has been used to construct them. Perhaps I shouldn't be too hard on the producers – many must have vast bank loans to pay back.

Napa is essentially a hot valley tempered in parts by sea air, allowing a whole range of styles to be produced. The southern end of the valley falls in the Carneros region and is cool. Here Chardonnay and Pinot Noir dominate, and the best are restrained, **complex** wines. The rest of the valley is all about Cabernet Sauvignon; some of the most profound examples worldwide are to be found here. The valley floor produces ripe, velvety examples while the cooler hillside sites show more **tannin** and **structure**.

Smaller regions within Napa, like the cool Howell Mountain and the hotter Rutherford, have also been mapped out. Both styles drink after only a few years but are capable of an extended stay in the cellar. My favourite 'cult' producers (tiny production, extraordinary wines, along with huge price tags and egos) are Bryant Family Vineyard, Harlan Estate, Philip Togni, Araujo, Opus One, Dominus and Screaming Eagle.

Sonoma Valley and Carneros

Carneros is, rather confusingly, part of both the Sonoma and the Napa Valleys, but the style of wines is firmly in the Sonoma camp. These are cool areas affected by the sea air, thus Chardonnay and Pinot Noir rule the roost, while excellent Zinfandels are made as well. The climate also allows for some fine sparkling wines. Most production happens in the

Try
🍇 **Chardonnay** p.192
🍇 **Pinot Noir** p.238

Ridge, Bonny Doon, Mount
Eden, Calera, Morgan,
Bernardus, Chalone,
Justin, Tablas Creek, Edna
Valley Vineyards, Au Bon
Climat, Qupé, Brewer-
Clifton, Jade Mountain,
Turley

northern part of the valley and here sub-regions such as the Russian River Valley make some of the most extraordinary Chardonnays I have ever tasted.

The south of Carneros is home to some largely unsuccessful projects of the big sparkling wine producers of the world. The Champagne house Taittinger and the Spanish Cava producer Freixenet invested heavily to make sparkling wine here, utilising the same methods and grapes as Champagne. The products are actually very good but remain a struggle to sell; many now are turning back to producing still white and red wine.

Central Coast

Diversity and, by Californian standards, value are the key to these areas. They lag a few years behind such regions as Napa in mapping out their own distinct regionality, but they are catching up. The Santa Cruz Mountains and the Santa Clara Valley are the first regions, south of San Francisco, of note.

Profound, long-lived Cabernet is grown in the coolest areas, along with fine Zinfandel. It is here that you get your first serious taste of a movement that has swept America in recent years: the so-called 'Rhône Rangers', which advocate the use of all grapes from this French region. They are generally a refreshing bunch, having little time for the more corporate side of Napa wineries. This stems from having struggled for years with varieties like Syrah to no avail. Now, with the grape in vogue, they realise better than many the vagaries of fashion. These are some of the most innovative, exciting and best-value (probably not for long, though) wines from the country.

Further south you come to the Monterey, a cool region where grapes can be hard to ripen. In the right spots restrained Chardonnay and Pinot Noir are made. Smaller niche areas such as Mount Harlan and the Carmel Valley produce profound examples of the same grapes.

Things get really rather exciting when you arrive in the counties of San Luis Obispo and Santa Barbara. These areas have only just started to take off since the mid-nineties. There is a diverse range of wine on offer and most you can actually afford to drink. Paso Robles in San Luis Obispo is famous for full-on Zinfandel, while there has been

much recent investment in all Rhône varieties. Excellent long-lived Cabernet Sauvignon is also found.

Edna Valley and Arroyo Grande lie in the southern end of the state; both are coolish regions turning out finely balanced Chardonnay, Pinot and spicy wines from Rhône varieties.

As you move into Santa Barbara, Pinot Noir and Chardonnay take centre stage. The Santa Maria and Santa Ynez Valleys are the main regions. As these cooler areas are further investigated the style of the wines is becoming increasingly balanced, **complex** and – dare I say it – reminiscent of fine Burgundy. Stunning Syrah is also produced that again harks back to France with its spicy style. This is a region constantly on the move, new sites and wineries spring up every year.

Try
🏵 Chardonnay p.192
🏵 Pinot Noir p.238, **Cabernet Sauvignon** p.224, **Zinfandel** p.247, **Syrah/Shiraz** p.243

Kendall-Jackson, Fetzer, Roederer

The Best of the Rest

Mendocino is a varied area north of Sonoma. The cool coastal areas produce one of the country's finest sparkling wines made by Roederer (of the Champagne house Louis Roederer). Inland, the heat allows excellent Cabernet Sauvignon and Zinfandel to be produced. It is also notable for containing two of California's best large operators; Kendall-Jackson, that admirably aims for diversity rather than homogeneity, and the all-**organic** Fetzer.

The inland area known as the Central Valley is where all the bulk production goes on. The Sierra Foothills and El Dorado, inland around the city of Sacramento, are both showing promise with their cool climate.

Try
🏵 Cabernet Sauvignon p.224, **Zinfandel** p.247

OREGON

Domaine Drouhin, Eyrie,
Amity, Bethel Heights,
Argyle, Ponzi, Beaux Frères

Try

🍇 **Chardonnay** p.192, **Pinot Gris** p.205

🍇 **Pinot Noir** p.238

Along with New Zealand, Oregon is touted as the answer to the Pinot Noir enigma. It requires an exacting set of conditions to be successful, and this is one of the few spots outside Burgundy so far found to be near its liking. Pinot producers are fanatics, love a challenge and perceive grapes such as Cabernet Sauvignon and Merlot to be uncouth and as easy to grow as weeds. By taking on an area very similar to Burgundy the growers have inherited the same major problem and that is to get the grapes fully ripe year in, year out. Unlike in California, it's important to take into consideration the vintage as they vary considerably.

The centre of wine production is the Willamette Valley. Pinot Noir is king here, the wines have fine **acidity** and, while approachable when young, have the **structure** for a few years' bottle age. There are also significant plantings of Chardonnay that have the same backbone but for some reason have left me less enthused than the Pinots.

Recently the growth Pinot Gris has soared; many are excellent, harking towards the rich spiciness of Alsace rather than an Italian Pinot Grigio. Many of these estates are tiny and prices are high, but so are those for fine Burgundy and quality across the board is higher.

Andrew Will, Château Ste Michelle, Cayuse, Woodward Canyon, Leonetti

Try

🍇 **Riesling** p.206, **Sauvignon Blanc** p.210

🍇 **Cabernet Sauvignon** p.224, **Merlot** p.234, **Syrah/Shiraz** p.243

These wines were until very recently rarely imported into the UK. Even now you will need to do some detective work to find them. It is, though, worth it as there seems to be a growing band (or maybe just more are being imported) of fine offerings; they have the considerable advantage of providing fine value compared with Oregon and California.

Bordeaux blends of Cabernet Sauvignon and Merlot seem to be particularly successful. In style they sit between the more voluptuous Californian offerings and Bordeaux. Syrah is the current 'it' grape across the States and I have tasted some excellent meaty, spicy examples that seem to be more Old World in style.

Chardonnay is of course planted but doesn't stand out. The cold-loving Riesling and Sauvignon Blanc make more exciting wines, with the former turning out some spectacular late-harvest stickies in the best years. Many wineries still blend grapes from across the state, so sub-region characteristics are often lost; one area, though, that is starting to shine for reds is the Walla Walla Valley.

WASHINGTON

THE GRAPES

WHITE GRAPES

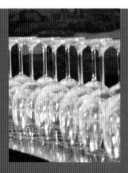

ALBARIÑO

Terras Gauda, Valmiñor,
Lasco do' Miño, Adegas
Galegas

Key Area
Northern Spain

Try
Rhône Valley p.84

Viognier p.218, **Muscat**
p.202, **Riesling** p.206,
Grüner Veltliner p.199,
Gewürztraminer p.198

Shellfish p.257, **Fish**
p.252, **Asian Food** p.281

This grape is a relative newcomer in the world of popular white grapes. Its home is in northern Spain, centred on Galicia. Light- to medium-bodied, it had the distinction of being the first unfortified Spanish white wine I enjoyed and it is still my favourite white from the country. Often likened to Viognier, Albariño does indeed share many of the same traits. Both have a floral, peachy nose, although Albariño has more **acidity** and never quite approaches the decadent heights of a great Viognier, but then nor does its price. The wines are all best drunk within one or two years. If you are on holiday in Spain, avoid the most expensive versions; these have suffered from a Spanish obsession with maturing wine in the barrel; **fresh** aromatic flavours like these do not marry with **oak**.

I love these floral, heady styles of wine as an aperitif. Otherwise try them with light, fresh seafood like squid, prawns and delicate white fish such as sole. Albariño also copes admirably with light foods such as those cooked with Thai or Chinese spices, if you feel so inclined.

A & P de Villaine, Goisot, Michel Bouzereau, Fichet

This grape is found in surprisingly large quantities in Burgundy, although it's always relegated to the worst vineyard sites. Aligoté is always distinguished from by the more noble wines made from Chardonnay by its name which will always appear on the label. This makes sense, as these wines are very different in style from a Burgundian Chardonnay – they will also sell for a lower price, so don't be confused into thinking you have suddenly found a bargain. The wines are high in **acidity** and generally low in flavour, and I am not a fan. Traditionally, the French add a good dose of Crème de Cassis (a sweet blackcurrant liqueur) to counter the swingeing **acidity** of this grape and I see no reason to disagree. As ever, there are always exceptions to the rule and top producers do make acceptable wines. Additionally, the tiny appellation of Bouzeron (the only one for Aligoté in France) somehow manages to fashion wines with added depths of flavour. Unfortunately, though, these are oddities, not the norm.

Key Area
🌐 **Burgundy** p.38

Try
🌐 **Loire** p.72

🍇 **Pinot Blanc/Bianco** p.204, **Chenin Blanc** p.194

🍴 **Shellfish** p.257, **Fish** p.252

The grape's only real attribute is its high **acidity** so keep it simple. Fresh shellfish and simple fish dishes.

Twenty years ago, if you wanted to drink a Chardonnay you had few options outside Burgundy. The everyday wines that people drank instead came from the lesser regions of Europe made from uninspiring workhorse grapes. Then along came the New World and in particular Australia. Chardonnay ripened beautifully there, producing accessible, fruit-driven wines and the climate was such that each year guaranteed a consistent wine. The British consumer loved the wines and there began a long-standing affair.

Giaconda (Australia),
Leeuwin Estate (Australia),
Kumeu River (New
Zealand),
Asso di Fiori (Italy),
Ramonet (Burgundy),
Carillon (Burgundy),
Sauzet (Burgundy),
Coche-Dury (Burgundy),
Comtes Lafon (Burgundy),
Jean Thévenet (Burgundy)

Chardonnay's spiritual home is Burgundy. Household names such as Chablis are all made from the grape, as well as some of the most sought-after whites from tiny villages such as Puligny-Montrachet. It is versatile and, while thriving in the relative cool of Burgundy, also works in the hotter New World growing regions. The worldwide demand for Chardonnay has seen plantings spring up everywhere, from the South of France, Italy and Spain to Chile and Argentina. It also plays a major part in the production of Champagne.

It is impossible to get to grips with the different flavours on offer without taking into account the effect of maturing Chardonnay in **oak** barrels, a process which adds extra dimensions of flavour. Many white and red wines are matured in this way, but for no other grape does it have such a defining influence. Chardonnay on its own is often light in colour with delicate flavours such as green apples and pears. Oaked examples, however, have a deeper golden colour with creamy, spicy flavours such as vanilla. The two often have little in common. I won't debate here the pros and cons of heavily oaked wines, but there is no doubt that the flavours often associated with this grape by many people are more than likely those of the **oak** rather than the taste of Chardonnay itself.

What I am trying to get across about this grape is the difficulty in categorising it. The range of flavours and weight between a light unoaked Chardonnay from France to a big **ripe**, oaky version from Australia is huge. If you enjoy a full-bodied Aussie Chardonnay, try other wines of this weight and don't just work your way through the Chardonnays of the world. The big bold wines might taste great after a sip but think about whether you'd want to be drinking it all night. As always, the more restrained examples are generally better matched to food.

Key Areas
Burgundy p.38,
Champagne p.64, **Italy**
p.104, **Spain** p.142,
Australia p.156, **New
Zealand** p.168, **California**
p.180, **Chile** p.167

Try
Northern Rhône p.86

Sémillon p.212, **Marsanne**
p.201, **Roussanne** p.208,
Pinot Gris p.205

This vast range of tastes can deal with anything the fishmonger can come up with and also make some surprising forays into the butcher's shop. Crisp, **un-oaked** wines partner shellfish, cod and any salad type things. The bigger wines like meaty fish; try monkfish, turbot and hake and a special mention for poached salmon and hollandaise, avoid too many strong herbs. Lobster and rich chardonnay is a decadent delight. These big wines will also be fine with roast chicken and lighter game.

If you fancy going 'off-piste', pair the best wines with a tender fillet steak or veal served in a rich cream sauce. This is a perfect illustration of why you should match the wine to the sauce first and foremost. The light **fresh** wines are a good match for goats cheeses while the rich stuff enjoys nothing better than a good smelly, runny number. The New World is thankfully reining in the **oak** in their wines, which is a good thing as the fat, over-oaked style is not food friendly.

Chenin Blanc is rather like a faded film star whose reputation has been tarnished by a series of bad TV movies. The grape's home is the Loire valley in France, where it makes long-lived dry whites and some of the most sublime and undervalued stickies in the world – this is Oscar level stuff. On the flat plains of South Africa, however, we have the made-for-television projects. Here the grape's natural propensity to produce vast quantities of wine is given free rein and unfortunately South African Chenin Blanc is some of the most uninspiring, dull, bulk-produced wine in the world. Please delete these wines from your wine-buying vocabulary. I must point out here that, on a recent trip to the area, I tasted some sublime Chenins from the Cape; the trouble is that we rarely see them in this country.

This grape has very high levels of natural **acidity** which, when grown in a cooler area like the Loire, means the wines often need a few years' bottle age to soften them. Here dry wine that can last for thirty years plus are made in places such as Vouvray and Savennières. It is also in the Loire that the grape makes some of the greatest and best-value sweet wines in the world. As with Riesling, the **acidity** of the grape marks it out and results in even the most intensely sweet wines having a refreshing **finish**. To put it another way, your mouth doesn't feel as if you have been eating neat sugar as it does after poor sweet wines. It is important to look out for the vintage, though, as this grape can be painful in years when it has not fully ripened.

Good **acidity** is a great commodity for rich creamy sauces. Drink the lighter wines with oily fish dishes. The medium-dry and heavier dry wines will stand up to chicken, veal and even some light game.

Drink the lighter, sweet wines with fruit-based desserts. The richer versions require nothing more than a glass.

COLOMBARD

I wasn't even going to mention this, the most lacklustre of white grapes. However, in today's wine world where marketing teams deem it vital to have a grape's name on the wine label, Colombard is increasingly being seen on our shelves. This is madness; the equivalent of advertising a car for sale without an engine. The wines have few redeeming features, being high in **acidity** and low in flavour – perfect, in fact, for distillation, thus it is widely utilised in Cognac and Armagnac production.

The Royal Tokaji Company,
Oremus, Disznókő

Key Area
Hungary p.103

Try
Alsace p.16

Grüner Veltliner p.199,
Pinot Gris p.205

This is one of the grapes responsible for the heavenly Tokaji in Hungary, which is now making a strong comeback after years in the Communist doldrums. I'll discuss the sweet wine later as its production methods are unique. Of late, though, some of the top producers of sweet wines have put their efforts into making good dry wine. These have a rich, spicy character and are generally excellent value for money, coming from such serious winemakers as they do.

Excellent with Asian foods, Furmint has the weight to stand up to Thai green curry provided you haven't overloaded it with the chillies.

FURMINT

GEWÜRZTRAMINER/TRAMINER

Bott-Geyl, Zind-Humbrecht, Schlumberger, Bruno Sorg, Schofitt, Hugel, Ostertag

Key Areas
Alsace p.16, **Italy** p.104, **Australia** p.156, **New Zealand** p.168

Try
Jurançon p.69, **Rhône Valley** p.84, **Austria** p.96

Grüner Veltiner p.199, **Pinot Gris** p.205, **Marsanne** p.201, **Roussanne** p.208, **Viognier** p.218, **Riesling** p.206, **Albariño** p.190, **Muscat** p.202

Light Game p.267

Gewürztraminer (France and the New World)
Traminer (Italy)

One of the four *noble* varieties grown in Alsace, this is another of those love-or-hate grapes. Rather like Riesling, Gewürztraminer's popularity suffers from its distinctly Germanic-sounding name. If you want delicate, subtle and restrained whites, please move on. At their best these wines have **ripe**, decadent, floral flavours, with lychees and rose petals often appearing in tasting notes. They have a golden hue and are interesting in that their nose is often misleading in giving clues as to how the wine will taste. The opulence of the smell leads one to think that the wine will be richer and sweeter than it actually is. So, although it can seem like an assault on the nasal passage, it is well worth persevering with.

The full-bodied *(Vendange Tardive)* and the sweet *(Sélection des Grains Nobles)* versions of Gewürztraminer produced in Alsace are stunners. Strangely, unlike Riesling and Pinot Gris, its other bedfellows in Alsace, Gewürztraminer hasn't made much of an impression around the world. New World versions from Australia and New Zealand lack depth and **balance**. Known as Traminer in Italy, it is picked early to retain freshness. Both these types, to me, defeat the object of what the grape is about, namely full-throttle flavour.

A magical food wine, try the driest versions with Asian foods. The richer *Vendange Tardive* wines from Alsace are beautiful with duck, goose and lighter game like partridge. No need for food at all with the truly sweet wines – just let them give your taste buds a good going over.

Prager, Schloss Gobelsburg

Key Area
Austria p.96

Try
Gewürztraminer p.198, Viognier p.218, Riesling p.206, Albariño p.190

Fish p.252, Cream Sauces p.284, Chicken p.265

Grüner Veltliner is a late entry to the white grape section. Until recently it was barely heard of outside its homeland of Austria. Now Austrian wines are undergoing a minor resurgence. The grape has similar floral notes to Gewürztraminer, but with more citrus flavours. It also has much better **structure** with a zippy **acidity**. Wines made from this grape are not easy to track down in your local bottle shop, but they have begun to make an appearance on wine lists at the better restaurants. They drink well when young but the top offerings from regions such as the Wachau age beautifully, revealing a **complex** minerality.

These are **complex structured** wines that are best served with food. They love fish, especially dishes with rich sauces, smoked fish also works beautifully. The bigger wines will work with roast chicken.

GRÜNER VELTLINER

MANSENG, PETIT AND GROS

Two varieties with similar attributes, both are grown down in the south-west of France. The most famous of the regions represented by Manseng is Jurançon. The wines range from the dry through to the intensely sweet: dry they have a floral, heady and aromatic excellent citrus **acidity**; as they move up the scale to full-blown sweeties they become honeyed and intense, but with the **acidity** always keeping the wines poised and **balanced**. The dry wines are best drunk young, and while the sweet ones will keep for ten years they also taste delicious in their youth. These wines always represent excellent value.

Dry Manseng wines will complement a range of fish dishes – look for them particularly to complement tricky herbs like tarragon and dill. The sweet ones have the requisite **acidity** to deal with a range of fruit-based puddings, but anything too sweet will overwhelm them. A good, ripe Brie or other runny cheeses also go down a treat.

Marsanne usually partners Roussanne in making some of the Northern Rhône's finest whites; Hermitage, Crozes-Hermitage and St Joseph. It makes big, oily wines with tropical-fruit flavours – in short it is a bit of a show-off. What it lacks is much **acidity** or **balance**, and this is where Roussanne comes in, lending a completeness to the blend. Lots of flavour and low **acidity** is unfortunately perceived to be a good selling point by many, though, and there has thus been an increase of Marsanne sold unblended. These wines, grown in the hot climate of the South of France, are high in alcohol and unbalanced. I call them one-glass wines as, after their initial showy flavours tire, this is all you'll want to drink.

These are rich wines and they can stand up to heavy fish and white meats. Avoid creamy sauces, though, as the grape generally has insufficient **acidity** to cut through them.

MARSANNE

Muscat (France), Moscato Bianco (Italy)

There are a huge number of variations on the Muscat theme, with many clones and sub-varieties. As they essentially have the same characteristics I'll deal with them all together and refer to them just as Muscat, and not confuse you with too many of the different names. They have two very distinct flavours associated with them. First, flowers, which is not unusual in wine, and secondly grapes, which oddly is...

Schofitt, Zind-Humbrecht
(Alsace), **Campbells**
(Australia), **Paul Jaboulet
Aïné** (Rhône Valley), **La
Spinetta** (Italy), **Marco de
Bortoli** (Italy)

Key Areas
Alsace (dry) p.16, **Italy
(sweet and fizzy)** p.104,
Spain p.142, **Portugal
(sweet)** p.142, **Australia**
p.156 **(sweet)**, **Rhône
Valley (sweet)**, p.84

**If you like the dry versions,
try**
Viognier p.218, **Albariño**
p.190, **Gewürztraminer**
p.198

**If you prefer the sweet
versions try**
Jurançon p.69

Fruit Puddings p.296,
Crème Brûlée p.295, **Hard
Cheese** p.291

This is the only grape whose juice produces wine that actually tastes like
the table grapes we eat. The best variety, called Muscat Blanc à Petits
Grains, is, rather inexplicably, one of the four *noble* varieties in Alsace.
The wines are deliciously fragrant but are not in the class of, say,
Riesling or Gewürztraminer. In the Southern Rhône it makes Muscat de
Beaumes-de-Venise, so loved by the English. The inferior Muscat
Alexandria is used to make the heavier and clumsy Muscat de
Rivesaltes.

The sweetness of Muscat de Rivesaltes is generated by
fortification, adding some stuffing to what is essentially a light,
refreshing grape. This method is repeated throughout Europe, with
Moscato in Italy and Moscatel in Portugal and Spain. The Australians
take it one step further, making sublime **fortified** Muscats, which are
usually treated like tawny Port, being released after five or more years in
the barrel and thus without a vintage. These are massively concentrated
wines, which ooze layers of sweetness, honey and orange peel. Hardly
seen in this country, they remain as yet fairly undiscovered by the wine
world in general and are thus stupidly good value. If you track some
down, do buy all you can.

Finally, a much maligned wine that is worth resurrecting is
Moscato d'Asti, produced in Northern Italy. The best of these are like
drinking fizzy grape juice. They must be drunk very cold, and preferably
with a bowl of strawberries in the summer. Low in alcohol with less fizz
than Champagne, I find a bottle each is usually appropriate...

The dry styles of Muscat are best served as aperitifs. The sweet versions
vary hugely in style, however, and should be treated accordingly. Serve
the lighter grapey versions with fruit-based desserts. You need to be
careful with richer styles with their intense flavours, which can
overwhelm many things. Crème brûlée likes the orange-tinged ones but
many are best drunk on their own. Treat the Aussie versions as tawny
Port and serve with hard crumbly cheeses like Cheddar or Cornish Yarg.

PINOT BLANC/PINOT BIANCO

Schofitt (Alsace), **Ostertag** (Alsace), **Jermann** (Italy), **Drius** (Italy)

Key Areas
Alsace p.16, **Italy** p.104

Try
Loire Valley p.72, **Bordeaux** p.24, **Soave** p.113

Pinot Grigio p.205, **Sauvignon Blanc** p.210, **Aligoté** p.191, **Chenin Blanc** p.194

Shellfish p.257, **Fish** p.252, **Salads** p.288

Pinot Blanc (France), Pinot Bianco (Italy)

Here is a grape that does lots of good work but never quite gets the blood pumping – it produces good, honest, **fresh** white wines that are enjoyable but rarely excite. Its home in France is Alsace. Here Pinot Blancs are rightly served as looseners for the more serious, flavour-packed wines to follow. They are clean, crisp and the best have mineral overtones; in short, the perfect aperitif. Italian Pinot Bianco is similarly **structured**. I am surprised that the Italian version has not found more popularity in this country, as I generally find the wines better **balanced** than the ubiquitous Pinot Grigio.

I like to drink these wines as an aperitif, or to partner them with light simple dishes of shellfish or grilled white fish and salads.

Ostertag (Alsace), **Alvaro Pecorari** (Italy), **Jermann** (Italy), **T'Gallant** (Australia), **Zind-Humbrecht** (Alsace)

Key Areas
Alsace p.16, **Italy** p.104, **Australia** p.156, **New Zealand** p.168

If you like the Alsatian style, try
Austria p.96

Gewürztraminer p.198, **Marsanne** p.201, **Roussanne** p.208, **Chardonnay** p.192

Pork p.273, **Asian Food** p.281

If you prefer the Italian style, try
Loire Valley p.72, **Soave** p.113, **Chablis** p.42

Pinot Blanc p.204, **Chenin Blanc** p.194

Antipasti p.287, **Fish** p.252

Pinot Gris, Tokay d'Alsace or Tokay Pinot Gris (France), Pinot Grigio (Italy)

This is another of the four *noble* grape varieties of Alsace, but it tends to get unfairly overlooked as it has neither the poise and **balance** of Riesling nor the full-on brashness of Gewürztraminer. Pinot Gris's flavour profile lies somewhere in between the two, with the best wines demonstrating a full-bodied, oily texture with smoky, spicy aromas. I love the Alsatian version; it has better **acidity** than Gewürztraminer and tends towards a drier, less opulent style, making it a more versatile wine. When conditions are right this grape can make sensational sweet wines, but these are not so widely produced as the Rieslings and Gewürztraminers.

What can I say about Pinot Grigio without offending the vast swathes of people who buy it? Not much, probably. The best versions, from Alto Adige or Friuli in Italy, are lovely wines, capturing some of the spice of Alsace but being much lighter in body and higher in **acidity**. They are good aperitifs and useful to wash down some simply grilled fish. Now to the other 98 per cent of wines masquerading under the Pinot Grigio label. These have all the flavour of alcoholic water. Italy has a peculiar obsession with harvesting white grapes very early to capture **acidity**. This, coupled with Italy's second national vinous pastime of seeing who can produce the highest **yields** per acre, leads to wines that are devoid of flavour.

   Some increasingly good versions of Pinot Gris are coming out of Australia and New Zealand at the moment. The former leans towards Alsace and the latter nods to Italy. America has also recently caught the Pinot Grigio bug. Their winemakers have responded by making some good but vastly overpriced versions that take Italy as their template.

Alsatian Pinot Gris loves to be matched with richer styles of Asian food. Its spicy **structure** also complements rich white meats such as sucking pig and wild boar.

   Italian Pinot Grigio goes best with vegetable antipasti and simply cooked fish.

The wine press and trade have been touting the comeback of Riesling for many a year in the face of general indifference from the wine-buying public. What can I say to change your mind? Probably not much, but it is my duty to open your eyes to the greatest white grape variety (yes, better than Chardonnay).

Trimbach (Alsace),
Zind-Humbrecht (Alsace),
Prager (Austria),
J. J. Prüm (Germany),
Egon Muller (Germany),
Grosset (Australia), Pipers
Brook (Tasmania)

Key Areas

Germany p.98, **Alsace**
p.16, **Austria** p.96, **Italy**
p.104, **Australia** p.156,
New Zealand p.168

Try

Loire Valley p.72, **Chablis**
p.42

Chenin Blanc p.194,
Sauvignon Blanc p.210,
Albariño p.190, **Grüner**
Veltliner p.199

Asian Food p.281, **Oily**
Fish p.252, **Chicken**
p.265, **Pork** p.273, **Veal**
p.276, **Pâté** p.273, **Fruit**
Puddings p.296

Britain is regarded as one of the most competitive and diverse wine markets in the world: there is no other country that can boast the array of wine we have on our shelves. It is to our credit that we buy such a range, but winemakers are baffled by our indifference towards this grape. This has not always been the case; in the first half of the twentieth century German Rieslings were highly prized, more so than white Burgundy. However, a new-found passion for all things dry, as well as a nose dive in the quality of German wine, abruptly ended our dalliance with Riesling. Now, though, our reputation as a cosmopolitan wine-buying country is on the line. Australians are bemused by the Poms' lack of interest in Riesling, and the French and Germans just shrug their shoulders and happily drink it all themselves.

I bestow the mantle of the 'greatest' variety on Riesling for a number of reasons. First, the grape covers every point on the taste spectrum, from bone-dry to decadently sweet. Second, and more important, is its poise; at whatever level Riesling is all about **balance**; the interplay between fruit, sweetness and **acidity** is key. The wines are hugely undervalued and, with no expensive **oak** barrels used in their production, are cheaper to make than your average Chardonnay. Last, they age magnificently; it is quite possible to go and buy a bottle for under a tenner that will happily sit in your cellar for ten years. The lighter styles make an excellent hunger-inducing aperitif, while the mid-weight wines are great with food (especially all things oriental). The sweeties, with their balance of sugar and **acidity**, are the perfect way to end a meal, although I advocate drinking them at any time of the day when your mood needs lifting.

Riesling's spiritual home is Germany, but for the uninitiated I would start elsewhere where the wines have usually been fermented to full dryness – say, just across the Rhine in Alsace, or northern Italy. Or you could sample some of the fabulous minerally examples now being produced in Austria. The cooler areas of Australia and New Zealand are also making top-notch Rieslings.

All the wines are a joy as an aperitif, especially any with a little bottle age. The light, young ones, with their fruit and touch of sweetness, are the answer to spicy Asian food. Richer versions will deal with almost anything: oily fish, quiches, roast chicken, pork and veal. Save the most decadent examples for pâté, foie gras and fruity desserts.

Qupé (California),
Beaucastel (Châteauneuf-
du-Pape), **Chave**
(Hermitage), **Chapoutier**
(Hermitage)

Key Areas
Rhône Valley p.84,
Australia p.156, **California**
p.180

Try
Chardonnay p.192,
Marsanne p.201, **Pinot
Gris** p.205

Fish p.252, **Chicken**
p.265, **Veal** p.276, **Soft
Cheese** p.292

A grape that is rarely vinified on its own. Roussanne's erstwhile partner is Marsanne and the two together make the heavyweight white wines of the Northern Rhône: Hermitage, Crozes-Hermitage and St Joseph.

It is also one of the four varietals permitted in the production of white Châteauneuf-du-Pape. Here the top estates like Beaucastel make some staggering white wines utilising a high proportion of Roussanne in the blend. Australia, with its high regard for all things Rhône, has significant acres of it under vine, while California has also become a player in the Rhône stakes. It has a fragrant, rich character, but also has the necessary **acidity** and affinity with **oak** to age gaining a honeyed **complexity**. I think Roussanne has lots going for it and wouldn't be surprised if we see more of this grape taking a starring role rather than just being a member of the supporting cast.

These are powerful, concentrated wines, so look to flavoursome fish dishes, roast chicken, veal and creamy cheeses.

Sauvignon Blanc is one of the most consumed white grapes in Britain. Yet the wine trade can be a bit sniffy about the wines made from it. At last year's International Wine Challenge – the equivalent of the wine Oscars – the grape won one solitary gold. The reason for this is that those in the know have come to the conclusion that Sauvignon is a one-dimensional grape and whisper quietly that it is 'dull'. This is plainly a load of old tosh. Those who advocate this view seem to have forgotten that while drinking wine can sometimes be a serious and cerebral exercise, most of the time it is not. I don't require subtlety when sitting outside on a summer afternoon with some mates; I want full-throttle refreshing fruit. Good Sauvignon from France or the New World should offer pure, simple pleasure – there, I've said it. You should stick your nose in the glass and think 'I am going to enjoy this'; none of this 'interesting, I wonder which side of the hill this is grown on ...' OK?!

Cotat (Loire Valley), **Neil Ellis** (South Africa), **Isabel Estate** (New Zealand), **Cloudy Bay** (New Zealand), **Dageneau** (Loire), **Jean-Max Roger** (Loire), **Henry Pellé** (Loire)

Key Areas

Loire Valley p.72, **Italy** p.104, **New Zealand** p.168, **Australia** p.156, **South Africa** p.174, **Chile** p.167

Try

Chablis p.42, **Soave** p.113

Riesling p.206, **Pinot Blanc** p.204, **Chenin Blanc** p.194, **Verdejo** p.215

Shellfish p.257, **Fish** p.252, **Goats Cheese** p.293, **Asian Food** p.281

Sauvignon likes the cooler regions of the world, hence its spiritual home in the Loire Valley in France. Here two *villages* in particular have made the grape famous, Sancerre and Pouilly-Fumé. They are also responsible for much of the harm done to this grape's image as there are many underwhelming and overpriced wines made here. Good French Sauvignon is characterised by its crisp, refreshing **acidity** and steely citrus flavours. Remember my mantra, though: regions don't make great wine, producers do.

Plantings in the New World and particularly New Zealand have brought the grape to a mass audience. Wines from the New World should give an explosion of tropical, zesty fruit flavours; in short, a souped-up and less restrained version of their European counterparts.

The main exception to this rule is the confusingly named Fumé Blanc from California. The name of the wine tells you that it is echoing the *village* of Pouilly-Fumé in the Loire, yet the wines taste nothing like them. They are big oily wines that to my taste are always over-oaked; my advice is to stay clear.

Sauvignon is a wonderful aperitif but is also a godsend when it comes to those tricky food and wine pairings. Like its very unfashionable brother, Riesling, the New World versions work a treat with spicy Asian food. European ones do also work, but here you should be thinking about regionality. For example, Loire Sauvignon and goat cheese is a classic match. 'Cheese and white wine?!' I hear you cry. Trust me, the French take their food much more seriously than we do, so if it weren't the most sublime match they wouldn't have been putting it together for years. It will also do a fine take on any light fish dishes, especially anything in a shell.

SÉMILLON

Sémillon is an unappreciated and versatile grape. Its home is Bordeaux where it is the main component of the region's sublime sweet wines, Sauternes and Barsac. It has a natural affinity with *botrytis*, the mould that concentrates the flavours of great sweet wine. However, it should be noted that these honeyed, caramelised delights are as much about the flavour of *botrytis* grapes as the inherent character of Sémillon. The dry whites of Bordeaux offer a glimpse of what it can do on its own. Those with a high proportion of the grape (unfortunately the more expensive ones) have a herbal, spicy character that is often enhanced by maturation in **oak** barrels. They tend to come into their own after a few years' bottle age, becoming honeyed and rich yet at the same time bone-dry. In the hotter areas of Australia, like the Hunter Valley, the grape has flourished, producing big, muscular, tropical-fruited wines that age superbly. I'm afraid, though, that the Aussies cannily kept most of these for themselves, so you need to work hard to track down the good bottles. Decadent sweet wines are made from the grape all around the world.

A good food wine, indeed the best when young, Sémillon can be a bit much without food. Try it with meaty fish like salmon and turbot; they'll easily stand up to any creamy sauce you throw at them. The older wines will take on chicken and tarragon, and even veal.

My honest opinion is that I like to drink all great sweet wine on its own; view it as pudding taken in liquid form. These ones, though, will work best with crème brûlée, tarte tartin and marmalade or treacle sponge; however, avoid tart, fruit-based desserts. Lastly, an odd but delicious combination is creamy blue cheese. The contrast of a slightly salty cheese and the sweet wine is heaven.

Sylvaner is most widely planted in Alsace. After the other aromatic joys that emanate from the region, it comes as a shock to find a truly dull variety. In the hands of the best producer the wines can have a crisp steeliness to them. Mostly, though, the grape is used to make high-yielding bulk wine that is low in taste.

Sylvaner's lack of inherent flavour limits you to drinking the wine as an aperitif or with veggie salads.

SYLVANER

Key Areas
 **France** p.14, **Italy** p.104

Try
Chablis p.42, **Muscadet** p.74

Pinot Grigio p.205, **Pinot Blanc** p.204

Salads p.288

Trebbiano (Italy), Ugni Blanc (France)

One of the dullest grapes planted in Europe, Trebbiano, or Ugni Blanc, is responsible for lakes of *Vin de Pays* in France and *Vino da Tavola* in Italy. It has little character apart from a fresh, zippy **acidity**. Its distinction is that it plays a part in two of Italy's most famous whites, Soave and Frascati. The best wines from these regions, though, include a proportion of varietals with a more interesting nature. In France it is also used to make the light acidic white wines necessary for distillation in Cognac and Armagnac.

These are good for washing down light vegetable-based salads, although 'wash down' rather than complement are the operative words.

Verdejo's home is Spain – more specifically a region in the north called Rueda. Here it traditionally made rich whites whose taste was heavily affected by the **oak** barrels it was matured in. These were highly regarded in Spain and fetched a high price. I have tasted some excellent wines in this style, but to my mind most are just over-oaked and **oxidised**. Either way, this style of wine is not what the international market demands.

Modern winemaking techniques have revolutionised how these wines are made. Fresh, fruity and aromatic whites are what today's producers strive for. As a result, the wines from the region are now arguably among Spain's best whites. Most are now designed for immediate consumption and remind me of a powerful Sauvignon Blanc, being full of fresh tropical fruits.

The lighter styles are great aperitifs, otherwise grilled vegetables and shellfish would be my preferred choice. Those that have seen a bit of barrel ageing are more robust and will stand up to all types of fish and simple chicken dishes.

VERDEJO

VERDELHO

Duckbill, David Traeger, Wordsworth

Key Areas
Portugal p.132, **Australia** p.156

Try
Alsace p.16, **Loire** p.72

Sauvignon Blanc p.210, **Riesling** p.206, **Pinot Gris** p.205, **Albariño** p.190, **Verdejo** p.215, **Vermentino** p.217

Fish p.252, **Asian/Fusion Food** p.281

Until recently this grape would only have warranted an entry as a postscript to a forgotten and dying style of wine. This is the grape responsible for the medium-weight style of Madeira. Recently though, it has been making a bit of a name for itself on the other side of the world. Australians, ever the innovators, have recently been seeking out more styles to add to their international palette of grapes. Verdelho has been seized upon and there are some excellent examples now being made across the country. The wines have an attractive lemony, tropical and oily character. They are never oaked and need to be drunk on release.

Verdelho makes a fine aperitif but also has reasonable weight, so it can stand up to most fishy things. Additionally, they match food that has an Asian/fusion slant.

Argiolas

Key Area
Italy p.104

Try
Alsace p.16, **Loire** p.72

Sauvignon Blanc p.210,
Riesling p.206, **Pinot Gris**
p.205, **Albariño** p.190,
Verdejo p.215

Antipasti p.287, **Salads**
p.288, **Pasta** p.278, **Fish**
p.252

Vermentino's home is Italy, where it makes **fresh** lemon-scented wine. It can be found throughout the country but the southern half is where it excels. The islands of Sicily and Sardinia in particular make **ripe**, creamy examples that always seem to encourage one to open that second bottle. The wines are generally light and **fresh** and need to be drunk as soon as they are released. Many Italian white varieties leave me cold, but good Vermentino though is one of my favourites.

Chilled right down they make great palate awakening aperitifs. Once you get to sitting around the table, drink them with grilled vegetable antipasti, salad starters, simple pasta dishes and all type of fish. These are not powerful wines, so simplicity rather than strong flavours should be your rule of thumb.

VERMENTINO

VIOGNIER

Viognier is essentially a show-off. It has heady aromas of peach blossom and spices, along with a puppy-fat texture, and there is no need for the words 'complex' or 'subtle' when describing these wines. In my view, when you are in the right mood they are a wonder to drink. Rather like Sauvignon Blanc, though, they are viewed with some suspicion in the wine trade. 'Where is the acidity to balance the wine?' the merchants cry, or they bemoan that the wines are shallow, only having one-dimensional primary flavours. Of course, the critics are right, but life would be infinitely duller if we only took a balanced approach to it – no more meals out that we couldn't afford or buying impractical fast cars. Bad Viogniers are made but no more so than any other variety.

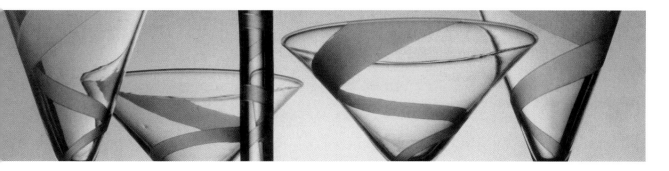

Bonny Doon (California),
Pierre Gaillard (Rhône),
Georges Vernay (Rhône),
André Perret (Rhône)

Key Areas
Rhône Valley p.84,
California p.180, **Australia**
p.156

Try
Gewürztraminer p.198,
Pinot Gris/Tokay d'Alsace
p.205, **Muscat** p.202,
Grüner Veltliner p.199,
Albariño p.190

The centre of Viognier production is in a tiny area called Condrieu in the northern Rhône. Here, on the steep valley sides, wonderfully fragrant, hedonistic wines are produced; the downside is that they are not cheap, and I suspect this is another reason why we, as a race, are sceptical of these wines. With our peculiarly British attitude towards ageing wine, we are unhappy at paying £20 for a bottle of Condrieu that will not benefit from any time in the cellar. I have never tasted a bottle of Viognier that has profited from more than a year or two in the bottle. In fact, I have drunk many that are over the hill.

The last five years have seen an explosion in plantings around the world and not always in the most suitable places. The grape needs heat, but also cool nights to retain its naturally low **acidity**. Australia, in particular, has been guilty of planting in the wrong areas; too much heat and the wines become excessively flabby and alcoholic. Italy is having particular success with Viognier as a blending tool, using it to pep up some of its blander wines. Please ignore the doomy pessimism, put on your brashest outfit, play your Pop Rivals CD, open a good bottle of Viognier and revel in being superficial.

I find that Viognier is often best drunk on its own because of its low **acidity**. The best have an aniseed character that works well with tarragon, which is useful as this is a tricky herb.

RED GRAPES

BARBERA

Elio Grasso, Braida,
Luciano Sandrone, Bruno
Rocca, Renato, Cigliuti,
Principiano

Key Area
Northern Italy p.104

Try
Syrah/Shiraz p.243, **Merlot**
p.234, **Zinfandel** p.247

Beef p.263, **Pork** p.273,
Stews p.275

Barbera's home is the north-east of Italy and in particular Piemonte, where it plays second fiddle to Barolo's grape, Nebbiolo. Its name will often be tagged on to the commune in which it is grown, such as Alba or Asti, and it makes darkly coloured rustic wine with rich flavours of plum and leather. It is low in **tannin** but high in **acidity** – a great commodity when pairing it with food. Most good Barolo producers make Barberas as well, but at a much more affordable price. These producers have been at the forefront of the grape's resurgence in recent years, reducing **yields** and experimenting by ageing the wine in new **oak** barrels. The top-end wines even have the stuffing for medium-term cellaring.

Barbera's high **acidity** and rusticity pairs best with good, hearty food. Beef stew, Italian sausages, wild boar and the like.

CABERNET FRANC

Charles Joguet (Loire),
Pierre-Jacques Druet
(Loire),
Couly-Duthiel (Loire),
Cheval Blanc (Bordeaux),
Viader (California),
Trinoro (Tuscany)

Key Areas
Loire Valley p.72,
Bordeaux p.24, **Bergerac**
p.22, **Australia** p.156

**If you like the lighter reds,
try**
Beaujolais p.60, **Loire
Valley** p.72

Gamay p.229, **Pinot Noir**
p.238

Fish p.252, **Chicken** p.265

**If you prefer the more full-
bodied versions, try**
South Africa p.174,
Australia p.156, **Bordeaux**
p.24

Pinotage p.240, **Merlot**
p.234

Lamb p.270, **Beef** p.263

This is one of the big three grapes that is used in the blend to make red Bordeaux. Unlike the other partners in the blend – Merlot and Cabernet Sauvignon – Cabernet Franc has never quite managed to make it on its own. It is, however, of particular importance to the soft Merlot-dominated wines of St Émilion and Pomerol.

On its own, Cabernet Franc is responsible for the best reds made in the Loire Valley, in places like Chinon and Bourgueil. These wines can be light and fruity; not dissimilar to Beaujolais and often chilled in the summer. If you want to drink some red wine with fish, these really work, and the best producers in the right vintage can make serious medium-bodied reds that will last ten years; and are more similar to Bordeaux in style. I often find myself not enjoying these wines, though, as unless the grapes are perfectly **ripe** they tend to have a vegetal, green pepper character to them that does not get on with me. I will probably incur the wrath of every red **vigneron** in the Loire now, but the best thing to do with Cabernet Franc is to buy a bottle and make up your own mind. The grape is pretty ubiquitous and has been planted everywhere in the world that makes wines utilising a Bordeaux blend. A recent development, in particular in Australia, is the production of wines made from 100 per cent Cabernet Franc. These are full of ripe, sweet fruit and in my opinion should see a great future.

The lighter reds work chilled with fish in the summer. The better Loire reds drink with red meat dishes, but avoid any heavy or rich sauces. These are medium not full-bodied wines.

CABERNET SAUVIGNON

The king of red grape varieties, Cabernet Sauvignon is now responsible for more of the world's greatest wines than any other grape. Royalty, though, can seem aloof and difficult to get to know, and this is certainly the case with Cabernet. The best of these wines are built for the long haul and, when tasted young, can seem unbalanced as they are very tannic and acidic. This is a grape for which trading up in your local wine merchant can lead to a great wine but one that is unready to drink. It is a thick-skinned grape and this accounts for the high level of tannins in the wine.

Vasse Felix (Australia), Moss Wood (Australia), Howard Park (Australia), Ridge (California), Bryant Family Vineyard (California), Léoville-Barton (Bordeaux), Léoville-Las-Cases (Bordeaux), Latour (Bordeaux), Ornellaia (Italy)

Key Areas

Bordeaux p.24, **Italy** p.104, **Spain** p.142, **Australia** p.156, **California** p.180, **Washington** p.185, **Chile** p.167, **Argentina** p.154, **South Africa** p.174

Try

Loire Valley p.72, **Italy** p.104, **Ribera del Duero** p.145

Merlot p.234, **Nebbiolo** p.237, **Cabernet Franc** p.223

Beef p.263, **Lamb** p.270, **Venison (roasted)** p.269

In cooler regions the grape is characterised by flavours of blackcurrants and pencil lead. In contrast, the hotter climes of the New World produce exuberant aromas of ripe black fruits and eucalyptus. The better wines will be matured in **oak** barrels, adding the **complexity** and power that Cabernet-dominated wines are all about. They may not have the immediate upfront appeal of some other varieties and to some palates weaned on soft, **ripe** New World red, the European Cabernets can seem austere. These wines have more **structure** and a dry, firm feel in the mouth. For those finding these offerings difficult, try them with a meal the first few times and you will find their **structure** is a real benefit when matched with food.

Cabernet's throne is Bordeaux and in particular the Médoc region, which encompasses such famous communes as Pauillac and St-Julien. Here, wines are made for the super-rich. Chateaux like Latour and Mouton-Rothschild make wines of astounding **complexity** and longevity – if you are ever offered any, practise drinking quickly beforehand. As people have colonised the world, so vines have travelled and Bordeaux has invariably been used as a blueprint for making fine red wine. Consequently, Cabernet Sauvignon is planted in practically every wine-growing region, from Australia to Chile. In Bordeaux, Cabernet Sauvignon is usually blended with Merlot and its half-brother, Cabernet Franc; these are often its partners outside Europe also, as winemakers seek to replicate the traditional Bordeaux blend. Increasingly, though, in the more innovative areas such as Australia, it is being mixed with grapes such as Shiraz. There are, however, many great wines made purely from 100 per cent Cabernet. It does not have the same need of a partner, especially outside Europe, as Merlot, its main rival in Bordeaux.

Structure is the key to pairing Cabernet with food. Take into account its assets of acid and **tannin** – young full-bodied reds will stand up to pretty much any red meat thrown at it, whilst burly, tannic wines do a great job of cutting through fatty rich sauces. The younger the wine the more rustic the dish can be.

Great, aged Cabernet requires simplicity to show off its nuances. For me there is only one meat to show off these flavours to the full, and that is lamb, simply cooked. The finer the bottle, the simpler the food. Avoid lots of garlic and other strong flavours.

CARIGNAN/CARIÑENA

Carignan (France) Cariñena (Spain)

Carignan is a red grape that you are more than likely to have drunk without knowing it. It plays a very important role in the wines of southern France, in particular in Languedoc-Roussillon and Provence. Under the guise of Cariñena it crops up throughout Spain. Carignan is one of those varieties that is easy to grow and it will turn out huge volumes of fruit. It is thus used to bulk out the lower end wines from these regions and has developed a rather shabby reputation. When **yields** are kept in check, however, some spicy, herbal, medium-bodied bottles can be made. Unfortunately producers who choose this path are few and far between.

On its own or as a major part of a blend, Carignan is fairly undemanding stuff, so I wouldn't ask it to deal with anything more than some simple meat dishes: grilled chicken and pork or, at a stretch, lamb chops or steak. The wines are low in **acidity** and **tannin** so avoid rich sauces and stews or casseroles.

DOLCETTO

Ca' Viola, Bruno Rocca, Braida, Roberto Voerzio

Key Area
Piemonte p.108

Try
Beaujolais p.60, **Loire Valley** p.72, **Bergerac** p.22, **Chianti** p.121, **Valpolicella** p.112

Sangiovese p.242, **Gamay** p.229, **Cabernet Franc** p.223

Chicken p.265, **Cured Meats** p.266, **Pasta** p.278, **Hard Cheese** p.291

Found almost exclusively in Piemonte, in the north-east of Italy, Dolcetto attaches itself to the name of a commune such as Alba and is made by many a great Barolo producer – rather like Barbera. At its best, the wine boasts fresh cherry fruits, is low in **tannin** and has comparatively soft **acidity**. Some, though, take on an earthy, almost burnt, smell that invokes either love or hate, and I'm afraid I fall into the latter category. These are the most forward wines of the Piemonte area, designed to be drunk within a year or two of release.

Not to be drunk with anything too heavy, Dolcetto suits roast chicken, tomato-based pasta dishes, cured meats and mild hard cheeses.

Paul Janin, Marcel
Lapiere, Jean-Charles
Pivot, Calot

This is the grape responsible for the much-maligned Beaujolais. The main culprit for its poor reputation is Beaujolais Nouveau, a wine that was in worldwide demand a few years ago but whose popularity is now in rapid decline. Traditionally the race would be on every year to get the first bottles to the UK. Many were not too bad, being light and fruity, and thus offering a perfect introduction to the joys of drinking red wine. The problem with this was that the race became such a cash cow for the producers that they neglected to make much effort to promote their more serious offerings. *Nouveau*, along with the rest of the fads of the eighties and early nineties, is now thankfully over, but many consumers are still blissfully unaware that Beaujolais produces any other wines. A great shame, as these are undoubtedly some of the finest-value French wines.

The versatility of Gamay is huge, the wines ranging from light, fresh, raspberry-scented numbers through to more full-bodied bottles with spices and black fruits. The former versions, in fact, are perfect after an hour in the fridge during the summer months. They have good natural **acidity**, a useful attribute when it comes to food; these wines are always low in **tannin** and so require no time in the cellar. Above all, Gamay is a joy to drink, offering uncomplicated pleasure. Those who deride the grape do not understand that wine does not have to be long-lived, expensive and rare to be great. Juicy, light examples can also be found from Touraine in the Loire.

Gamay is a wonderfully versatile food grape on account of its low **tannin** level and fresh **acidity**. The light examples are the perfect answer for those who want to drink red with fish, as after an hour or so in the fridge, they go perfectly with heavy, oily fish like salmon. Moving up the scale, wash them down with roast chicken or any rich chicken casserole (the French knock back copious quantities with coq-au-vin). The fruit complements, while the **acidity** cuts through, salamis and cured hams. Cheese-wise, stick to **ripe**, creamy numbers. If you absolutely must have some red with your Indian, this is one of the better options.

Key Areas

Try

GAMAY

Grenache (France and New World), Garnacha (Spain)

Grenache has a multifaceted character. It belongs to the Rhône club where the wines range from light, quaffing reds, with a cherried fruit character, to big, peppery, black-fruited wines. It also – rather unsuitably in my view because of its high natural alcohol level – is used to make much rosé. It is lighter and lower in tannin and acidity than Syrah or Mourvèdre. The breadth of flavours attributed to Grenache is a result of the grape's popularity among the bulk producers of the world. In Southern France and Spain in particular it is much abused, partly because it is easy to grow and it produces high yields. If you owned ten acres of land down in southern Spain and wanted to produce as much wine as possible from it, Grenache would be your first port of call when visiting the local garden centre.

Clos Mogador (Priorat),
Rayas (Châteauneuf-du-
pape), Château des Tours
(Vacqueyras), Mas d'en
Compte (Priorat)

Key Areas
Southern France p.14,
Sicily and Sardinia p.128,
Spain p.142, **Australia**
p.156

Try
Syrah/Shiraz p.243,
Mourvèdre p.236, **Pinot
Noir** p.238, **Sangiovese**
p.242

Chicken p.265, **Beef**
p.263, **Lamb** p.270,
Barbecued Meat p.262,
Liver p.271

Grenache plays a major part in the blends of most Southern Rhône reds like Châteauneuf-du-Pape and Côtes du Rhône. Unfortunately, some of the worst examples of these wines are caused when a large proportion of high-yielding Grenache is used. The same can be said of Spain's most famous region, Rioja, where Grenache also plays a part. At the other end of the spectrum, however, when **yields** are kept in check it makes some wonderful wines. One only has to look at the wines of Priorato in Spain or Château de Tours in Vacqueyras (run by the Reynaud family of Château Rayas fame in Châteauneuf-du-Pape) to see what can be achieved. Being part of the Rhône family Grenache has begun to establish itself alongside Syrah in Australia. While Syrah – or Shiraz – is now internationally acclaimed, Grenache has been largely ignored. It does perform brilliantly in the Aussie heat, though, the extra sun seeming to compensate for the dilution caused by high **yields**. Again, in Australia it usually forms part of a blend, but it is possible to track down some wonderful wines made from 100 per cent old vine Grenache. The wines don't carry the same kudos as Shiraz would on the label and so are great value.

The lighter wines made from this grape need no more than chicken, while the spiciness of a good Côtes du Rhône is useful for anything barbecued. The best wines like all red meats that are cooked in a rustic fashion, so throw in lots of herbs.

MALBEC

Colomé (Argentina),
Achaval Ferrer (Argentina),
Coss-Maisonneuve
(Cahors), **Château du
Cèdre** (Cahors)

Key Area
Argentina p.154, **Cahors**
p.62

Try
Bandol p.20, **Madiran**
p.80, **Bordeaux** p.24,
Provence p.88

Syrah/Shiraz p.243,
Mourvèdre p.236, **Merlot**
p.234, **Cabernet
Sauvignon** p.224

Beef p.263, **Lamb** p.270,
Stews p.275

Until a few years ago Malbec would only have warranted a passing mention as a historical footnote to the wines of Bordeaux. One of the five permitted varieties used in the region, it now plays practically no role in the blend. This is because it rarely ripens fully in Bordeaux's climate. It is a thick-skinned grape that produces inky black juice, which is great when ripe but bitter and green when not. Consigned to the dustbin in Bordeaux, it has made a strong comeback on the other side of the world. Just as Australia has become synonymous with Shiraz, and Chile with Merlot, so has Argentina with Malbec. The country has a good collection of older vineyards and this, coupled with the unfortunate recent economic situation in the country, has made for some excellent-value wines. The wines have a deep, almost purple colour and flavours of soft black fruits; the best have an earthy wild character. I am a big fan of Malbec as these are wines of real character at an affordable price. The French wine of Cahors, famously called the 'black wine', utilises large quantities of Malbec. These are big, chunky wines that often need a few years in the bottle. Flavours of earth, tar and herbs dominate.

Argentinian Malbec is good with rare red meats and copes with the strong flavours of barbecues. Cahors needs big meaty rustic dishes such as herb-infused stews.

MERLOT

Merlot verges on being a tart. It will seduce you with immediate, voluptuous fruit and a silky texture, but underneath the flashy exterior there often lies a hollow and one-dimensional core. Only in a few cases around the world does Merlot produce truly profound wines on its own. The rest of the time another grape or two will be playing an important back-up role.

Château Pétrus (Bordeaux), Château Clinet (Bordeaux), Château Pavie (Bordeaux), Matanza's Creek (California), Château Trotanoy (Bordeaux), Duckhorn (California), Masseto (Tuscany), Valtellina (Tuscany)

Merlot was a beneficiary in the major shift to red wine consumption that took place ten years ago. This movement was largely driven by the American market and influenced by a medical report extolling the health benefits of consuming red wine. Winemakers needed to find an easy-drinking red grape for palates used to white wine and Merlot was the answer; it is naturally low in **tannins** and **acidity**, both things that those new to red wine tend to dislike. The fruit characteristics of the grape are also universally appealing, being dominated by flavours of plums and ripe red fruits. This, coupled with lavish helpings of oak, seemed to give consumers exactly what they wanted. As Merlot mania reached fever pitch it was being bottled all over the world as a single variety. Increasingly in the New World, however, other varieties are appearing where you used to see just Merlot on the label but a blended wine is much harder to sell than a wine whose grape appears on the label.

Merlot is hugely important in the blending process of wines from Bordeaux. Even a small proportion of the grape added to the Cabernet Sauvignon-dominated Médoc wines adds charm and suppleness. On the other side of the Gironde river, Merlot takes centre stage in St Émilion and Pomerol – the latter region is home to the fabled Château Pétrus, whose vineyards are planted with 95 per cent Merlot. (A bottle from a great vintage will leave your tongue and mind greatly enriched, but the wallet empty.) This time it is the addition of a small proportion of Cabernet Sauvignon or Cabernet Franc that adds **complexity** and backbone to the immediate charm of the grape.

In France flavours of plums, cedar wood and tobacco dominate, while in the hotter regions of the New World I find the components to be more one-dimensional. This is most evident in California. Here wineries have become victims of their own success in selling the brand Merlot. Super-ripe grapes are lavished with a long period in new **oak** barrels and, while the first mouthful can take the breath away, your palate becomes bored by the end of the first glass. On a trip to California I felt that many winemakers would prefer to make blended wines, à la Bordeaux, but were unwilling to take the plunge and try to sell a blended rather than a varietal wine.

Key Areas
Chile p.167, **Australia** p.156, **California** p.180, **Bordeaux** p.24

Try
Loire Valley p.72, **Ribera del Duero** p.145

Cabernet Franc p.223, **Cabernet Sauvignon** p.224, **Barbera** p.222

Lamb p.270, **Beef** p.263, **Curry** p.280

Merlot makes naturally very juicy wines, which work well with most red meats. Avoid anything too heavy or with rich sauces, though, as reds with more **acidity** and **structure** are needed for these.

The soft, low-acid, juicy New World versions are one of the better things for standing up to spicy food.

Mourvèdre (France), Monastrell (Spain), Mataro (Australia, California)

I love this grape for its uniqueness. There are no polite introductions here, more a punch in the solar plexus. These are deeply coloured wines that can be high in **acidity** and **tannin**, so they need some time in the cellar. As I am sure you will have gathered, I believe wine should offer enjoyment but also stimulation – I don't like wine that is made to fall into the 'please everyone' category. Mourvèdre cannot be accused of this; given to friends it inspires equal amounts of love and loathing. This is excellent, far better than everyone saying they all *quite* liked it.

In France, Mourvèdre reaches its apex in Provence and in particular in Bandol. These are big wines, stuffed full of character, exuding smoky aromas of herbs and black fruits. The top producers of Châteauneuf-du-Pape also utilise a significant proportion to add stuffing to the final blend. Grown widely in Spain, Monastrell is turning out some fine, value wines from the south. The New World offerings are more polished, with the black fruit character becoming more pronounced. Any good-value wines made in California tend to be from the more esoteric grapes, like this.

Hearty, earthy wines like these require a similarly rustic style of food. Stews and roasted meats with lots of herbs are the order of the day.

Gaja, Aldo Conterno,
Giacomo Conterno, Roberto
Voerzio, Cigliuti, Luciano
Sandrone

Key Area
Piemonte p.108

**Try: Young Barolo is really
like nothing else. Once it
has aged**
Old Burgundy p.38, **or old
Northern Rhône** p.86,
Bandol p.20

Syrah/Shiraz p.243

Pork p.273, **Lamb** p.270,
Stews p.275, **Light and
Dark Game** p.267, **Runny
Cheese** p.292

As Italy's greatest variety, this deserves to be up alongside Cabernet Sauvignon and Pinot Noir in the world rankings. Nebbiolo only really exists in, and is indigenous to, Piemonte, in the north-west of Italy, where it most famously produces Barolo and Barbaresco. The reason why it hasn't travelled the world is that it makes monstrously uncommercial wines. Early drinking? Instantly appealing? Absolutely not. A quick glance at a young Nebbiolo cannot prepare you for what's actually in the glass. Fairly light in colour, one could confuse it with a Pinot Noir, but oh, how wrong can you get?! They are tongue-curlingly tannic and acidic in their youth, and even today's modern winemaking techniques have failed to tame them. Many are not approachable for five years and I have tasted plenty at ten years that seem to have defied time. Top-quality wines from a great vintage will effortlessly last thirty years. These are wines full of character and individuality, and should be cherished in this day and age when the homogeneity of wines is in danger of becoming the norm. Nebbiolos, Barolos and Barbarescos are rarely seen in restaurants or on the high street because of their inaccessible youth. When young they have aromas of cherries, leather and spice. As they age and shed their tannic clothes they become gamy and have a character not unlike fine old Burgundy with a little added spice. Their scarcity means these wines are not cheap, but they are something you should buy a few bottles of, stick away in the cellar and forget about.

Young Nebbiolo needs a good stretch in the decanter and some seriously rich food to counter the acid and **tannins**. Fatty meats like duck, pork belly or knuckle, lamb shanks and oxtail have got the balls. Once they have aged, like red Burgundy, they love game: roast grouse or partridge, pheasant stew, rabbit, and runny creamy cheese.

NEBBIOLO

Frankly, this is the most bloody annoying grape to get to grips with. Sometimes I almost wish it didn't exist as I spend more money and have more disappointments looking for great bottles of Pinot Noir than any other grape. Wine growers freely admit it is a pig to grow (the words they actually use are not printable in a family book). Its thin skin makes it susceptible to just about every problem going, it needs an exacting set of weather conditions to grow successfully and it is fussy when it comes to soil types. All this adds up to expense for the buyer – great and even mediocre wines do not come cheaply. 'Fantastic,' I can hear you all say, 'thanks for the warning, we'll cross this off the shopping list.' Absolutely not, I love, adore and am quite probably obsessed by this grape. For me it is unequivocally the greatest red grape in the world. There is as yet no magic formula to grow this grape, unlike, say, Chardonnay or Shiraz, where with enough care and attention world-class wines can be made every year. Pinot Noir's spiritual home is Burgundy in France but there are just as many, if not more, disappointing bottles from here than anywhere else.

Dujac (Burgundy),
Armand Rousseau
(Burgundy), **De Vogüé**
(Burgundy), **Barrat**
(Australia), **Felton Road**
(New Zealand), **Gibbston**
(New Zealand), **Calera**
(California), **Bouchard-**
Finlayson (South Africa)

Key Areas
⚅ **Burgundy** p.38, **Beaujolais**
p.60

Try
⚅ **Loire Valley** p.72,
Beaujolais p.60

🍇 **Sangiovese** p.242,
Cabernet Franc p.223

🍴 **Fish** p.252, **Chicken**
p.265, **Feathered Game**
p.267, **Soft Cheese** p.292

Why do the growers and drinkers persevere, then? Well, when it all comes together there is nothing else like it. Pinot Noir has an amazing capacity for **complex**, seductive flavours; at its best it has rich, mouth-filling flavours yet the wines are not full-bodied. These wines are all about silky texture, **complexity** and getting in touch with your feminine side. The best will age but the beauty of this grape is that even the best stuff is approachable when young. I am, in fact, a huge believer in drinking these wines in their youth, more so than any other red grape, and I think that great Pinot Noir suffers more than any other wine because of our peculiarly English obsession with ageing wine. Burgundy suffers the worst because its wines are not cheap, and we seem to believe that because something has cost us dear it must last and even improve with a good few years in the cellar. The French, who make most of the Pinot in the world, don't have much truck with this rule, so neither should we.

As I have already discussed, Pinot is a fussy plant preferring coolish climates, so Burgundy remains the major source of Pinot in the world. Unlike, say, Syrah from the Rhône – which has been exported to Australia with great success, under the guise of Shiraz – Pinot does not travel well from France. The most exciting areas outside Europe in which it is being grown on are only just starting to come into their own. Cool-climate areas such as Tasmania and Otago in New Zealand are examples, as well as Oregon in the States, where, until fairly recently, the climate was perceived to be too cool for successful grape production.

The grape's wines are characterised by bright cherry fruit flavours that become sweeter and taste of raspberries in hotter regions. Having good natural **acidity**, it is a fine food wine.

Light, young, basic Pinot can easily be drunk with richer fish dishes and chicken. Put it in the fridge for half an hour beforehand to freshen up the fruit flavours. These wines are also great for those who want to drink red as an aperitif.

Great Pinot is a traditional and fantastic partner to feathered game. Here it is worthwhile having one with a few years' (but not too many) bottle age. The earthy, vegetal flavours work fabulously with the bird – another match where both the wine and the food enhance each other's flavour. Runny, smelly cheese with Pinot is also an old classic.

PINOTAGE

Warwick Estate, Grangehurst

Key Area
South Africa p.174

Try
Bandol p.20, **Loire Valley** p.72

Cabernet Franc p.223

Beef p.263, **Lamb** p.270, **Pork** p.273, **Stews** p.275

Pinotage is a cross between Pinot Noir – the delicate, elegant Burgundian grape – and Cinsault, a workhorse grape from the Southern Rhône. Not a match made in heaven you'd think, and I'm afraid you'd be correct. I dislike – in fact, I loathe – Pinotage. Even if I were stuck on a desert island with only this grape to drink I would stick to coconut milk. This is my own personal opinion, however, there is nothing inherently wrong with the grape – its flavours just don't agree with me. The home of Pinotage is South Africa and this is partly the problem, as for too many producers it is a workhorse grape, rather than one used for quality wine. In the most flattering terms possible – to avoid hate mail from the Pinotage Society – the wines are deeply coloured, having black fruits and a smoky tobacco element. It is the last bit I don't like, as too often I find these smoky flavours overpowering, becoming bitter and excessively rustic.

The rusticity of this variety can be overcome with some good, hearty food. Barbecued food works well, especially spare ribs and strongly flavoured stews.

A Mano, Tomaresca

Key Area
Puglia p.128

Try
Barbera p.222, **Zinfandel** p.247

Stews p.275, **Barbecues** p.262

A grape that has long been the workhorse of many southern Italian reds, Primitivo is now starting to make a bit of a name for itself in Puglia (the heel part of the boot). There, in the right hands, it is turning out big, dark-fruited wines full of blackberries, earth and spice. To put it politely, southern Italy has never threatened the quality end of the market before, so these new-wave offerings are great value. This grape was often thought, in the past, to be the same as Zinfandel in California and they do indeed share many similarities apart from price.

These are not sophisticated wines, so go for big rustic flavours, such as barbecues and stews.

PRIMITIVO

SANGIOVESE

Lamborghini, Michele Satta, Querciabella, Isole e Olena, Dei, Lisini, Argiano, Costanti

Key Area
Tuscany p.120

For younger, simple wines try
Valpolicella p.112, Beaujolais p.60

Pinot Noir p.238, **Light Cabernet Franc** p.223, **Dolcetto** p.228

Pasta p.278, **Cured Meats** p.266

For older, stronger wines try
Pinot Noir p.238, **Tempranillo** p.245, **Nebbiolo** p.237, **Syrah/Shiraz** p.243

Lamb p.270, **Beef** p.263, **Pork** p.273, **Light Game** p.267, **Mushrooms** p.287

Sangiovese has been much abused over the years: overproduced, poorly vinified and then shoved into a bottle with a wicker basket round the outside. To make matters worse the bottle, once empty, was immortalised in student digs by being fashioned into a lamp. You should have guessed by now that this grape is one of the main components of Chianti. Things are changing in Chianti, though; it has had huge amounts of investment poured into it. There are some outstandingly good wines now being produced, most of which are ridiculously undervalued. A modern phenomenon has been to blend Sangiovese with a non-Italian varietal like Cabernet Sauvignon or Merlot; these wines are commonly known as 'super-Tuscans'.

Slightly bigger in style are those from further south towards Umbria, such as Brunello di Montalcino, which is produced solely from Sangiovese. Small pockets of plantings have started to emerge around the world, notably in California, but I wouldn't be surprised to see these expand rapidly.

The Sangiovese grape is characterised by red fruits like cherries and redcurrants. It has the tell-tale **acidity** of an Italian red but with relatively low **tannins**. As **yields** are reduced for the best wines, deeper colours occur and many will spend time in new **oak** barrels. These offerings reek of morello cherries, leather and herbs. Styles range from early-drinking Chiantis to Brunellos that can be cellared for twenty years. As it ages, this grape reveals wonderful plum and truffle aromas.

It's no coincidence that these wines found their way into your local trattoria back in the seventies. The everyday wines work brilliantly with Bolognese sauce, tomato and vegetable pastas, and cured meats. The more serious wines, when young, need red meat – try roast lamb with rosemary or rib of beef.

As they age the flavours become more delicate and **complex**, so don't overwhelm them – lighter game like partridge and quail is perfect, and the truffle character marries beautifully to anything containing wild mushrooms, like a risotto or polenta. Better still, stuff some pork with *funghi* and sage.

Jean-Louis Chavé (Rhône), **Paul Jaboulet Aîné** (Rhône), **Guigal** (Rhône), **Tardieu-Laurent** (Rhône), **Auguste Clape** (Rhône), **Torbreck** (Australia), **Jim Barry** (Australia), **Henschke** (Australia), **Qupé** (California)

Key Areas
Northern Rhône p.86, **Languedoc and Roussillon** p.70, **Australia** p.156, **South Africa** p.174, **California** p.180

Try
Barbera p.222, **Mourvèdre** p.236, **Grenache** p.230, **Malbec** p.232, **Sangiovese** p.242, **Zinfandel** p.247

Beef p.263, **Lamb** p.270, **Stews** p.275, **Barbecues** p.262

Elegance, subtlety and restraint are words not to associate with this grape. The trend to homogenisation of the taste of wine has severely affected Syrah, as winemakers have started to tone down its wild earthy flavours. This is akin to trying to turn a well-hung grouse into a skinless chicken breast. If you don't like big, robust, strongly flavoured red wines, don't drink Syrah.

This grape is called Shiraz in Australia and South Africa. Syrah's spiritual home is in the Northern Rhône, France. Here *villages* such as Hermitage and Côte Rôtie produce some of the most profound and long-lived wines in the world. The grape has travelled well, though, in particular to hot areas like Australia, where full-bodied, super-concentrated Shiraz's have become famous. The prices for some of the cult **cuvées** of Shiraz, such as Penfolds Grange Hermitage, have now overtaken their French counterparts.

In the cooler climate of Europe Syrah is distinguished by its peppery, earthy, baked-fruit flavours. In hotter areas such as Australia, it retains some of its spicy character while also having lots of dark, sweet fruit flavours. The extra ripeness of the New World Shiraz's means they drink well when young while also being capable of ageing. Good Syrah from France needs a few years in the bottle to tame the wilder flavours that are evident when young.

The top wines from both these areas are wonderful but the best thing about this grape is that at the lower level it packs in lots of flavour for your money. The lesser regions in the Rhône (see Crozes-Hermitage and St Joseph) are producing wines of stunning value. Indeed, between the £5 and £10 mark the Northern Rhône is in a different league from areas such as Bordeaux. Juicy, fruit-driven Shiraz from Australia, along with their Chardonnays, is the reason we spend more on wine from this country than any other.

Syrahs have big hearty flavours and so need strong foods to go with them. The lesser wines are great with a barbecue and on their own. The top stuff, though, should bring out the carnivore in you – think stews and big chunks of roasted red meats.

TANNAT

Berthoumieu, Château
Boucassé, Château
Montus, Château La
Rosée, Château La Tyre,
Château Meinjarre

Key Area
Madiran p.80

Try
Bandol p.20, **Cahors** p.62,
Barolo p.109, **Barbaresco**
p.109

Malbec p.232, **Nebbiolo**
p.237, **Mourvèdre** p.236

Venison p.269, **Oxtail**
p.264, **Beef** p.263, **Lamb**
p.270

Tannat deserves a mention for its fearsome reputation as one of the components in making the Madiran from the south-west of France. Those with a high proportion of Tannat are big, tannic brutes that need a few years in the cellar to pull all the flavours together. They are **complex**, unique wines with dark black fruits, herbs and a smoky earthiness to them.

Young Madiran needs big simple flavours to stand up to it – venison stew, oxtail, that kind of thing. They become **complex** with age so at the later stage keep it simple and let the wine do the talking, think of simple roast beef and lamb.

Pesquera, Pingus, Bodegas
Alion, Vega Sicilia, Roda,
Allende, Palacios Remondo

Key Areas
Spain p.142, **Argentina**
p.154

Try
Chianti p.121, **Burgundy**
p.38

Sangiovese p.242, **Pinot
Noir** p.238, **Merlot** p.234

Chicken p.265, **Veal**
p.276, **Barbecues** p.262,
Lamb p.270, **Beef** p.263

Tempranillo is Spain's premier grape for fine wine. It is a key component in Rioja and the wines of Ribera del Duero, but can also be found in nearly every other region of red wine production. It is characterised by juicy red fruits like strawberries, and its moderate **tannins** and **acidity** means it can be drunk fairly young. The best Tempranillo-based wines are blended with another red grape with more guts. Helped along in this fashion the wines become candidates for mid-term cellaring, with the top ones lasting for twenty years. Herbs and spices mark out these older wines.

Traditionally Rioja has been aged in American **oak** barrels that produce its much-loved sweet, toasty flavours. Remember, though, that this is the taste of oak, not Tempranillo.

The grape is starting to get a toehold abroad, particularly in South America, and in Argentina it produces deeply coloured, fruity examples.

On its own Tempranillo will do a pretty versatile job for you. The fairly low **acidity** means it will work with a range of light meat dishes – roast chicken and veal – and its juicy fruit makes it a good quaffer at barbecues. The better wines from Rioja and the Ribera del Duero need something with more stuffing, though, such as roast lamb or beef. They do not generally have the guts to take on big rich stews or fatty cuts of meat.

TEMPRANILLO

TOURIGA NACIONAL

Quinta de la Rosa, Quinta dos Roques

Key Area
Portugal p.132

Try
Australia p.156, **Northern Rhône** p.86

Syrah/Shiraz p.243, **Barbera** p.222

Beef p.263, **Chocolate** p.294, **Hard Cheese** p.291

Touriga Nacional is the most important grape in making the finest Ports. As you'd expect, it turns out deeply coloured wines that are full of blackberries, spices and leather. They are generally low in **tannin** but have good **acidity**. Recently it has been touted, with some success, as the answer to Portugal's red wine problem, and more and more producers are turning to it to make almost New World-style reds of great ripeness.

Big wines require big food. I'd drink these wines with big slabs of steak and even the wine humbug, chocolate. If you've got Port, I prefer it with hard cheeses like Stilton, rather than the soft numbers.

Doug Nalle, Helen Turley, Ridge

Zinfandel has been the subject of hot debate recently within the wine trade. California has long claimed this grape as her own, disputing the assertion that it was in fact the Italian grape Primitivo. Science has now apparently solved the issue: Zinfandel is genetically similar to an unpronounceable Croatian variety, which only goes to show that the precocious Californians should have quit while they were ahead and made do with the more glamorous associations of southern Italy.

Arguments aside, Zinfandel does certainly have an Italian feel to it, being full of black cherries and spices. Its naturally good **acidity** gives the wines admirable **balance** in the hotter California climes, where it is almost exclusively grown. The best will happily age for ten years, although they taste great when young.

Key Area
🧭 **California** p.180

Try
🧭 **Puglia** p.128, **Piemonte** p.108, **Chianti** p.121

🍇 **Primitivo** p.241, **Barbera** p.222, **Syrah/Shiraz** p.243, **Sangiovese** p.242

🍴 **Stews** p.275, **Lamb** p.270, **Beef** p.263, **Chocolate** p.294, **Hard Cheese** p.291

Warning:
This grape has suffered more than its far share of abuse. For example, Blush Zinfandel rosé is a horrid, sickly affair. I know we have all drunk it (even me, although I was a student, it was late and nothing else was available...), but please never drink it again. The other major problem is that most Californian wine retailing at under a tenner is not worth it, so don't drink these either. This is only a grape to enjoy if you buy the best stuff.

The top wines are positively Port-like and thus can take on chocolate, the bête noire of most wine. Otherwise go for big hearty dishes; stews made with shin of beef, lamb shanks and duck cassoulet. Zinfandel loves good, hard, crumbly cheeses like Cheddar and Wensleydale.

FOOD

Matching food and wine is often perceived as a grandiose affair and something that only goes on in the finest restaurants where sommeliers rule the roost. The perception is that certain wines and foods need to be drunk and eaten together for maximum enjoyment. All this adds to the mystery and pomp that surrounds wine, and what should be a pleasurable indulgence gets touted as an art form that alienates many.

Let's blow away a few myths. Many of the greatest food and wine matches are the most simple. The concept of pairing wine and food does not originate from three star Michelin restaurants; rather, many matches result from regionality and work right down to the level of sustenance food. The downmarket trattoria in Tuscany will give you a far better idea of which foods suit the local Sangiovese grape than any of the region's fancy restaurants.

Food undoubtedly affects the taste of wine and vice versa. Unconvinced? Next time you open your favourite crisp white have a slurp. Then find any old piece of chocolate and have a bite before returning to the wine. Not only will you not taste it, but you might now find you don't actually like it; the wine will taste acidic and bland.

'What are the rules?' I hear you cry. White with fish and red with meat is as far as most people get, and I'm afraid I can't be any more specific. The chocolate example is one of the few absolutes, but even the most predictable-seeming foods can cause problems. A piece of beef today might come grilled in the form of a steak, or sliced into a Thai green curry. It doesn't take a lifetime of working with wine to realise that these dishes need different wines.

The role of wine today is often to be fruity and accessible as soon as the bottle is opened and in this country we drink many (often New World) bottles without food. This is not so on the Continent, where wine is rarely designed for consumption without a meal. Here we come to the nub of the issue: **structure**, meaning **acidity** for whites and **tannin** and **acidity** for reds.

Structure is not something our modern palates are accustomed to. I won't go so far as to say that New World wines don't have any **structure**, but generally they have much lower levels of **acidity** and **tannin**. At many tastings I hold with friends, **structured** wines lose out in the pre-dinner tasting but, to the surprise of most, they are clear winners when drunk with a plate of food. Acid and **tannin** act as counterpoints to food, especially rich dishes. A hefty stew needs some red with bite to cut through it, and your favourite New World Cabernet Sauvignon is just going to taste flabby, while each mouthful of food will taste increasingly heavy.

All the following suggestions are just that – your tongue is the final judge and jury. Build up a set of your own rules through tasting and use my suggestions as guidelines, all the while trying to think why a match works and remembering each wine's style. You'll be surprised how quickly you find your palate demanding **fresh** simple wines with the most delicate foods, robust young wines to stand up to the most demanding dishes, and simple food to show off old fancy bottles.

Many suggestions are best-case scenarios, but plenty of other wines will work. Occasionally I am rather strident, as there are a number of matches that are just so good they can't be ignored, and in such a situation you can end up with something whose whole is much greater than the sum of its parts. Remember, though, this shouldn't all be taken too seriously. Enjoy the tasting and experimentation, but don't forget that, at the end of the day, your guests' and your enjoyment is the only scale by which to measure success.

COOKING FISH

The taste of fish is affected by the way it is cooked and, while your cooking method will not be the deciding factor in which wine to serve, it will have an influence. Steaming always produces the subtlest flavours. If I had a truly great bottle of white to show off I'd steam or poach some fish; salmon done in this way is the ultimate vehicle for fine Chardonnay. This is also the easiest way to cook a piece of fish and keep it moist. You don't need any fancy kit like a fish kettle. Just use the method popularised by Jamie Oliver – wrap the fish in some tin foil with some form of liquid and bung it in the oven.

Roasting, grilling or pan-frying all throw up more pronounced flavours. Using the salmon example, I might still serve a Chardonnay, but not the best bottle in the cellar. I'd plump for a good, fruit-driven New World number rather than a more complex version from Burgundy.

Cook your fish over a naked flame on the barbecue and a smoky, burnt flavour comes to the forefront. This will overwhelm delicate whites and override the complexities of finer bottles. I'd maybe go for a simple, fruity New Zealand Sauvignon with lighter fish. For salmon and suchlike I might plump for some ripe Sémillon or a rich Pinot Gris. Light, fruity reds from the Loire or Beaujolais would be just as satisfactory, as would some good rosé.

LIGHT FISH

Try

Chablis p.42, **Loire Valley** p.72

Unoaked Chardonnay p.192, **Sauvignon Blanc** p.210

I like to cook all this type of fish (cod, seabass, bream) as simply as possible – grilled, steamed or baked with a wedge of lemon. I don't think that delicately flavoured flesh warrants rich sauces or strongly flavoured accompaniments. Thus the answer for wine is to keep it fresh and simple. If I were in a Chardonnay mood, it would be an unoaked one from the New World or something fresh from Burgundy: Chablis or something from the Mâconnais or Chalonnaise would be the answer. While in France I'd make a beeline for the Loire. Muscadet has an affinity with anything fishy, but it is the Sauvignon Blanc-based wines at the other end of the valley that excel.

Try

Italy p.104

Albariño p.190, **Verdejo** p.215, **Riesling** p.206, **Pinot Blanc/Bianco** p.204, **Pinot Grigio** p.205

Fruity Sauvignon from around the world might be a better bet if you start to introduce any sauces or spices to the dish. In a similar vein, Italy's crisp whites are just the ticket. Albariño and Verdejo from Spain are also excellent partners. Riesling, as ever, works a treat although I'd stick to light examples – the really oily examples from around the world can be overpowering. For this reason I would avoid the truly heady grapes like Gewürztraminer and Pinot Gris.

Try
Burgundy p.38, **New Zealand** p.168, **Australia** p.156, **California** p.180

Chardonnay p.192

For whites try
Australia p.156, **South Africa** p.174, **Loire Valley** p.72, **Alsace** p.16

Chardonnay p.192, **Sauvignon Blanc** p.210, **Chenin Blanc** p.194, **Riesling** p.206

For reds try
Beaujolais p.60, **Loire Valley** p.72

Gamay p.229, **Cabernet Franc** p.223, **Pinot Noir** p.238

OILY AND MEATY FISH

This description covers the strongest-tasting forms of fish. As well as their pronounced taste, they all have a firm or oily texture, demanding wines with good acidity. I don't want to seem down on New World wine, but many are simply too flabby to work with this type of food. They might taste great on their own, but with rich fish the combination will just seem clumsy and heavy. Thus, if I recommend a New World Chardonnay, find one that comes from the cooler regions, as these will have that essential, food-friendly acidity.

Salmon used to be the most luxurious of all fish; now, due to intensive farming, it is cheaper than the great British stalwart, cod. If you are lucky enough to know someone who fishes or is sufficiently wealthy to afford wild salmon, treat it with respect. Poach it and serve with a little hollandaise and the finest bottle of Chardonnay you can possibly lay your hands on: Burgundy in France, or examples from New Zealand, Australia and California. This is one of the greatest of all matches and, like many, so simple.

Farmed salmon has a high fat content, so I prefer something with a bit more zip. Chardonnay will still do the trick but also try New World Sauvignon Blanc, Verdelho from Australia, top Chenin Blanc from the Loire or South Africa, and rich Riesling from Alsace, Austria or Australia. Rosé is also a fine partner and for those who only do red, this is not a problem. Gamay from the Loire or Beaujolais suits salmon, as does light Cabernet Franc or Pinot Noir; make sure you stick them in the fridge for an hour or so before serving. Trout is generally lighter, so I would steer towards the Sauvignon Blancs.

Sardines and mackerel have a stronger taste than salmon or trout. The Spanish adore grilled sardines and love to wash them down with Fino Sherry. It's a great match – the wine deals admirably with the smoky flavours created by grilling the fish and it has all the necessary oomph to cut through the oily flesh. Try the same combination with mackerel or look for some Pinot Gris, especially if you cook the fish on the barbecue. The light reds listed above will also do the job, and you can even go more full-bodied if you start serving the fish with a strong accompaniment like ratatouille; try junior Chianti or Valpolicella.

Turbot and monkfish have a meaty texture but mild flavour, so you need to rein in the wines. Simply cooked, serve them with some Sauvignon Blanc, lighter Rieslings, or, if you are feeling adventurous, maybe some Albariño from Spain. Being expensive, premium fish, you will often find them served in restaurants with rich cream sauces or meat reductions. With these you need to match the wine to the sauce; the former will enjoy some Chardonnay while the latter will benefit from some soft, fruity red like a Pinot Noir, or even some juicy young Right Bank Bordeaux.

Tuna and swordfish are some of the meatiest fish around; indeed, a good piece of tuna will actually look similar to a fillet steak. For something light like a Tuna Niçoise salad, look to some restrained Sauvignon Blanc or delicate Riesling. The rarer you cook fish like this, the fuller the wine needs to be, so crack open some rich Chardonnay, fine Sémillon, oily Viognier or a top Chenin Blanc. Rosé and chilled Valpolicella or young Chianti are sometimes a better match if you are serving the fish with other strong, rich flavours.

PRESERVED FISH

This category contains some pretty extreme flavours that throw up a heap of challenges for wine. Apart from smoking, the two main ways of preserving fish are to immerse them either in salt or in vinegar. Both methods can destroy most wines you might drink with them, so you need to think outside the box and entertain combinations that wouldn't seem to work on the face of things.

Rollmops and other pickled fish are tricky because of vinegar's acidity. This style of food comes from Scandinavia and with no tradition of wine drinking you can't even fall back on local knowledge. Choose whites whose acidity is in line with the food and that don't have strong flavours which might clash with the herbs and spices used in the pickling process. Try Muscadet, Pinot Bianco, Loire Sauvignon and Chenin Blanc.

Go to Spain and the anchovy will offer you a great combination with that old food stalwart, Fino Sherry. How it copes with nosh as diverse as chorizo and rollmops I don't know, but it does. Spaniards wolf down plates of the beautiful little silver fish in Tapas bars, where the only thing to drink with them is a chilled glass of Fino. It will even do a passable job at seeing to the brown salted anchovies that come in tins.

Salt cod can look deeply unattractive until it has spent twenty-four hours soaking in a bath of water, resembling as it does a plank of wood rather than a fish. Even having been soaked and taken on some semblance of a fishy appearance, it will have a salty flavour. It is then most often puréed with olive oil and garlic to be turned into a powerful paste that the French call *brandade*. Try Muscadet and Loire Sauvignon Blanc, that will not mind being an afterthought on your taste buds. Bolder whites too often clash, but surprisingly, lighter reds do the trick. Try the usual suspects like Beaujolais or even lighter versions of Southern French reds like Minervois or Corbières. The similar dish in Spain would be washed down with Fino or some light Tempranillo.

Try
- Loire Valley p.72
- Pinot Bianco p.204, Sauvignon Blanc p.210, Chenin Blanc p.194

Try
- Fino Sherry p.148

For whites try
- Loire Valley p.72, Fino Sherry p.148, Spain p.142
- Pinot Bianco p.205, Sauvignon Blanc p.210, Chenin Blanc p.194

For reds try
- Beaujolais p.60, Minervois p.81, Corbières p.68, Spain p.142
- Gamay p.229, Tempranillo p.245

SHELLFISH

The beauty of most shellfish is the simplicity of its serving. There are not often many sauces or other flavours incorporated, and so there are fewer problems for wine. Unadorned like this, shellfish have a delicate taste that is often reminiscent of the sea itself. Unsurprisingly, then, the best wines for this food are light, unobtrusive whites, which complement rather than overpower.

Oysters eaten raw encapsulate the taste of the sea better than anything. The French have a long love affair with this mollusc, so as ever we should begin traditionally. Muscadet from the Loire Valley is the logical answer. The vineyards are situated near the town of Nantes on the coast and here the consumption of oysters and Muscadet by the locals takes on heroic proportions. On its own it can be a refreshing if uninspiring wine; paired with oysters it magically comes into its own. The best have a creamy, salty tang that is unforgettably good with a local Brittany oyster. Muscadet is always cheap and so has the added advantage of making the bill palatable if you have indulged in an oyster binge.

Don't stop there, though, as Muscadet loves all manner of things in a shell: mussels, clams and tiny little winkles. Remember, though, that all this works only in its simplest form. Other wines to look at are Chablis, Loire Sauvignons like Sancerre, and light, steely Riesling from Alsace, Australia or New Zealand. Italian whites like Pinot Bianco, Lugana and Gavi di Gavi will all provide the necessary freshness, while Manzanilla Sherry's famed salty taste does a star turn with creamy, rich, native oysters.

Moving on to richer, meaty shellfish like prawns, scallops, langoustine or lobster, the above will all work but I tend to prefer something with a bit more weight. Think about fruitier versions of Sauvignon Blanc from Australia, New Zealand, Chile and South Africa. Riesling from Germany, with a touch of sweetness, is also an excellent partner.

Try

🍴 **Burgundy** p.38, **New Zealand** p.168

🍷 **Chardonnay** p.192, **Sauvignon Blanc** p.210

Lobster and scallops are the richest form of shellfish, so you need to entertain creamy Chardonnays; acidity in these wines is of paramount importance to cut through the rich flesh. Both are special-occasion foods, so treat them to a fine bottle of Burgundy, the best of which will have a minerality to them that will complement the sea taste of the shellfish. If you want to go for some New World bottles be sure to pick ones that are not too oaky and have the necessary acidity.

Try

🍴 **Australia** p.156, **New Zealand** p.168, **Burgundy** p.38, **Bordeaux** p.24, **Rhône Valley** p.84, **Alsace** p.16

🍷 **Chardonnay** p.192, **Sémillon** p.212, **Chenin Blanc** p.194, **Riesling** p.206, **Pinot Gris** p.205, **Gewürztraminer** p.198

Once you start adding sauces and spices to the above you need to think about the additional flavours. Moules Marinières will contain cream and garlic, so it needs a punchier white than Muscadet – think about some New World Sauvignon or some richer Riesling. Scallops can come with a plethora of flavours: bacon, cream sauce, even black pudding. Crank up the power of the whites for these dishes and go for full-throttle Chardonnay, Sémillon, top Chenin Blanc and ripe Riesling.

Mix in some meaty flavours and rosé, or even some very light chilled reds can be the answer. Lobster with hollandaise or any other rich sauce demands the best Chardonnay you can lay your hands on. Shellfish stews like bouillabaisse will contain strong garlic, saffron and tomato elements. You are now essentially matching the wine to the sauce rather than the fish; try rich white Rhônes, Pinot Gris and Gewürztraminer. For any Thai or Asian influences in the dish, look up the section on that style of cooking.

SMOKED FISH

Try

🍴 **Loire Valley** p.72, **Chile** p.167, **New Zealand** p.168, **Spain** p.142, **Italy** p.104, **Burgundy** p.38, **Alsace** p.16

🍷 **Sauvignon Blanc** p.210, **Verdejo** p.215, **Albariño** p.190, **Pinot Gris** p.205, **Chardonnay** p.192, **Riesling** p.206

Smoking fish is the traditional way to preserve them in this country. Like curing meat, the process has developed much further into something that adds flavour to the final product. While the Italians, French and Spanish can argue among themselves as to who produces the finest cured meats, we, along with the Scandinavians, can justly claim to be the masters of smoking anything that comes out of water.

Scottish smoked salmon is revered all over the world. I used to work with a fabulously surly Frenchman who had nothing but disdain for most British foods (he once looked at me incredulously when I suggested that parsnips were a great vegetable, claiming that in France

only the pigs ate them). He did, however grudgingly, admit that we knew a thing or two about smoking fish – eels were his particular favourite.

The flavour of smoked fish is a strong one and can sit uncomfortably with many wines, although salmon is not usually a problem as the smokiness is never that pronounced. You can go down one of two paths here. First, serve a crisp Sauvignon from the Loire Valley or, better, with their fruitier flavours, those from the New World. Any other crisp, fruity white will do – Spanish Verdejo, Albariño, good Pinot Grigio or Riesling. All these wines will cut through the oily fish. I generally prefer to take the second option, though, and complement the richness of the fish. Fine Chardonnay from Burgundy or around the world works. The absolute match made in heaven, however, is Pinot Gris either from Alsace or the ripe versions that Australia and New Zealand can turn out. These are rich wines that have a smoky character and are lip-smackingly good with smoked salmon.

For whites try
Alsace p.16, **Burgundy** p.38

Pinot Gris p.205, **Gewürztraminer** p.198, **Sémillon** p.212, **Chardonnay** p.192, **Chenin Blanc** p.194

For reds try
Beaujolais p.60, **Rhône Valley** p.84

Gamay p.229, **Grenache** p.230

Other fish that often end up in the smoke house are mackerel, herrings (kippers) and eels. All these have a much smokier taste so you need to go down the rich oily route for white wine. Pinot Gris is number one; Gewürztraminer, Sémillon, Chardonnay and Chenin Blanc will all stay the course but only in their most full-blown guises. Don't be afraid to turn to some lighter reds for help – fruity Beaujolais or some light Côtes du Rhône will do a far better job than any light white wine can.

SUSHI

Sushi is one of my favourite ways to consume fish. I remember eating it for the first time in a restaurant in Hong Kong when I must have been about twelve. I had been taken out for a meal with the 'grown-ups' and was determined not to let the side down. However, being confronted by a plate of raw fish was not what I had in mind. I so expected to be sick on the spot that I don't remember the first mouthful, but after that I was converted to its silky texture and delicate flavour.

Raw fish in its most pure form is actually very easy to match wine to. You want a light, fresh white to be in the background while your tongue enjoys the subtlety of the meat. Muscadet, Chablis or any other light, innocuous white will do.

Sushi, however, is usually served with three strong flavourings that play havoc with wine. Pickled ginger, wasabi and soy sauce constitute a three-pronged attack that many bottles cannot survive. Ginger is fragrant and vinegary, wasabi is horseradish hot and soy is very salty. You need to head for unfashionable grapes and regions to find help: Riesling and, in particular, those from Germany which have a touch of sweetness (*Kabinett* and *Spätlese* level), but are also fresh. Other versions from around the world will do but they don't have quite the same poise. Other grapes to look for are Pinot Gris (nothing too oily, though), New World Sauvignon Blanc and Spain's Albariño. Good rosé will also do the job, but I'm afraid full-blown red wine is out.

Try
Loire Valley p.72, **Soave** p.113, **Chablis** p.42

Unoaked Chardonnay p.192

Try
Germany p.98, **New Zealand** p.168, **Chile** p.167, **Spain** p.142

Riesling p.206, **Pinot Gris** p.205, **Sauvignon Blanc** p.210, **Albariño** p.190

MEAT

COOKING MEAT

The method used to cook a piece of meat, while not being the overriding factor in swaying your wine choice, should influence it. Roasting in the oven is the most common way of cooking large chunks of meat and, provided you don't burn the outside, you need to adjust your normal wine choices. However, take a piece of steak or a lamb chop and cook it over any type of open flame and you have an altogether more rustic meal. Red will still be your choice of wine, but whereas I might have served a complex, fine bottle with the same meat if roasted, I would now look for a full-throttle, less subtle wine to counter the smoky, burnt flavours of the cooking process.

Slow cooking and braising gives meat a melt-in-the-mouth texture. Additionally, cuts cooked in this way are often fatty, like lamb shanks or pork belly, so you'll be looking for something with a bit of extra acidity.

How you like a steak to be cooked comes down to personal preference and wine-wise you don't need to worry too much. Generally, I like to drink ripe, full-bodied reds with juicy rare meat. The sweetness and fruit of New World reds is particularly good in this area provided any sauce in the equation is not too heavy.

BEEF

Rather like lamb, you might think that cows were invented purely to show off red wine. I can think of very few bottles that don't go with beef and all the recommendations below are my favourites, rather than absolutes.

A traditional Sunday roast of beef is an excuse to produce the finest bottle of red Bordeaux you can muster. Don't get put off by the upper-class image of drinking claret and beef; you don't need a huge wine cellar, a country mansion or, indeed, gout to enjoy one of the most sublime food and wine matches. Cook the meat simply, avoid strong flavours (horseradish is essential, I know, but avoid the stuff that makes your eyes water) and let the complexities of the wine do the talking.

Wines that utilise the same grapes from around the world will also do the trick. Fine Cabernet Sauvignon or Merlot from Margaret River or Coonawarra in Australia, Bolgheri in Italy, or California. Bordeaux is my preference, but any other fine reds from around the world will also work. The key is that the meat should let the nuances of fine wines shine through.

With old and delicate wine I cook the most subtly flavoured cuts, like fillet, with a minimal amount of other flavourings. It thus follows that I'll serve the younger wines that have more pronounced tannins and acidity with the meatier cuts like rib. The bloodier the meat, the sweeter and juicier I like the wine; thus I might look to a Merlot-dominated wine from Bordeaux or California.

Beef in its rarest form is steak tartare in France, or carpaccio in Italy. In its raw form beef has a surprisingly delicate flavour. Try soft, fruity reds like Beaujolais, any Pinot Noir, or light Sangiovese from Italy. You can even drink rich, oily whites, especially with steak tartare, as it can be strongly flavoured with capers and mustard. White wine with beef may sound strange, but in France I have greatly enjoyed a rare fillet of beef with creamy mushroom sauce, with which our host served a rich, fine white Burgundy. It was a great example of the benefits of matching wine to the sauce of a dish rather than simply the meat underneath.

Try

Southern Italy p.104,
Spain p.142, Portugal
p.132, Argentina p.154,
South Africa p.174

Malbec p.232, Tempranillo
p.245, Pinotage p.240,
Shiraz/Syrah p.243,
Grenache p.230

In its more everyday guise, beef might come in the form of a burger or a steak grilled on the barbecue. This requires a good, robust, juicy red that won't mind any pickles or mustard you might use. Southern Italian red, Portuguese or Spanish country wine, and spicy southern French blends will all perform admirably, as will most New World wines: Argentinean Malbec or Tempranillo, South African reds (I would even countenance Pinotage) and any Aussie Shiraz or Grenache-based wine.

Try

Southern Rhône p.90,
Bandol p.20, Minervois
p.81, Provence p.83,
Piemonte p.108

Mourvèdre p.236, Syrah
p.243, Barbera p.222

Stewed or braised beef is your next port of call. Here you need to be led by the herbs and spices that will go into the dish. Good stew with herb dumplings loves all hearty southern French reds – lesser Rhône, Bandol, Minervois and Provence. I adore oxtail, but it is one of the truly fatty cuts of beef. The above wines will do but I prefer the extra acidity of Italian reds – all things from down south, or maybe some leathery Barbera from Piemonte.

CHICKEN AND TURKEY

Chicken is a versatile meat for showing off wine. Many dishes are equally happy with white or red, which is a bonus for those who want to match food and wine but have a particular dislike of one wine colour.

Simple roast chicken is one of my favourite dishes. In the summer, served with a salad, I would eat it with a rich Chardonnay from either Burgundy or the New World. An oily Pinot Gris, Riesling or Gewürztraminer would be better if you are going to introduce lots of herbs like thyme into the equation. Tarragon has a particular affinity with chicken but its aniseed flavour can cause problems for wine; I have always found a ripe Viognier to be the answer. Alternatively, I chill some decent Beaujolais, light Pinot Noir, fruity Chianti, or a Loire Cabernet Franc like St Nicolas de Bourgueil.

Once you get into winter and serve your roast with gravy, red is better. Any mid-weight Pinot Noir from around the world, top-cru Beaujolais like Moulin-à-Vent, Valpolicella, or Dolcetto will do the trick. Cold roast chicken is delicious although the breast meat can be a little dry; I counter this by serving a lightly chilled, juicy red, although fine rosé will also fit the bill. If you were to knock up a coronation chicken with the leftovers, though, I'd go back to the white camp, in particular anything from Alsace or some Riesling to marry with the light curry flavours.

Choosing wine to suit any kind of chicken casserole all depends on what's in the sauce. In Alsace, for example, a traditional coq-au-vin might be white-wine-based, so look no further than their rich whites. Burgundians, on the other hand, would only marinate the bird in red, so a Pinot Noir is called for. Remember, the richer the sauce the more important it is to have a wine with good acidity to cut through the fat. If you get more exotic and need some wine for curry or any Asian-type chicken, have a look in the Spice Route section.

I only eat turkey at Christmas and even then I try to avoid it. They are amazing birds to look at but in my view would be better off left alive

For whites try
Burgundy p.38, **Alsace** p.16, **Australia** p.156

Chardonnay p.192, **Pinot Gris** p.205, **Gewürztraminer** p.198, **Viognier** p.218

For reds try
Burgundy p.38, **Beaujolais** p.60, **Tuscany** p.120, **Loire** p.72

Gamay p.229, **Pinot Noir** p.238, **Cabernet Franc** p.223

Try
Burgundy p.38, **Beaujolais** p.60, **Valpolicella** p.112, **Piemonte** p.108

Pinot Noir p.238, **Gamay** p.229, **Dolcetto** p.228

For whites try
Alsace p.16

Pinot Gris p.205, **Riesling** p.206

For reds try
Burgundy p.38

Pinot Noir p.238

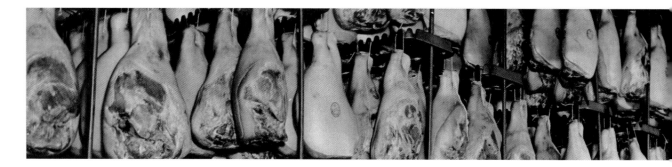

rather than ending up on my plate. Even the best-bred organic birds are fairly tasteless. Wine-wise treat them as a chicken. As they are usually eaten at Christmas, red seems to be the prevailing choice. Dig out the best bottle of Burgundy you can find and then at least your tongue will be excited by what you are drinking. Better still, spare the turkey and hunt down a goose.

CURED MEAT

Try
🍷 **Loire Valley** p.72, **Beaujolais** p.60, **Australia** p.156, **Chile** p.167

🍷 **Cabernet Franc** p.223, **Gamay** p.229, **Cabernet Sauvignon** p.224, **Shiraz/Syrah** p.243

Curing meat has come a long way from simply being a method of preserving any leftover fresh stuff that could not be consumed. There are now many different methods of doing it and various flavours that can be introduced in the process. Good British ham needs some fruity red like a Loire Cabernet Franc or proper Beaujolais. The saltier versions still require a fruity wine but something with more body. Look out for some New World Cabernet Sauvignon or Shiraz, but not the inkiest black heavyweights.

For whites try
🍷 **Alsace** p.16, **Austria** p.96, **Australia** p.156

🍷 **Riesling** p.206

For reds try
🍷 **France** p.14, **Italy** p.104, **Sherry** p.148

🍷 **Gamay** p.229, **Pinot Noir** p.238, **Merlot** p.234, **Sangiovese** p.242, **Dolcetto** p.228, **Tempranillo** p.245

Cured pork like Parma, Bayon or Serrano ham has an inherent sweetness to it. Again, these are best suited to fruity, mid-weight reds, but ones with European levels of acidity that will cut through the richness of the meat. Cru Beaujolais is a winner – try also Gamay from Touraine, light Pinot Noir from the Loire or Burgundy and the basic Merlot-dominated wines from Bordeaux's Right Bank.

In Italy, look for entry level Chianti, Valpolicella, Dolcetto and Freisa from the north. Lighter styles of Rioja from Spain will also do the trick. Don't be afraid to put any of these reds in the fridge for an hour or so before serving. While in Spain, you will find that Fino Sherry's remarkable ability to work with all manner of food does not disappoint. The unique, tangy taste of the wine contrasts beautifully with the sweet meat. Other whites don't satisfy so well, but fat Rieslings from Alsace, Austria or the New World will all do a passable job. Cured duck or beef, like *bresaola*, can be slightly richer, so use the heavier of the recommendations above.

Try
- Italy p.104, **Spain** p.142, **France** p.14
- **Barbera** p.222, **Nebbiolo** p.237, **Sangiovese** p.242, **Primitivo** p.241, **Tempranillo** p.245, **Grenache** p.230, **Mourvèdre** p.236

Salami is rich and fatty and, being flavoured with things like fennel, has an altogether more rustic, less subtle taste than some cured meats. Fattiness needs acidity and tannin to balance it, while the strong flavours need to be mirrored by the wine if it is not to be overwhelmed. Don't get carried away and serve the finest wines, though, as the salami is always going to do the talking in this combination.

In Italy think about Barbera and Nebbiolo from the north, good Sangiovese and hearty southern grapes like Primitivo or Negroamaro. In Spain try Tempranillo but from the lesser regions like Toro; beefy blends including Monastrell, from places such as Jumilla, also work well. In France wines from the Southern Rhône and those that use the same grapes, like Languedoc and Provence, are the answer. Again, stick to country rather than fine wines.

Fiery, spicy *chorizo* is the most potent of salamis. The chilli heat plays havoc with red wine so go back to the best food all-rounder in the game, Sherry. Chilled Fino or Manzanilla has all the zip necessary to cut through its fat and the weight to counter its fiery taste.

FEATHERED GAME

Try
- Burgundy p.38, **Beaujolais** p.60
- **Chardonnay** p.192
- **Gamay** p.229

I love all types of game. The taste is fantastic and there are some wine matches to be had that get me all worked up. Most game is still only available seasonally, which makes things all the more exciting for the few months that it's around. I also like the fact that a partridge from your local butcher looks like a proper bit of meat. I bought some recently that had not only a smattering of feathers but also their feet still on. In the feathered world, this is as far away as you can possibly get from a tasteless, watery, skinless chicken breast.

I'll start with the most chicken-like of game and work towards the darker meats. It is important to note that the taste for all these birds will not be uniform and will often depend on how old they are and how long they have been hung for. The more gamy, well-hung birds will require wines from the stronger end of the spectrum.

Quail is now widely farmed in this country and tends to be the lightest in flavour of the game birds. Treat them like good roast chicken and serve with some rich Chardonnay or a light, Beaujolais-like red. I also view guinea fowl in the same way.

Try

🥄 **Burgundy** p.38, **Australia** p.156, **New Zealand** p.168, **California** p.180, **Piemonte** p.108, **Tuscany** p.120, **Northern Rhône** p.86

🍷 **Pinot Noir** p.238, **Nebbiolo** p.237, **Sangiovese** p.242, **Syrah** p.243

Time for one of the all-time classics now. Pinot Noir could really have been invented to help you consume birds like pheasant, partridge and – best of the lot – grouse. Young wine is fine but anything with a few years' bottle age verges on the sublime. This is special-occasion, no-holds-barred food, so buy the best bottle you can. Outside Burgundy, Australia, New Zealand and California are all going to help out. However, none of these regions has yet produced wines that age into earthy complex numbers that, as one famous wine critic noted, 'should smell like shit'.

The flavours of these wines marry wonderfully with the wild ones of fine game. Get some wild mushrooms involved in the dish and things will just get better. The complexities of aged red are the answer and other ones to look for are Nebbiolo from Barolo or Barbaresco, any Sangiovese like Chianti or Brunello and, surprisingly, fine old Northern Rhône Syrah. If you are going to pull the stops out on the wine, it is important not to confuse the issue and overdo the herbs and spices. Just roast your preferred bird, and serve it along with some bread sauce and maybe a few roast potatoes.

Try

🥄 **Bordeaux** p.24, **Northern Italy** p.104, **Bandol** p.20, **Languedoc** p.70, **Provence** p.83

🍷 **Merlot** p.234, **Cabernet Sauvignon** p.224, **Mourvèdre** p.236

Roast duck and wood pigeon, with their dark powerful meat, can overwhelm fine old Pinot so I'd stick to the younger bottles. Any juicy red will do the trick – Right Bank Bordeaux, New World Merlot and Cabernet Sauvignon. Barbera and Amarone from the north of Italy get a special mention with duck. If you are confronted with duck confit or any type of cassoulet think of rustic wines – spicy Rhône reds or those from further south like Bandol, Languedoc and Provence. All things Italian are safe bets when dealing with these fatty dishes.

Try

🥄 **Burgundy** p.38

🍷 **Pinot Noir** p.238, **Merlot** p.234

Goose is rapidly becoming a Christmas favourite in the UK, replacing the terminally dull turkey. Treat it to some fine Pinot Noir of the fuller style – the best Burgundy has to offer or, more realistically price-wise, fat New World bottles. Other juicy reds or any Merlot-dominated wine will also hit the spot.

FURRY GAME

Try
Bordeaux p.24, **Spain** p.142, **Australia** p.156, **Chile** p.167

Merlot p.234, Tempranillo p.245, **Cabernet Sauvignon** p.224

I am always undecided as to whether or not I actually enjoy venison. A well-hung piece can be just a little over the top and too gamy for my liking; I prefer it when it hasn't been sitting around for too long. It is dark meat, so red wine is needed to balance it. Venison is also lean and so does not require the high-acidity reds that you might buy to take on something like pork. Due to its leanness, it only requires cooking to pink when in the form of a joint; otherwise it will become dry and tough. This will affect your choice of wine.

I like juicy, full-bodied reds. From Bordeaux I would look for the Merlot-dominated wines of the Right Bank, or the great Tempranillo of Ribera del Duero or Rioja. New World reds also work a treat, although I would be inclined to stick to the more restrained flavours of Merlot and Cabernet Sauvignon rather than a wild, powerful Shiraz.

Try Northern Rhône p.86, **Bandol** p.20, **Tuscany** p.120, **Piemonte** p.108

Syrah/Shiraz p.243, **Sangiovese** p.242, **Nebbiolo** p.237, **Barbera** p.222, **Grenache** p.230

As soon as you make a venison casserole Syrah should come into the picture. Juniper is a favourite spice to serve with venison and it has a very pronounced flavour, needing the big bold bottles. Try any Syrah from the Northern Rhône, Bandol and all things southern French. Italian wine loves this kind of food – all Sangiovese-based wines and anything made from Nebbiolo in the north, or Barbera. Now is also the time to uncork that New World Shiraz or Grenache.

Try
Burgundy p.38, **Australia** p.156, **New Zealand** p.168, **USA** p.178, **Loire Valley** p.72

Pinot Noir p.238, **Sangiovese** p.242, **Cabernet Franc** p.223

Wild boar gets a mention because I love it, although it is rarely seen in this country. Italians, on the other hand, worship all things hoglike. When on holiday there, treat it pretty much like pork but err on the side of strong wines as the meat is darker and has a more intense flavour.

Rabbit and hare are delicate, light meats but with a gamy flavour. Although they don't have wings, when choosing wine I tend to treat them like game birds. Pinot Noir is therefore my starting point: Burgundy first, but those from Australia, New Zealand and the States will do just as well. More budget-orientated reds like basic Chianti and Loire Cabernet Franc will also hit the spot.

Try

🐟 Alsace p.16, **Bordeaux** p.24, **Rhône** p.84

🍷 Gewürztraminer p.198, **Pinot Gris** p.205, **Riesling** p.206, **Sémillon** p.212, **Marsanne** p.201, **Roussanne** p.208

Rabbit often gets served up as a stew, which means a rich sauce, so be sure to pick wines with good acidity. Fine, concentrated white will also do the trick, and Gewürztraminer or Pinot Gris from Alsace would be the perfect partner for any kind of mustard and cream sauce. Riesling from around the world would be fine and I'd also try some rich Sémillon from Bordeaux or Australia. Lastly, the unusual white grapes from the Rhône can help out. Viognier is too light, but white Hermitage would be an excellent choice. Marsanne and Roussanne grapes that produce Hermitage-style wine are also grown successfully in Australia and will leave the bank balance in a happier state.

LAMB

Try

🍖 Bordeaux p.24, **Spain** p.142, **Italy** p.104, **Austria** p.96, **USA** p.178

🍷 Cabernet Sauvignon p.224, **Merlot** p.234

Lamb is the ultimate vehicle for showing off great red wine. In addition, apart from Port and very light wines, I can't really think of any red that doesn't work with lamb. The following are only my favourite selections, so don't get upset if you can't get the perfect match. Fine cuts of simply roasted lamb cry out for anything that is akin to the wines of Bordeaux. Rack of lamb, with its subtle flavour, loves aged Cabernet Sauvignon, whether from the Médoc, Spain, Italy, Australia or the USA. If the wine is young, veer towards juicy, Merlot-dominated ones from the Right Bank in Bordeaux or any of the above countries. Younger Cabernet Sauvignon won't hurt a rack of lamb but prefers the meaty, fattier cuts like roast leg or shoulder.

Try

🍖 Bandol p.20, **Languedoc** p.70, **Rhône Valley** p.84, **Australia** p.156

🍷 Grenache p.230, **Mourvèdre** p.236, **Shiraz/Syrah** p.243

As ever, the more complex and fine your wine is, the more simply the dish needs to be cooked; use garlic by all means, but in moderation. Once you start introducing strong flavours, those in the wine need to be more pronounced. Roast lamb is an art form in Provence, with lots of herbs and garlic or studded with anchovy and lemon peel. This needs butch, southern French wine – try Bandol, all Rhône reds, Languedoc and Shiraz from Australia.

Try

Italy p.104, **Spain** p.142,
Southern France p.14

Sangiovese p.242,
Tempranillo p.245,
Grenache p.230, **Primitivo**
p.241, **Touriga Nacional**
p.246, **Monastrell** p.236

Once you get to slow-cooked, flavoured roasts, or lamb shanks – one of my all-time favourites – you need to think about acidity. These cuts have a high fat content, which the meat absorbs in the slow cooking process. The Italians and Spanish are masters at this so in Italy look for Nebbiolo in the north or any good Sangiovese such as Brunello di Montalcino. From Spain try Rioja or any Garnacha/Grenache-based wine (Priorato if you are feeling flush). Once the dish gets really rustic – maybe a rich lamb shank stew with olives – don't go overboard on the wine. Stick to earthy, full-bodied bottles like some Touriga Nacional from Portugal, Monastrell from Spain, Italian bottles from Puglia or Sicily, Corbières or Minervois from France.

OFFAL

Try

Burgundy p.38, **Alsace**
p.16

Chardonnay p.192, **Pinot
Gris** p.205, **Gewürztraminer**
p.198, **Riesling** p.206

Gamay p.229

Calf's liver aside, there is something satisfyingly frugal about eating offal. It is usually cheap and I like the thought that nothing is going to waste. Deep-fried calves brains are surprisingly delicious and creamy, and to go with them I'd plump for some fine rich Chardonnay or a light fruity red like a Gamay. Sweetbreads are only really seen on brave restaurant menus; they have a subtle flavour and rich white would again be my first choice, whether from Burgundy or Alsace.

Try Burgundy p.38, **Tuscany**
p.120, **Bordeaux** p.24

Pinot Noir p.238,
Sangiovese p.242, **Merlot**
p.234

Into the realms of reality now. Liver comes in many guises but generally needs red wine. Calf's has the most delicate flavours, but even these are earthy. I'd go for some Pinot Noir, even better if it has a few years' bottle age; Chianti is also an option and mid-weight Merlot might help out.

Try

- Rhône p.84, **Provence** p.88, **Southern Italy** p.104, **Spain** p.142
- Grenache p.230, **Mourvèdre** p.236, **Dolcetto** p.228

Lamb's and pig's livers have stronger, rustic flavours so I might open a Southern Rhône bottle or anything from Provence and the surrounding area. I'd think also about hearty southern Italian wines and anything from regions like Jumilla in Spain. These kinds of butch reds are what I would have in mind for kidneys, even more so if they were immersed in a rich sauce or a steak and kidney pie.

Tripe in Italy is more likely than not to come in a rich tomato sauce, so I'd aim for a Dolcetto or a Freisa to cut through the richness but not be overpowering.

- Try **Alsace** p.16, **Loire Valley** p.72, **Australia** p.156, **Piemonte** p.108
- Gamay p.229, **Merlot** p.234, **Barbera** p.222

Terrine made from chicken livers is dealt with in the pâté section but, fried with some salad, you'll want some light red like a Loire Gamay or some oily white from Alsace to go with them. Duck livers are richer and darker so I'd stick with some sweetly fruited, uncomplicated New World Merlot or Barbera from Italy.

Try

- Bordeaux p.24, **Loire Valley** p.72, **Alsace** p.16
- Chenin Blanc p.194, **Riesling** p.206, **Sémillon** p.212

The moral rights and wrongs of foie gras and its production are well documented. It is, though, undeniably delicious stuff, even if I do feel slightly guilty for eating it too often. Rather like game with Pinot Noir, it plays a role of one of the all-time great matches with sweet wine. Sweet Bordeaux is an obvious start, although you should stick to bottles that don't have the orange tinge of a heavily affected botrytis wine. Sweet Loire Chenin Blanc and Alsatian Riesling, with their palate-cleansing acidity, are two others that are guaranteed to have you and your guests cooing with delight.

PÂTÉ

Try

- Beaujolais p.60, **Burgundy** p.38, **Loire Valley** p.72, **Italy** p.104
- Gamay p.229, **Pinot Noir** p.238, **Cabernet Franc** p.223, **Sangiovese** p.242

I just love pâté, terrines, parfait, rillettes and all other members of this family. A stick of French bread, a pot of Dijon mustard and some crunchy cornichons transport me to foodie heaven. The French are the undisputed masters of pâté and thus it is from them that we should take our lead in terms of what wine to drink. Red would seem the obvious choice as most of these dishes have a red meat feel to them. Don't uncork anything too gutsy, though, and remember to pick something with that all-important acidity to counter the richness.

I'd start with the Gamay grape, either from Beaujolais or the Loire. Its big brother Pinot Noir also works, but don't get anything too fancy – young, fruity and fresh is the answer. Staying in France, Loire Cabernet Franc is a good choice, but again, choose the fruity, early-drinking bottles. Around Europe, light Italian reds are fine, in particular the lesser Sangiovese-based wines.

Try
Northern Rhône p.86, **Jurançon** p.69, **Loire Valley** p.72, **Alsace** p.16

Chenin Blanc p.194, **Riesling** p.206, **Gewürztraminer** p.198, **Pinot Gris** p.205

Decadent fat whites with pâté, however, provide a match made in heaven. For those who like the unusual there is Jurançon and the Northern Rhône. The Chenin Blanc-based whites of the Loire are a joy – medium-dry and sweet Vouvray comes out top, but mid-weight Coteaux du Layon would also fit the bill. Alsace, though, is where it really all happens – *Vendange Tardive* (late harvest) Riesling, Gewürztraminer or Pinot Gris are almost too good to describe.

PORK

Try
Piemonte p.108, **Tuscany** p.120

Nebbiolo p.237, **Barbera** p.222, **Sangiovese** p.242

After lamb, pork is my favourite meat to eat with wine. While lamb is the answer for complex sophisticated reds, pork likes bottles that pack a punch. The meat has a high fat content and thus tastes rich, the wine you serve needs to act as a counterpoint to this. Good acidity and a helping of tannin is the key. This rules out a fair number of New World wines, only those grown in the coolest areas have the necessary punch to cut through the fat.

Pigs are perhaps revered most by the Italians so it is no surprise that their reds are a joy to drink with them. Roast your cut as they might utilising herbs like sage. If you are feeling rich go for Barolo or Barbaresco in the north. Barbera will also do the trick. Move further south and serious Chianti, Brunello di Montalcino, Vino Nobile di Montepulciano, or any of the host of other Sangiovese-based wines will do the job admirably.

Try Rhône Valley p.84,
Languedoc p.70, **Bandol**
p.20

Grenache p.230,
Mourvèdre p.236

For whites try
Burgundy p.38, **Bordeaux**
p.24, **Loire Valley** p.72

Chardonnay p.192, **Sémillon**
p.212, **Chenin Blanc** p.194

For reds try
Burgundy p.38, **Loire Valley**
p.72, **Northern Italy** p.104

Pinot Noir p.238, **Gamay**
p.229, **Cabernet Franc**
p.223, **Dolcetto** p.228

Try
Alsace p.16, **Germany**
p.98, **Austria** p.96

Pinot Gris p.205, **Riesling**
p.206, **Grüner Veltliner**
p.199

Moving to France I favour the more rustic wines from the south. Good, earthy Châteauneuf-du-Pape or any other Southern Rhône blend from there, or down to places like the Languedoc. Bandol always has balls to cope with any amount of fat or herbs you might throw at it.

Once you get to the more delicate cuts of pork like loin fillet you need to take a different approach. As the fat content is lost you essentially have a white meat, so more delicate styles of wine need to be introduced. Think of lighter reds, like Pinot Noir, Beaujolais, Loire Cabernet Franc, Dolcetto and Valpolicella. Moving towards creamy sauces, white wines can enter the fray. Full-bodied Chardonnay can be a fine match, but if you want to go New World make sure they have good acidity. Another good match would be rich Sémillon from Bordeaux or Australia, or one of the underrated dry Chenin Blancs from the Loire. After a few years' bottle age their honeyed flavours love any dish with cream, while they have all the structure to work with white meats.

Alsatians love a bit of pork and so their whites are good to consider. Pinot Gris is excellent and Riesling, with its fine acidity, really hits the spot. Those from Alsace are great, as are *Spätlese* or *Auslese* level German Rieslings or, if you can find them, Austrian examples or even some Grüner Veltliner. Ripe, tropical New World Riesling will also do the job. Once any Asian influences enter the equation these whites are definitely your best bet.

SAUSAGES

Try
Rhône Valley p.84,
Southern France p.14,
Italy p.104, **Spain** p.142,
Portugal p.132

A good sausage should have been made from meat with a high fat content, which keeps them moist as they cook, so you need to select a good beefy red that has fine acidity to cut through the high fat content. In France, I'd look to all things from the Rhône. Syrah in the north might be my choice for a grandiose wild boar sausage, while some from the south would provide the answer to a fine, herby Cumberland. Bandol, Minervois, Languedoc or Corbières would also do the job. Italian

Syrah/Shiraz p.243, **Malbec** p.232, **Grenache** p.230, **Primitivo** p.241, **Touriga Nacional** p.246, **Zinfandel** p.247

Try
Spain p.142, **Italy** p.104, **Beaujolais** p.60, **Fino Sherry** p.148

Sangiovese p.242, **Gamay** p.229, **Tempranillo** p.245

Try
France p.14, **Spain** p.142, **Italy** p.104, **Argentina** p.154, **Australia** p.156

Cabernet Sauvignon p.224, **Syrah/Shiraz** p.243, **Grenache** p.230, **Mourvèdre** p.236, **Malbec** p.232, **Barbera** p.222, **Primitivo** p.241, **Touriga Nacional** p.246

country reds would be my next port of call and, in particular, the dark, brooding wines of Puglia. Portuguese reds such as Touriga Nacional and everyday Spanish reds from the likes of Toro or Somontano will be just right. In the New World I would stick to the less polished wines like Shiraz, Grenache, Zinfandel or Malbec.

French and Italian sausages have firmer textures and more powerful flavours than British ones, so match them with the strongest of the recommendations above. Reds often stumble a bit when they hit upon Merguez or Chorizo. Rein in the power of these sausages and try something lighter like some basic Chianti, Valpolicella, Beaujolais or cheap Tempranillo. The finest match for fiery Chorizo is actually some chilled Fino Sherry.

STEW

I love all forms of meat cooked in this way. There is nothing more satisfying than getting a great big pot to cook your vegetables in, then adding meat and some lubrication in the form of wine, stock or beer and slowly cooking the whole lot for a long time. Shin of beef, lamb shanks and my all-time favourite, oxtail, are ideal for serving large numbers on a budget. The end result is hearty, warming and satisfying, requiring only some creamy mashed potato and red wine.

If you are making a British-style stew, you will end up with a rich, dark sauce that might have been flavoured with some bay or rosemary, but nothing too strong. All you need to do is concentrate on finding a good, beefy red to stand up to the sauce. Bordeaux and Cabernet Sauvignons from around the world will work but they seem a bit too sophisticated for this kind of fare. I would look further south in France. The Rhône Valley rarely takes any prisoners and everything from there to the border works a treat; staunchly uncommercial wines like Bandol or Madiran come into their own.

Hop over to Spain and any of their rustic wines from the likes of Jumilla or Toro will be just the ticket. Touriga Nacional and other grapes native to Portugal are equally excellent. Italian wine always comes up trumps when some acidity is needed to cut through a rich sauce, but don't go for anything too fancy. Barbera or something from Langhe would be good, or anything from down south in Puglia, Sicily or Sardinia, as they usually have the unsubtle flavours we're after here. Meaty Shiraz from Australia or Malbec from Argentina would be my pick of the New World options.

VEAL

For reds try
🌐 **Burgundy** p.38, **Rhône Valley** p.84, **Bordeaux** p.24

🍇 **Pinot Noir** p.238, **Syrah/Shiraz** p.243, **Grenache** p.230, **Mourvèdre** p.236

For whites try
🌐 **Loire Valley** p.72, **Australia** p.156

🍇 **Chardonnay** p.192, **Riesling** p.206, **Pinot Gris** p.205, **Sémillon** p.212

Veal is still an emotive issue in the UK and is rarely seen in any but the best butchers. The French have never had these qualms, hence veal is available in all the supermarkets. Having once improvised and cooked some veal on a grill over the log fire in France, I concluded that a Rhône wine took the edge over a fine red Burgundy, on account of the smoky flavours the steaks had taken on in the fire. Cooked less aggressively, though, Pinot would be my first port of call, especially if, like the Burgundians do, I got some mushrooms involved in the dish. Juicy, Merlot-dominated Bordeaux is also a fine choice.

Veal is often served with a cream sauce and whites will do surprisingly well with its delicate flesh. Think about serious Burgundy or a fat New World Chardonnay; also, oily Riesling, Pinot Gris, or Sémillon. The hugely underrated dry whites of the Loire come into play here too; Vouvray or Savennières have all the acidity and weight required.

PASTA

This is a rather general heading, but if ever a type of food illustrated the importance of regionality in food and wine matching this is it. Italy is, of course, the home of pasta, so it's not surprising that their home-grown wines are the first you should consider.

Try Italy p.104

Pinot Grigio p.205, **Soave** p.113, **Pinot Bianco** p.204

The simplest of pasta dishes might just have some olive oil, garlic and a few pine nuts tossed in it, or maybe some grilled vegetables. Light, fresh white is what you need to think of – Pinot Grigio et al. Go for something a bit richer to try to stand up to the pungency of a pesto.

Try Tuscany p.120, **Piemonte** p.108, **Puglia** p.128, **Sicily** p.128

Sangiovese p.242, **Nebbiolo** p.237, **Barbera** p.222

Rich tomato sauce and bolognese call for some red, but nothing too serious. Structure is important to counter the food's inherent richness, and Sangiovese- or Nebbiolo-based wines are the answer. Richer meat sauces including pork or wild boar might call for something with a bit more clout – perhaps some Barbera or a sweetly fruited bottle from the south.

For whites try Italy p.104, **Australia** p.156, **New Zealand** p.168

Sauvignon Blanc p.210

For reds try Northern Italy p.104

Dolcetto p.228, **Barbera** p.222

Ravioli, tortellini and cannelloni filled with meat generally require something lighter, so try Dolcetto or Valpolicella. Stuffed with cheese, you could stick with these reds or try richer whites like a good Soave, Arneis, Tokay or any of the international grapes, like Sauvignon.

PIZZA

The two basic components of pizza that affect your choice of wine are a rich tomato sauce and cheese. If you then choose to slap on Tandoori chicken, pineapple and jalapeños I can't help. However, pizza in the Italian sense of the word uses small amounts of simple toppings like salami, capers, spinach or possibly an egg. Even with these combinations you are looking at a wide range of powerful tastes. This is simple rustic cooking so you should look for wine that is in the same mould.

Try

🍷 **Puglia** p.128, **Sicily** p.130, **Piemonte** p.108, **Tuscany** p.120

🍷 **Primitivo** p.241, **Cabernet Sauvignon** p.224, **Sangiovese** p.242

The richness of melted cheese and a tomato sauce demands red with some stuffing. It doesn't have to be the most full-bodied, inky black affair, but it must have a good backbone of acidity; some tannin wouldn't go amiss either. Fruity, low-acidity reds might taste great on their own but they are not up to the job for this kind of food. It's no surprise, then, that Italian wines are just the ticket. Don't push the boat out, though, as a hearty bottle from down south will do the trick – try Puglia or Sicily. Any Sangiovese-based wine would also be great, as would Valpolicella or Freisa from the north.

Try

🍷 **Spain** p.142, **Portugal** p.132, **Southern Rhône** p.90, **Australia** p.156, **South Africa** p.174

🍷 **Tempranillo** p.245, **Grenache** p.230, **Syrah/Shiraz** p.243, **Mourvèdre** p.236, **Pinotage** p.240

In Spain I'd try any Tempranillo or a beefy Rhône-like blend from Jumilla. Portuguese red is also sufficiently rough round the edges to go down a treat. If you wanted to go to France, I would stick to the south and all those areas that mimic the Southern Rhône. Polished New World reds don't seem to work so well, although spicy Shiraz from Australia's cooler regions can work and this is one of the few occasions when I might drink some Pinotage from South Africa.

CURRY

For whites try
Australia p.156, **New Zealand** p.168, **Chile** p.167, **Austria** p.96, **Alsace** p.16

Riesling p.206, **Gewürztraminer** p.198, **Pinot Gris** p.205, **Sauvignon Blanc** p.210

For reds try
Australia p.156, **Chile** p.167

Grenache p.230, **Pinot Noir** p.238, **Merlot** p.234

Curry and wine are not the happiest of bedfellows. Partners can be found that will get on, but marriage is never likely to be in the offing. The first main hurdle is the strength of the spices used in this kind of cooking. The likes of cardamom and cumin have intense flavours that can overwhelm wine, but the biggest problem by far is the heat of chillies.

I love hot food and find the pain-pleasure thing of an eye-wateringly hot curry irresistible. However, hot food essentially numbs your palate to the intricacies of wine. Worse still, while you will not be able to detect the wine's taste, you will be able to sense its acidity and – for reds – any tannins that are present. Thus the wine will taste astringent and bitter. If you just can't resist ordering the hot dishes I'm afraid I have to throw up my hands in surrender and suggest you stick to water or beer.

Red wine is particularly troublesome with this type of food. The best options are soft, fruit-driven reds. From Europe try Beaujolais, Loire reds, Valpolicella from Italy. New World reds that are generally low in tannin and acidity do surprisingly well. Don't go overboard and get the biggest wines, but try some Grenache, Pinot Noir and even juicy Merlot. Whites are a better option, although you need to stick to unfashionable grapes like Riesling; the rich versions from the New World, Austria or Alsace are the best. Gewürztraminer and Pinot Gris will also stay the course admirably, as will ripe, fruity Sauvignon Blanc from places like New Zealand. The rule of thumb for both whites and reds is to not splash out – the subtleties of expensive fine wine will be lost in the curry cauldron.

MOROCCAN

Tagines are Morocco's most famous contribution to the culinary world. The flavours used in them are strong: spices, olives and preserved citrus fruits like lemons or oranges. When confronted by such bold flavours, the wine you choose is always going to take a back seat to the food. A rich sauce is another important factor. If fish were the main component I'd like something crisp and fruity. Those varieties that work well with Asian food should be your first port of call: Riesling from around the globe, ripe New World Sauvignon Blanc, good Pinot Grigio from Italy and Gewürztraminer. Look for fruity examples but not the best – full-bodied, fragrant examples will just end up fighting against the flavours of the food.

Chicken and lamb are the most common forms of tagine. The above recommendations will be fine for chicken if you feel like white. For red I would choose an honest fruity red now, however, with good acidity to deal with the rich sauce. Some crisp Gamay from the Loire or Beaujolais is a good start. Entry level red Burgundy would be an excellent but not very economical choice. My next stop might be the Southern Rhône for a light Côte du Rhône as the inherent spices in these wines will complement the fragrance of the dish. Don't choose anything too serious though; too big a wine will clash with the food. Dolcetto, Freisa and Valpolicella from northern Italy are like all the country's reds, blessed with fine acidity and the fruitiness we are looking for. New World reds can be an excellent choice, but avoid the really inky black wines and look for something from the cooler zones with more acid. The grapes I would favour are Pinot Noir, Cabernet Franc and Grenache, rather than the heavier ones like Shiraz or Cabernet Sauvignon.

For whites try

Italy p.104, **New Zealand** p.168, **Chile** p.167

Riesling p.206, **Sauvignon Blanc** p.210, **Pinot Grigio** p.205, **Gewürztraminer** p.198

For reds try

Loire Valley p.72, **Beaujolais** p.60, **Southern Rhône** p.90, **Northern Italy** p.108

Gamay p.229, **Pinot Noir** p.238, **Cabernet Franc** p.223, **Grenache** p.230, **Dolcetto** p.228

CHINESE, THAI AND FUSION FOOD

Thai food and what is known as 'fusion cooking' or 'Pacific Rim' provides a whole heap of challenges for wine. The latter two styles are a modern phenomenon that were very much in vogue five years ago,

Try

New Zealand p.168, **South Africa** p.174, **Chile** p.167, **Australia** p.156, **Loire Valley** p.72, **Italy** p.104, **Spain** p.142

Sauvignon Blanc p.210, **Verdejo** p.215

essentially combining eastern ingredients with more traditional styles of European cooking. Our enthusiasm for them has waned recently, however; the critics rightly pointed out that some chefs had got a bit overexcited and tried to fob us off with wacky combinations that simply didn't work. Kept simple, though, it can be the most wonderfully fresh food to eat. These styles, unlike European cooking, have no history of being consumed with wine. Thus, starting with a clean slate, any number of combinations can be entertained.

The first hurdle to overcome is chilli. Wine does not enjoy the palate-numbing effects of this vegetable. If you are cooking the meal use them by all means, but in moderation. If the recipe calls for an eye-watering number (many Thai dishes are authentically very hot), I can't help – stick to beer and lots of water. Red wine, especially with any tannin, is particularly vulnerable to tasting vile when consumed with a hot chilli dish and the reds I recommend will only go with the mildest of dishes.

The second element in much of this style of cooking is the abundance of differing fresh flavours. Lime leaves, lemongrass, galangal and sweet basil all have a pungent fragrancy to them. Lastly, consider the wildly different tastes you encounter with each mouthful – a chunk of lemongrass in one chew, followed maybe by a creamy slurp of chilli-hot coconut milk the next. Contrast this to eating a traditional European meal where the extremes of flavour are far smaller.

All this requires one to think outside the box a little. Wine is never going to take centre stage with this type of food, so forget about getting out fancy, complex bottles; their nuances will be lost. What are required are ripe, fruity, uncomplicated wines with good acidity. Oaky wines don't work, as their inherent spiciness clashes rather than complements.

Unburdened by any regional bias, you are free to trawl the wine world. Good, ripe Sauvignon Blanc is an excellent start, so look at New Zealand, South Africa, Chile and Australia. Examples from Europe would naturally include wines like Sancerre from the Loire Valley, although these only work in the hottest, ripest years. You might be better off having a go at those from Italy. Good Verdejo from Spain would also be a fine choice.

Try

🍇 **Australia** p.156, **New Zealand** p.168

🍇 **Riesling** p.206, **Verdelho** p.216

I've eased you in gently but now it's time to head to more unfashionable zones. Riesling has all the right characteristics – fruit, acidity and even (in some) a touch of sweetness that is great for standing up to chilli heat. Australians are credited with having invented fusion cooking and it is no coincidence that many of their restaurant wine lists major in Riesling. If you have a phobia against Riesling try the Aussie and New Zealand versions first, as they are generally bone-dry. While you are in Oz, have a go at any Verdelho you might come across.

Try

🍇 **Germany** p.98, **Alsace** p.16, **Italy** p.104, **Australia** p.156

🍇 **Riesling** p.206, **Gewürztraminer** p.198, **Pinot Gris** p.205

Your next port of call should be Germany. Revel in being a trendsetter; try the mid-weight wines (*Spätlese* and *Auslese*); the sweetness works particularly well with any dishes containing coconut milk. If German wine is just a step too far, nip over the border to Alsace, where their Rieslings are richer and mostly dry. However, it is the two other grapes grown in this region that really stand out: Gewürztraminer and Pinot Gris. The former breaks one of my rules as it is low in acidity but gets away with it because of its flamboyant fragrance. Pinot Gris is a bit more restrained but still does the trick. Italy's Pinot Grigio is generally too light, but fine ripe examples from Australia can be found and will do the trick admirably. Good fruity examples of these two grapes are among the finest matches for Asian food.

Try

🍇 **Beaujolais** p.60, **Loire Valley** p.72, **Valpolicella** p.112

🍇 **Gamay** p.229, **Cabernet Franc** p.223

Red is much more tricky and less satisfactory. If you must have a glass you need to look for the same attributes as with whites, namely ripe fruit flavours. It is imperative not to serve red that has any tannin with anything hot. This rules out much of Europe where tannin is key to so many of the wines. In France good Beaujolais and ripe Cabernet Franc from the Loire can be useful, as is proper Valpolicella from northern Italy. Medium-weight juicy New World reds are also good.

Try

🍇 **Australia** p.156, **New Zealand** p.168

🍇 **Pinot Noir** p.238, **Grenache** p.230

Your best bet is sweet, ripe Pinot Noir from Australia or New Zealand; Grenache from the former will also work. Pinot, though, is never a cheap option and remember that many of the wine's subtleties will be lost to the food. When serving these reds with this type of food, I find they always benefit from an hour in the fridge as it helps to accentuate their fruit flavours.

CREAM SAUCES

Cream equals rich. Regardless of any flavours you add to it, your wine must have good acidity to cut through cream's texture. If you were looking for some white to partner a cream-heavy fish dish I'd start with Chardonnay. Good, ripe examples of this grape have often spent some time maturing in oak barrels. This will give the wine a buttery rich texture that complements cream. Examples from the New World will often be the most pronounced; as ever, though, make sure they have good acidity – oily, fat Chardonnay with a cream dish will be too much. I might look to the Adelaide Hills in Australia, cool Sonoma County in California and all New Zealand's offerings. I also find good Sémillon a fine match so try Australia or those from Bordeaux.

Once you start to increase the flavours in the sauce – perhaps by adding some mustard or a strong herb like tarragon – I'd look to classic food helpers like Riesling and Pinot Gris. Good Viognier or other Rhône whites such as Marsanne or Roussanne have the right flavour profile but they can lack the necessary zip. If you are feeling adventurous track down some Grüner Veltliner from Austria or even a full-bodied Albariño from Spain.

Bring some meat into the fray and you'll want to start entertaining some red. Big, heavy, bruising reds don't enjoy this kind of food, so even if you do have a juicy piece of steak under your sauce I'd stick to something fairly light. Pinot Noir, with its freshness, is always a good option as would be many mid-weight Italian wines: Valpolicella, Dolcetto or Chianti (but not the top stuff). Proper Cru Beaujolais or even some Gamay from the Loire would also work, and while you are there, check out the reds made from Cabernet Franc, some Chinon or St Nicolas de Bourgueil in a ripe year would do the trick.

Don't be afraid to break with conventional wisdom dictating that you should always drink red with meat and vice versa, as you should essentially be matching the wine to the sauce. Indeed, for creamy pork or chicken dishes, I would always steer towards white.

MEATY SAUCES

Sauces made with stock from meaty bones all have one thing in common: they are rich. Heavily reduced ones can become very intense and almost overpowering. The key to dealing with this richness is to match wines with good structure; whites with fine acidity and reds with a helping of acid and tannin.

With a reduction of chicken stock, I would think about some big Riesling – Alsatian or New World rather than Germany, whose wines are more fragrant than powerful. For reds I'd have a look at Gamay, Pinot Noir, Cabernet Franc, light Tempranillo and Italian food stalwarts like Chianti or Dolcetto; some mid-weight Merlot from Bordeaux would also work.

Sticky red meat reductions can be positively sweet and need a gutsy red to act as a counterpoint. I tend to start off thinking classically – Bordeaux if lamb or beef is involved, or Burgundy if the sauce is accompanying game. Bordeaux grapes grown in Spain, Italy or the New World can be just as good, but remember that soft, fruity, commercial styles are not the answer.

Meaty sauce served with fish is not uncommon in France and for this I'd go back to some of the lighter recommendations. Don't be afraid to drink red with fish if it is accompanied by a meaty reduction.

Introduce strong herbs into the equation and you can entertain spicy southern French wines, beefy Portuguese reds, Spanish country wines, Australian Shiraz and all manner of things Italian. Above all, serve your fine complex wines with the simple dishes and the bruising bottles with the rustic dishes.

ARTICHOKES

Artichokes are delicious things but they are one of the few foods that really don't like wine at all. They will kill most wine dead in the water, especially if you do as the Italians do and dunk the raw leaves in olive oil.

Cooked and marinated is how you are most likely to encounter artichokes; even then they do wine no favours. Light and innocuous white is what they need. Think of Pinot Grigio, Pinot Bianco or Soave from Italy. Basic Loire whites like Muscadet or Sauvignon de Touraine can be fine, as would a Sylvaner or a Pinot Blanc from Alsace. Oaky whites or fruity wines from the New World just seem to clash, and I'm afraid red is not an option. The real rule of thumb here is not to spend too much money, as the wine should always take the back seat.

ASPARAGUS

I just adore this stuff and in the rural heaven that I have constructed in my mind, I would have an asparagus bed of at least an acre (apparently it's a bitch to grow and requires hard work and lots of attention to detail, so this dream is unlikely to become reality). The thick spears you can buy all the year round are perfectly satisfactory. However, the thin, altogether greener stalks produced in this country during asparagus's distressingly short season have more flavour, so seek them out in springtime.

Unhappily for wine, this delicious vegetable has a particular dislike of many things vinous. Along with artichokes it will do a pretty good job at destroying wine, so don't serve your finest bottles; the answer is fresh and ultimately simple whites. Sauvignon Blanc from the Loire is a classic match but fruitier ones from the New World work just as well, especially if you have knocked up some hollandaise. Pinot Blanc from Alsace, Pinot Grigio and Bianco from Italy, Muscadet and light Rieslings will all be fine. Avoid rich or oaky white, and I'm afraid reds are a no-no.

MUSHROOMS

Try

🍷 **Burgundy** p.38, **Italy** p.104

🍇 **Pinot Noir** p.238, **Sangiovese** p.242, **Nebbiolo** p.237

The grape that loves all things fungal is Pinot Noir – any bottles with a few years' age will just make them even better. Fine Pinots, especially those from Burgundy, have an earthy, complex taste, not unlike many wild mushrooms. The French love to serve morels with a good chicken, in which case you should immediately reach for the Burgundy; grilled ceps and any game, ditto.

Italians pair their porcini with pork. Pinot will work a treat here, but even better, look for an aged bottle of good Chianti or some venerable old Nebbiolo from up north. Being a traditionalist at heart, I feel better drinking Italian wine with Italian food, so bottles of the above would be my first choice if confronted by a mushroom risotto. These wines, when aged, take on the same complex truffle character as Pinot. Of course, other wines will work, but if you have gone to the trouble to secure some wild mushrooms, why settle for second best with the wine?

ANTIPASTI

Try

🍷 **Northern Italy** p.104

🍇 **Sauvignon Blanc** p.210, **Pinot Bianco** p.204

These two methods of cooking change the way many vegetables taste. Steamed carrots are a different prospect from the roasted version, and raw peppers are something I have never been able to get to grips with; roast them, however, and they are delicious. Aubergines, courgettes, onions and tomatoes cooked in this way all feature in classic Italian antipasti and are great, simple starter-fare in the summer.

These roasted vegetables have a sweetness to them that is not apparent in their raw or steamed form, and there is a range of wines you can drink with this kind of food. I often let the situation dictate the bottle I am going to quaff as much as what is on the plate. Roasted vegetables as a starter or light lunch just remind me of the summer, and I'd look for some light fresh Italian white to cut through the sweetness of the vegetables while not getting in the way of their delicate flavour: Verdicchio, Vernaccia di San Gimignano, Lugana, Pinot Bianco are all classic examples.

For whites try Soave p.113, **Burgundy** p.38

Chardonnay p.192

For reds try Beaujolais p.60, **Tuscany** p.120

Gamay p.229, **Sangiovese** p.242

A roasted aubergine, perhaps studded with some garlic and rosemary, is an altogether meatier thing and something I might contemplate on a winter's evening if I wanted some comfort food. All the above whites would do the trick but they lack that warming factor, so I might veer towards some serious, creamy Soave or even a lightly oaked Chardonnay. A soft, fruity red such as anything made with Gamay or Sangiovese would also hit the spot.

SALADS

Try

Italy p.104, **Loire Valley** p.72, **Alsace** p.16, **Germany** p.98, **New Zealand** p.168, **South Africa** p.174, **Australia** p.156

Pinot Grigio p.205, **Pinot Bianco** p.204, **Sylvaner** p.213, **Riesling** p.206, **Sauvignon Blanc** p.210

Salads seem the most innocent of things and as such would seem easy to match with wine. After all, a cucumber slice or a lettuce leaf is hardly stuffed full of flavour. Problems arise, though, with the dressing you choose to splash on it. A good slug of fine olive oil and a squeeze of lemon is no problem. However, a strong vinaigrette might contain garlic, mustard and, of course, vinegar, which is high in acidity. For such a dressed salad you need to be wary.

Thankfully, the ingredients now available, mean that a salad no longer just means some shredded watery iceberg and a few slices of cucumber. French and Italian salad leaves have altogether more flavour – think of the bitterness of endive or radicchio. We have also learnt that some chopped green herbs can enliven proceedings considerably – tarragon, parsley, chervil and basil might all make an appearance. Chuck in a few nuts and you suddenly have a cornucopia of different tastes.

All this is excellent news for our taste buds, but the acidity of a dressing, bitter flavours from the leaves and various herbs all add up to a bit of a headache for wine. In this instance the salad is always going to do the talking, so you need something light and neutral to wash it down with. Red wine is out, as is strongly flavoured oaky white. European styles are going to be favoured as they have the requisite acidity levels to match the dressing. Try Pinot Grigio, Verdicchio, or Pinot Bianco from Italy, basic Chablis, all dry Loire whites, Pinot Blanc or Sylvaner from Alsace and basic low-level Riesling from Germany. New World-wise your best bet is going to be Riesling or Sauvignons from cool areas in New Zealand, South Africa and Australia.

TOMATOES

For whites try Loire Valley p.72, **Northern Italy** p.104

Chenin Blanc p.194, **Sauvignon Blanc** p.210, **Pinot Blanc** p.204, **Pinot Grigio** p.205, **Chardonnay** p.192

For reds try Tuscany p.120, **Loire Valley** p.72, **Beaujolais** p.60,

Sangiovese p.242, **Gamay** p.229

Try
Bordeaux p.24, **Australia** p.156, **California** p.180, **Chile** p.167, **Northern Italy** p.104, **Spain** p.142

Merlot p.234, **Dolcetto** p.228, **Barbera** p.222, **Tempranillo** p.245

Until I visited Italy for the first time, I was always fairly indifferent to the tomato. Sun-ripened plum tomatoes sliced with good olive oil, some balsamic vinegar and basil may sound like a clichéd salad, but when the ingredients are top-notch, it is food heaven.

Unripe tomatoes – as often sold in the UK – are high in acidity, causing havoc with wine and reds in particular. You need to drink light, innocuous whites with the same levels of acid. Try Loire Chenin or Sauvignon Blanc, Pinot Blanc or Grigio and even some of the duller white grapes of the world like Trebbiano and Colombard. Find some deep-red ripe ones and you can entertain richer whites like some good Soave or unoaked Chardonnay, but avoid oaky, flabby bottles. Light, fruity reds like basic Chianti, and Gamay from the Loire or Beaujolais are excellent.

Once you cook tomatoes, either by roasting or by adding them to a pasta sauce, they become miraculously sweet and rich. Reds are best, but nothing too serious or heavy. Try the reds above or some lightweight, juicy Merlot from Bordeaux or the New World. Dolcetto and light versions of Barbera from northern Italy, along with any sweetly fruited Tempranillo, will all be fine.

CHEESE

You could write a whole book about cheese and wine matching and still not do it justice. The range of cheese on our shelves from Europe and from our own shores is now huge. The spectrum of taste from mild creamy goats cheese to a salty mature blue, like Roquefort, is poles apart. Unfortunately this is one area we seem to be generally confident in when food and wine matching. Full-bodied red or Port is the thing to serve with cheese, right? This might have been true twenty years ago when the only thing likely to be found on a cheese board was Cheddar and some Stilton if you were feeling adventurous. Today, though, it is categorically not the case.

Red wine is still an all-round winner, but it doesn't need to be the heaviest kind. Port is simply too rich for many cheeses. Some of the finest matches are to be found with white wines and even sweet wine. If you don't believe me ask the French. They take the appreciation of cheese very seriously indeed. White wine with many of their finest cheeses is not some recent invention; rather, it has the backing of hundreds of years of gastronomic history. Eyebrows will be raised, especially among the more traditional, but by serving some great sweet wine with a blue cheese or a crisp Loire Sauvignon with goats cheese, you will not only cause a stir but also have the perfect match.

HARD CHEESE

🍷 **Try Bordeaux** p.24, **Australia** p.156, **Chile** p.167, **California** p.180, **Piemonte** p.108, **Portugal** p.132

🍇 **Cabernet Sauvignon** p.224, **Merlot** p.234, **Barbera** p.222

Mature hard cheese tends to have some of the strongest flavours, so here you are perfectly entitled to indulge in full-blooded red wine and Port. Red Bordeaux – or claret, as we like to call it – is a great foil to the tang of fine crumbly Cheddar, although I prefer the Merlot-dominated wines of the Right Bank, with their sweeter fruit. This classic blend of Cabernet Sauvignon and Merlot is replicated around the world.

Good examples from the New World can often be an even better match as their ripe fruit contrasts with the sharp taste of the mature cheese. Port-wise I prefer to stick to the lighter styles, especially tawny. The sweetness of New World Cabernet, Merlot and Port do a great job also and are better suited to our more crumbly cheeses like those from Cheshire or Lancashire. Barbera from Italy also works admirably.

🍷 **Try Burgundy** p.38, **Beaujolais** p.60, **Loire** p.72, **Valpolicella** p.112

🍇 **Pinot Noir** p.238, **Cabernet Franc** p.223, **Gamay** p.229

Move abroad and many Continental hard cheeses have a waxy texture and a more delicate taste than our native ones. Tomme from France, Gouda from Holland and Emmental from Switzerland are better suited to lighter reds. Pinot Noir is a favourite but juicy Cabernet Franc from the Loire, Beaujolais or even Valpolicella will do the trick.

🍷 **Try Piemonte** p.108, **Tuscany** p.120, **Amarone (Valpolicella)** p.113

🍇 **Barbera** p.222, **Dolcetto** p.228, **Sangiovese** p.242

Good Parmesan is something that should be eaten more in its own right and not just grated over pasta. It enjoys Italian wine with its fine acidity and sweet fruits – try Barbera and Dolcetto from the north and any Sangiovese from Tuscany and Umbria. Along with mature Cheddar it is one of the few cheeses that packs the necessary punch to deal with Italy's unique Amarone.

🍷 **Try Bordeaux** p.24, **Montalcino (Tuscany)** p.120

🍇 **Cabernet Sauvignon** p.224, **Merlot** p.234, **Sangiovese** p.242

Less mature hard cheeses like Cornish Yarg or a medium Pecorino from Italy are a better bet if you want to show off an old bottle of something. Their delicate flavours are less intrusive on the complexities of an old Bordeaux or fine Brunello from Tuscany.

SOFT AND RUNNY CHEESES

For white wines try
🍷 Alsace p.16, **Rhône** p.84

🍇 **Pinot Gris** p.205, **Gewürztraminer** p.198, **Chardonnay** p.192

For red wines try
🍷 **Burgundy** p.38, **Beaujolais** p.60, **Spain** p.142, **Tuscany** p.120, **Piemonte** p.108, **Loire** p.72

🍇 **Pinot Noir** p.238, **Tempranillo** p.245, **Gamay** p.229, **Cabernet Franc** p.223

Cheeses in this category run the full gamut of flavours from creamy Brie through to the pungency of Munster. While the general rule of thumb for hard cheese is red, full-bodied wine, soft ones prefer lighter reds and white wine.

Pinot Noir is the absolute king of the soft-cheese world. It is no coincidence that Burgundy, the grape's home, also produces two of the world's finest runny cheeses. No matter how tightly you think the Vacherin and Epoisses might be sealed in your fridge, it's guaranteed to reek of them for days after you've eaten them. Drink young, fresh Pinot or Beaujolais with the former and something a bit older with the latter, and the smell will seem a small price to pay.

Grapes with similar characteristics to Pinot also work well so try Tempranillo, Sangiovese and – if you are lucky enough to have any – aged Barolo or Barbaresco. Good, oily Pinot Gris or Gewürztraminer from Alsace, or maybe rich Rhône whites, will also hit the spot. Munster, which takes the word 'smelly' to a new plane, particularly enjoys over-the-top Alsatian white.

With less pongy affairs like Brie, Reblechon, or Stinking Bishop, I prefer the white option. If you demand red, have something light like a Loire Cabernet Franc or some Gamay – don't be afraid to put the bottles in the fridge for an hour or so before you serve them. Rich Pinot Gris, whether from France or the New World, is a particularly fine experience. Good, rich Chardonnay, whether from Burgundy or the New World, is an excellent match for the creamier cheese but nothing too pungent.

BLUE CHEESE

Try
🍷 **Jurançon** p.69

🍇 **Chenin Blanc** p.194, **Riesling** p.206

It's time now to introduce you to one of my favourite and most odd food and wine combinations. Salty blue cheeses like Roquefort, Fourme d'Ambert and Stilton taste utterly delicious with sweet wine. The match works on the same principle as any dish that has a sweet-and-sour element to it. The sharp, salty taste of the cheese is a perfect foil to a decadent sweet wine. To be specific, my top choices are sweeties made from Chenin Blanc and Riesling, and those rare but delicious wines from Jurançon. The extra acidity of these grapes cuts through the creamy blue cheese such as Dolcelatte and Blue Brie.

Try

🍷 **Port** p.132, **Banyuls** p.71, **Maury** p.71

🍇 **Sémillon** p.212

The all-round sweetness of a botrytis Sémillon, whether from Bordeaux or elsewhere, is better with stronger blues like Stilton. If sweet wine is not your thing, then get traditional and serve some Port, which is in effect a sweet red wine and works well for the same reason. Try also France's version of Port from down south in the guise of Banyuls or Maury.

Try

🍷 **Alsace** p.16, **Australia** p.156, **California** p.180, **Amarone (Valpolicella)** p.113

🍇 **Pinot Gris** p.205

🍇 **Shiraz** p.243, **Zinfandel** p.247

Rich whites from Alsatian varieties like Pinot Gris are fine for the light, creamy blues but will get lost with the heavy-duty stuff. If only red will do, pick ripe, full-bodied bottles; Australia excels at Shiraz that has the consistency of Port, as does California with its Zinfandel. Closer to home, the monstrous Amarones from northern Italy will more than suffice.

GOATS CHEESE

Try

🍷 **Loire Valley** p.72, **New Zealand** p.168, **Chile** p.167, **Australia** p.156, **Northern Italy** p.104

🍇 **Sauvignon Blanc** p.210, **Verdejo** p.215, **Pinot Grigio** p.205, **Pinot Bianco** p.204

Washed down with chilled Loire Sauvignon Blanc, this is one of the all-time great food and wine matches. Good crisp examples from the cooler sites around the world work just as well. Try those from New Zealand, South Africa, Chile, Australia and, closer to home, those from northern Italy. You can venture outside Sauvignon if it doesn't agree with you. Some Spanish Verdejo, good Pinot Grigio, Pinot Bianco or Pinot Blanc will all suffice.

Try

🍷 **St Nicolas de Bourgueil (Loire)** p.76, **Beaujolais** p.60, **Valpolicella** p.112

🍇 **Pinot Noir** p.238, **Gamay** p.229

With the older more pungent examples of goats cheese I prefer to drink some red, but nothing too heavy. If you want to stay local, a mid-weight fruity Cabernet Franc like some St Nicolas de Bourgueil will do the trick, or some Gamay from Touraine. Otherwise Beaujolais, any light Pinot Noir, or even Valpolicella will be fine. If you are lucky enough to be eating outside on a hot day, don't be afraid to stick the reds in the fridge for an hour or so before serving.

CHOCOLATE

Try
Portugal p.132, **Southern France** p.14, **Australia** p.156, **South Africa** p.174, **USA** p.178

More wine is ruined by being drunk with chocolate than by any other food. By calling sweet wine dessert wine we have misled ourselves into believing that it will go with all puddings. There are very few certainties in food and wine matching, but the fact that a rich chocolate pudding will destroy the taste of nearly all wine is one of them. Like the yolk of an egg, chocolate coats the taste buds and doesn't allow much else through. You will find that the flavour of the wine is lost but that you can detect its acidity, which leaves a bitter, unpleasant taste in the mouth. Sadder than this taste experience is the waste of a fine bottle. Sweet wine is never cheap, so treat it with respect.

The number of options open to you here is small. What's needed is the equivalent of a vinous sledgehammer to get through to your tongue. Sweet red wine is a good place to start, with Port being the most obvious choice. The best match is some good Ruby Port or a young vintage one – you need really ripe fruit, so don't waste the complexities of a fine mature bottle. Better value can usually be had from France's answer to Port – Maury and Banyuls from down south, both of which are usually served chilled. For fine value look for wines made in a Port style from Australia, South Africa and the USA.

Try
California p.180, **Australia** p.156, **Italy** p.104, **Sherry** p.148

Zinfandel p.247, **Shiraz** p.243, **Muscat** p.202

The sweetness of these wines is one element of why these matches work, the other is the high alcohol content. This gives a clue to more potential pairings. Thick, treacly Sherry is wonderful stuff in its own right but it also has the guts for chocolate, so seek out some fine Pedro Ximénez or Moscatel.

Your next stop should be super-heavyweight reds. Many of these lumbering monsters are too cumbersome for other food, and what they all have in common is huge flavours and high alcohol. Try overripe Californian Zinfandels, bruising Shiraz from Australia (the Barossa in particular), and Italy's uniquely powerful Amarone. You can get away with light wines like some fortified Muscat de Rivesaltes if you serve a light, fluffy chocolate mousse.

CHRISTMAS PUDDING AND MINCE PIES

Try
Port p.132, **Sweet Sherry** p.148, **Marsala** p.131, **Madeira** p.138, **Banyuls** p.71, **Maury** p.71

Christmas is not one of my favourite culinary times of the year. Anything made with mincemeat sends shivers of apprehension done my spine, fruit cake leaves me cold and marzipan should be reclassified as a swear word. However, what one drinks with these festive puddings gets me altogether more excited. These are big flavours; add a dollop of brandy butter and things only get bolder.

Christmas is a time when we let tradition rule the roost, but I am afraid this doesn't work for sweet wine. Your fine old bottle of Sauternes will be wasted. You need to think bigger and blacker. Intensely sweet Sherry is a good place to start (this will also keep great-aunt happy) – Pedro Ximénez and Moscatel look like black treacle and taste like liquefied raisins.

If you're having Port with the Stilton you can just get started a little earlier, as this also works a treat. Better still would be some old liqueur wines from Australia or South Africa. Back to Europe, sweet Malmsey or Bual Madeira, Marsala or Moscato di Pantelleria, and the south of France's answer to Port – Maury and Banyuls – have all got the power for the job.

CRÈME BRÛLÉE AND CREAMY PUDDINGS

Try
Barsac and Sauternes p.31, **Monbazillac (Bergerac)** p.23, **Jurançon** p.69, **Germany** p.98, **Hungary** p.103, **Italy** p.104

Sémillon p.212, **Riesling** p.206

For me, crème brûlée is the perfect way to end a meal – decadently rich, sweet custard with a micro-thin topping of caramelised sugar. Additions of dates, rhubarb, lemongrass and even Earl Grey tea can all work, but I prefer mine au naturel.

Orange-tinged, *botrytis*-affected stickies are what you should be thinking about with this kind of pudding. Great to try are sweet Bordeaux or their cheaper cousins, Monbazillac and Saussignac, thick Aussie Sémillon, *Beerenauslese* or *Trockenbeerenauslese* Rieslings, honeyed Jurançon, Tokaji from Hungary and last, but not least, Vin

Santo from Italy. All these wines have the weight to cope with the sweet custard, and also the burnt caramel flavours to complement the dessert's sugary cap.

FRUIT DESSERTS

Try

🍷 **Champagne** p.64, **Northern Italy** p.104, **Germany** p.98, **Alsace** p.16, **Loire Valley** p.72, **Jurançon** p.69

🍇 **Muscat** p.202, **Riesling** p.206

Fruit-based puddings can range from a light, fresh summer salad to the good old winter crumble that will be sloshing around in fine home-made custard. We'll start light and get progressively heavier.

Fruit, in its raw, unadulterated form, is not artery-cloggingly sweet and generally has high levels of acidity. Your choice of wine needs to reflect this; medium sweet with fresh acidity is best. I would avoid sweet wines that have been heavily affected by botrytis, as you are looking for concentrated fruit flavours rather than the caramel and marmalade notes that are generally found in botrytis-affected sweet wines.

Strawberries or raspberries with cream is the most quintessential of British summer puddings. The most decadent match for this is demi-sec (slightly sweet) Champagne or, alternatively, some fine fizzy Moscato from Italy. I'd open either of the above for fruit salad and also some fresh, sweet wines – young Auslese Riesling from Germany, Vendange Tardive from Alsace or, best of the lot, any Loire sweet wines. Don't splash out and get the heaviest vintages – look at the lesser, cheaper regions like Coteaux du Layon. Sweet Jurançon would also be a fine choice, but again, stick to the lighter versions.

Try

🍷 **Barsac and Sauternes** p.31, **Australia** p.156

🍇 **Sémillon** p.212, **Chenin Blanc** p.194

As you cook fruit it becomes sweeter. More elaborate desserts will introduce flavourings, some cinnamon in stewed apples or a red wine reduction with poached pears. Any strong alcohol flavours like brandy or calvados also need to be taken into account. I'd stick to the fuller versions of the above with most things. Strawberry cheesecake, for example, would need something from a good ripe vintage, although I would still favour the something in the fruity and fresh mould. Fruit tarts require the same type of treatment but again, let the fruit's acidity and tartness guide you.

Pear and almond tart moves towards the fruity, rich end of the scale while lemon tart wants something light and fresh. Most crumbles will be happy with the above fruity options, but really tart fruits like gooseberries need something with the equivalent level of acidity so the fresher the better. Rhubarb is probably the greatest ingredient for crumble, but unfortunately it is not a lover of wine. Unless you have the most succulent of young stalks, most will contain tannin, which plays havoc with wine. Keep it simple and don't bring out your best bottles.

Stewed fruit like a baked apple may have been caramelised with some brown sugar. In this case I would want the orange tinge of a botrytis sweet wine, so anything from Bordeaux or Aussie Sémillon would be good.

TARTE TATIN AND CARAMELISED DESSERTS

Try

Australia p.156, **Bordeaux** p.24, **Loire Valley** p.72, **Germany** p.98, **Austria** p.96, **Tuscany** p.120, **Hungary** p.103

Sémillon p.212, **Riesling** p.206

Sweet wines essentially fall into two categories: those that are made from very ripe grapes and those that have been made from *botrytis*-affected berries. The former have rich, sweet, fruit flavours while the latter have caramel and marmalade flavours. It doesn't require a degree in food and wine matching to work out which goes best with a sticky pudding. Rather than going for contrast, this is all about the flavours in the wine and food being similar and thus complementing each other.

A tip – if you are choosing a sweet wine and are unsure which camp the bottle falls into, check the colour. A wine that has an orange tinge to it has, more often than not, been affected by *botrytis*. Sweet Sémillon from Australia is a good-value place to start, then head to Bordeaux. Top Loire stickies like Coteaux du Layon are also a joy. If money is no object, German *Beerenauslese* and *Trockenbeerenauslese* are decadent treats, although the same level of sweetness can be had for a more realistic price from Austria. Vin Santo from Tuscany will help out, but a special mention must go to Hungary's unique Tokaji – drunk with an apple tarte tatin and a blob of vanilla ice cream I can think of no better way to finish a meal.

I have chosen a few recipes (a big thank you to Jeremy in the Big Apple for penning them) to try to illustrate the points I have been making about pairing food and wine. None are too complicated and all can be enjoyed with a range of bottles to suit all budgets. My perfect wine choices are just that, so don't be afraid to experiment.

PAN FRIED BASS WITH BROWN BUTTER LEMON AND HAZELNUTS

The combination of fish, brown butter and lemon has been used around Europe for many years. Skate and Dover Sole are favourites but almost any firm non-oily white mild-flavoured fish goes well. The simplicity of this dish allows any wine you serve with it full rein to show off. Fine white Burgundy would, wallet permitting, be my first choice. Good New World Chardonnay would do just as well. Almost any rich white will work, though, a great Alsace Riesling, an unctuous Rhône white or an Aussie Sémillon.

(Serves 4)

For the Fish
4 150-g 1-cm-thick
   skinless fillets of bass
   or firm white fish
all purpose flour
salt and pepper
1 lemon cut in half
75 g butter
60 g crushed toasted
   hazelnuts
1 tablespoon chopped
   parsley

For the Spinach
300 g baby spinach
300 g rocket
1 clove of garlic, cut in
   half
1 teaspoon of butter

For the Fish: Heat a couple of tablespoons of oil in a large sauté pan. Season the fish and lightly flour the fillets on one side. When the oil starts to smoke add the fish flour side down and sauté for 2 minutes on both sides. Remove the fillets and place each one on a bed of spinach.

Wipe out the pan and place it back on the heat. Add the butter and cook until it starts to turn brown, squeeze in the lemon juice and add the hazelnuts. Remove the pan from the heat and finish the sauce with the parsley, season with salt and pour a generous amount over each fish fillet.

For the Spinach: Heat butter in a large sauté pan and add the clove of garlic. Sauté for 1 minute before adding the spinach and rocket. Sauté for a further 2 minutes or until all greens are wilted. Split equally on to four warm plates.

Best Wines: Chardonnay, Riesling, Sémillon

ROAST PORK SHOULDER WITH MUSHROOM RAGOUT

Comfort food doesn't get much better than some nice roast pork on a Sunday afternoon. In this recipe it's best to use either the belly or a rolled boneless shoulder, as these cheaper cuts are easier to cook and have infinitely more flavour. The fat content in both cuts makes the meat deliciously tender and tasty when slow-roasted. Look for wines with good acidity to tackle the rich meat. Italy has some good matches – try Piemonte or Tuscany.

For the Roast Pork

2 kg joint of rolled, tied shoulder or boneless pork belly
2 sprigs rosemary, roughly chopped
2 tablespoons olive oil
$1/_2$ litre chicken stock
10 sage leaves
salt and pepper

For the Mushroom Ragout

300 g sliced shitake mushrooms
300 g oyster mushrooms
3 sliced shallots
2 mashed garlic cloves
1 teaspoon fresh marjoram, chopped
1 teaspoon sherry vinegar
olive oil

Preheat the oven to 325f/160c/gas mark 3. Take the scored joint of meat and rub olive oil, rosemary and sage into the skin, then season liberally with salt and pepper. Place the meat on a rack in a roasting pan. Raising the meat off the pan like this will stop any burning or drying out of the underside of the joint. Put in the oven, basting every 45 minutes to an hour for 3-4 hours. To test whether the joint is done, stick a knife into the centre: if it goes in and out with little to no resistance the meat is ready. Remove the joint from the oven and rest for 20 minutes before carving, keeping the meat juices aside.

The mushroom ragout can be made while the pork is roasting. Try to use fresh marjoram as it loses its beautifully floral tones when dried. In a pan containing a generous amount of olive oil, sauté the mushrooms in small batches until they are golden brown, seasoning at the end. When the mushrooms all are cooked and resting on a tray, add the garlic and shallots to the pan and sauté on a medium heat for 2-3 minutes or until they have a light golden colour. Pour the sherry vinegar into the pan, then add the mushrooms and marjoram. Cook on a medium heat for a further minute; give it a final taste, season with salt and pepper, then set aside. Before serving, add the chicken stock to the juice from the pork and reduce to a gravy-like consistency, before pouring over the mushrooms.

Best Wines: Piemonte, Sangiovese

BEEF AND ALE STEW

Stew is good proper British cooking, generally involving strong flavours and a warming rich sauce. Slow cooking often utilises those funny cuts of meat that no one seems to want, it is thus a cheap way to feed a large horde. Wines need to be red, big and for want of a more delicate word, butch. The Rhône Valley and Southern France come up trumps in this area, and they are also producing France's finest-value fine wines. These will thus, along with the dish, make you feel satisfyingly frugal. The same grapes (Syrah, Grenache and Mourvèdre) grown around the world will do just as well.

(Serves 6)

1.5 kg beef shin, cut into 2-inch cubes
175 g unsmoked bacon, cut into 1 inch lardons
2 tablespoons flour
2 red onions, diced into $1/2$-inch pieces
3 shallots, diced into $1/2$-inch pieces
4 cloves of garlic, thinly sliced
2 carrots, diced into $1/2$-inch pieces
2 sticks of celery, diced into $1/2$-inch pieces
500 g of mushrooms, stemmed and quartered
2-tablespoons tomato paste
250 ml Guinness
1 litre beef stock
2 bay leaves
1 tablespoon fresh thyme leaves
1 teaspoon chopped fresh rosemary

For the Stew: Preheat the oven to 275f/140c/gas mark 2. In a large bowl season the beef with salt and pepper. Add the flour and lightly toss until all the beef is coated. Add 2 tablespoons of oil to a large sauté pan and brown the meat on all sides. Be careful not to overcrowd the pan, or you will end up boiling rather than caramelising the outside of the meat. Remove the beef when browned and, in the same pan, separately sauté the mushrooms, carrots and bacon. Set them aside, wipe the pan and add two fresh tablespoons of oil. Sauté the shallots, onions, garlic and celery on a medium heat until lightly coloured, then add the tomato purée, bay leaves, thyme and rosemary, then cook for a further 2-3 minutes. Add the ale and reduce to a syrup consistency. Put the meat back into the pan and cover with the stock. Bring up to a slow simmer, season with salt and pepper, cover and place in the oven. Cook for 1 hour, then add the carrots, bacon and mushrooms. Replace the lid and cook for a further 45 minutes. If you find the stew becomes too dry, add more stock as it is cooking. Remove the lid and check to see if the meat is done. The sauce should be rich and the meat should be melt-in-your-mouth tender. Do not worry if it needs to be cooked for longer, as it will only get better as it cooks.

Serve with creamy mashed potato.

Best wines: Rhône Valley, Bandol, Corbières, Languedoc, Provence, Shiraz, Grenache.

MONKFISH YELLOW CURRY

This recipe is based on perhaps one of Thailand's mildest curries. It uses a moderate amount of chilli and a fairly high proportion of spice and herbs. The deep yellow colour comes from the turmeric. This dish goes well with almost any white firm fish, prawns, lobster or scallops. Wines need to be white and fruity but avoid oaky bottles. It is also time to be adventurous with my beloved Riesling and all things Alsatian.

Yellow Curry Paste

4 red chillies (seeded)
1 tablespoon coriander seeds
1 teaspoon cumin seeds
2 tablespoons chopped
    shallots
2 tablespoons chopped garlic
1 2-inch thumb of ginger
1 chopped stick of
    lemongrass
4 kaffir lime leaves
1 tablespoon of turmeric
1 tablespoon mild curry
    powder
60 ml peanut oil

For the Curry

600 g monkfish
3 tablespoons plus 1
    teaspoon yellow curry
    paste
2 tablespoons peanut oil
4 medium-size waxy potatoes
300 ml coconut milk
1 tablespoon fish sauce
1 teaspoon of light-brown
    sugar
Soy sauce to taste
Fine-chopped spring onions
    to garnish

For the Yellow Curry Paste: Take all the ingredients and blend in a food processor until a smooth paste is formed. The colour should be a deep yellow. You can freeze any leftover paste.

To Prepare the Curry: Cut the monkfish fillets into 1-inch pieces and marinate in 1 teaspoon of curry paste and 2 tablespoons of peanut oil. Set aside for 30 minutes. Cut the potatoes into 1-inch cubes and boil in salted water until just tender. It is very important not to overcook your potatoes, as they will break in the final sauce creating a grainy texture. While the potatoes are cooking sauté the fish on one side for 2 minutes. Turn the fish, add the remaining curry paste and cook for one more minute. Then add the coconut milk, sugar and fish sauce. Season with soy sauce if needed, add the potatoes and cook for a further 2 minutes. Finish the curry with a pinch of sliced spring onions.

Serve the curry with steamed jasmine rice.

Best Wines: Riesling, Gewürztraminer, Grüner Veltliner, New World Sauvignon Blanc

CROUTON WITH CHAVIGNOL GOAT CHEESE MOUSSE AND APPLE-BEETROOT RELISH

If you are fond of rich, creamy cheese there is no better place to be than the Loire region of France. The region's most famous cheese is Chavignol goats cheese. Goat milk has a high fat content and thus produces a smooth cheese that is rich but delicately flavoured. Most reds will overpower goats cheese. Crisp white is the answer and it comes as no surprise that from Chavignol come some of the Loire's finest Sauvignon Blancs, in the form of Sancerre.

Relish
100 g peeled and finely diced
   Granny Smith apple
1 medium beetroot
1 sprig thyme
10 g butter
50 g finely diced shallots
60 g sugar
60 ml red wine vinegar
pinch of salt

Crouton
16 $1/2$-cm slices of baguette
2 cloves of garlic cut in half
50 ml extra virgin olive oil
2 teaspoons of fresh thyme
   leaves

Mousse
225 g young chavignol goats
   cheese (at room
   temperature)
75 ml double cream
$1/2$ tablespoon finely chopped
   parsley
$1/2$ tablespoon finely chopped
   chives

For the Relish: Wrap the beetroot in foil with 1 sprig of thyme, a pinch of salt and 1 teaspoon of butter. Place it in the oven at 180c/350f/gas mark 4 and roast for about 1 hour, until tender when pierced with a knife. Allow the beetroot to cool and finely dice it. Put all the relish ingredients except the beetroot in a pan and cook over a very low heat for 15 minutes. Add the finely diced beetroot and cook for a further 15 minutes or until all the moisture has evaporated. Cool and serve. This relish will last for up to a week covered in the fridge.

For the Croutons: Take the slices of baguette and rub a piece of garlic over each one. Brush each piece with olive oil and lay them out on a backing tray. Sprinkle with thyme and salt, and bake in the oven on 160c/325f/gas mark 4 until crisp and golden.

For the Mousse: Note that it is important to use the younger form of Chavignol goat cheese in this recipe, as we are making a mild and creamy mousse. While the croutons are cooking, take the goats cheese, remove the rind and crumble the cheese into a food processor and blend it until smooth. Turn the processor off and gradually fold in the cream until all is incorporated. Fold in the parsley and chives, then season the mousse with salt and pepper to taste.

Place a generous amount of mousse on a crouton, top with the relish and a few chopped chives.

Best wines: If you feel traditional stick to Loire Sauvignon Blanc, although other versions from around the world will do just as well.

MACERATED STRAWBERRIES WITH SHORTBREAD AND CLOTTED CREAM

This recipe is a simple collection of three classic British foods: shortbread from Scotland, thick, gooey clotted cream from the south-west of England and the quintessential English summer fruit, strawberries. These are warm-weather beasts, so they should always be served at room temperature for maximum flavour. This is a dessert but not in the fully sweet scheme of things. It does not enjoy super-sweet stickies, preferring medium wines with a healthy zip of acidity. Sweet Chenin Blanc from the Loire or mid-weight Riesling is fine. However, slightly sweet fizz is a decadent delight that will only add to the volume levels when you serve this outside in the summer.

For the Shortbread
(makes 18 biscuits)
150 g unsalted butter
75 g fine caster sugar
180 g sifted flour

For the strawberries
400 g strawberries
6 mint leaves, roughly
    chopped
2 tablespoons sugar
juice of half a lemon
Clotted cream to serve

For the Shortbread: Using a food processor, cream the butter and the sugar together until light and smooth. Slowly mix in the sifted flour. Roll the dough into a long cylinder 3-4 cm wide and wrap it in either greaseproof paper or cling film. Once tightly wrapped, cut into _-cm discs and lay on a non-stick or buttered baking tray. Preheat the oven to 350f/180c/4 and bake for 15 minutes or until golden.

For the Strawberries: Combine all the ingredients and allow the strawberries to macerate for 1 hour at room temperature.

To serve: Serve a small bowl of strawberries at room temperature with a dollop of clotted cream and a couple of pieces of shortbread.

Best Wines: Loire Valley, Alsace, Germany (*Auslese* level), *demi-sec* Champagne, Moscato d'Asti.

The aim of this section is to describe general terms that appear on wine labels or in the text. Terms that are specific to one area can be found in the index.

acidity Acid is present in all forms of wine. White wines with high levels of acid will often be described as refreshing and will leave your mouth salivating. Wines from hot countries generally have lower acidity. Consider acid levels when matching wine and food.

azienda agricola An Italian term for a producer that is the equivalent to a French *domaine*.

balance A tasting term referring to a wine's overall quality. A balanced wine has all its components – such as tannin, acidity and fruit – in harmony.

barrel-fermented This indicates a white wine that has undergone its fermentation in an oak barrel rather than in a stainless steel tank. The resulting wines are generally rich and creamy.

barrique A French term for an oak barrel.

biodynamic A new fad that is sweeping the wine industry. Not only are the vines looked after organically, but the whole approach in the vineyard and winery is led by the teachings of Rudolph Steiner, the godfather of bio-dynamism, incorporating the effects of planetary cycles and magnetism on viticulture. Some of the world's most exclusive producers are now embracing this seemingly strange idea.

bodega A Spanish term for a wine-producing estate.

botrytis cinerea Also referred to as 'noble rot', this is one of the more peculiar techniques in winemaking. Botrytis is a mould that attacks grapes and feeds on the water inside them, thereby concentrating the flavours. The resulting wines are intensely sweet and have an orange tinge.

breathe A wine that is left in a decanter or glass before drinking is given the chance to 'breathe'. This exposure to oxygen allows the wine's subtleties to develop.

brut A French term for 'dry', usually relating to Champagne.

cépage A French term for the grape or grapes that make up a wine.

claret A British term for the red wines of Bordeaux.

commercial A term I use liberally, it defines soft, fruity, crowd-pleasing wines. There's nothing wrong with this at entry level, but I believe it has become too common among fine wines.

complex A positive way to describe a wine that has many differing nuances.

co-operative The name for a winery that is owned by a number of different people who have pooled their resources. This can be a good way to make fine value wine, but more often than not though it is a byword for mediocrity. I would be particularly wary of Italian co-operatives.

corked Not, as Basil Fawlty noted, a wine containing pieces of floating cork, but rather one that has been spoiled by a faulty cork tainted with a bacteria called TCA. Hence the development of plastic corks and Stelvin closures.

Cru or Cru Classé	A confusing term on French wine labels as its meaning changes depending upon what region you are in. In wine terms it refers to a vineyard – in Burgundy and Champagne these will be owned by a number of growers. In Provence it refers to an estate. In Bordeaux Cru Classé refers to a property's rank within a classification system.
crémant	A French term for a sparkling wine.
cuvée	A loose term that literally means blend. Most producers make more than one wine; these different bottlings will often be referred to as cuvées.
decanting	This is the process of removing a wine from the bottle into a larger container. It is done for two purposes: firstly, to remove any sediment that might have formed in red wine or port; secondly, it aerates the wine by exposing a greater proportion to oxygen. The process is overused for old wine, as there is a danger of it going over the hill in the decanter. Unless you know the wine, far better to pour an old red with a steady hand. You can always leave it in the glass to breathe. It is underused for young wine; a good stint in the decanter will soften the tannins and acidity of a wine in its infancy.
demi-sec	A French term for an off dry wine, most commonly from the Loire Valley or Champagne.
domaine	A French term, of particular relevance to Burgundy, indicating an estate that owns the vineyards that it produces wine from. It thus has complete control over the quality of the final product.
en-primeur	A French term, although it is now applied around the world, for wine that is offered for sale before it is even bottled. In theory, this allows customers to secure allocations of rare wine at a bargain price.
fermentation	The fundamental basis of all wine production. It is the process by which yeast transforms the sugar in grape juice to alcohol.
finish	A term referring to the taste left in your mouth after a wine has been swallowed. A good finish will leave a pleasant taste and last for some time.
fortified	A wine described as fortified has had a neutral spirit added to it. The final alcohol level will usually be higher than an unfortified wine. Sherry and Port are two good examples.
fresh	A tasting term used to describe a wine, often white, that has good acidity. The indication is that the wine is refreshing.
fût de chêne	A French term used to indicate a wine has been matured in oak barrels.
Grand Cru	A French term used to describe a region's best vineyard sites. It is of particular importance for Burgundy, Alsace and Champagne.
jeunes vignes	A French term indicating a wine made from young vines. Some top producers will make a cuvée from young vines that will be sold at a more accessible price.
late harvest	This refers to grapes that have been given extra time to ripen on the vine. They have higher sugar levels and usually make sweet wines.
lees	These are dead yeast cells that sink to the bottom of the fermentation vessel. Leaving them with the wine for an extended period of time imparts flavour. The most famous example is Muscadet 'Sur Lie'.

legs	A tasting note reference to the rivulets of wine that pour down the inside of a glass after it has been swirled. The more prominent the legs the greater the alcohol content of the wine.
length	A tasting term that refers to the amount of time a wine's taste stays in the mouth after you have swallowed it – the longer the better.
moelleux	A French term for sweet wine.
monopole	A French term that usually relates to Burgundy. It indicates that the vineyard in question is owned by one single producer.
mousseux	A French term for sparkling wine.
négociant	A French term for a producer who buys grapes from growers to make wine. They do not often have full control over the end quality of the product.
noble rot	See *botrytis cinerea*.
organic	The grapes used to make these wines will have been grown in accordance with national guidelines for organic agricultural production. Potentially of higher quality, these wines are often more expensive to produce.
oak	The maturation of wine in oak barrels imparts extra flavour to the final taste. Only some grape varieties and the best wines are suitable for this process.
oxidised	A wine that has generally been spoiled by contact with the air. A white wine might be darker than expected or have an orange tinge and smell like sherry. A red one might look older than expected and have a brown hue, due to its being stored incorrectly. Wines like Sherry and Madeira are deliberately oxidised and the flavours imparted form part of the wines' final tastes.
ripe	When used as a tasting term this is positive and implies a wine is juicy, fruity and of a high quality.
riserva	An Italian term to indicate that a wine has undergone an additional period of maturation in oak barrels. This treatment is reserved for only the best wines and they generally require a few years in the cellar to be at their best.
sec	A French term for a dry wine.
stelvin	Another name for a screw cap. This recent development eliminates the possibility of a wine being corked. Traditionalists (most of Europe) turn their nose up at them, while the New World is pushing for their wider use. Those who think they are cheap and tacky should bear in mind that they cost more than cheap cork and should be regarded as a sign of a producer's dedication to quality.
structure	A tasting term referring to the framework of a wine. For a white this will take into consideration the wine's acidity and, for reds, both acidity and tannin. A wine with good structure should indicate a potential for ageing and is essential for matching with food.
tannin	This is the mouth-drying effect left by some red wines. Unsure about what I mean? Bite into a banana skin, that's tannin. A component of a wine's structure, it contributes to the ability of red wines to age and is also a useful foil against the rich foods.

tears	See legs.
terroir	A French term that is now used globally. *Terroir* is the essence of a wine's regional identity. The idea is that in a specific location a combination of soil, weather and geography come together to produce something unique. This is the essential ethos behind the French *appellation contrôlée* system, that where a wine is produced is more important than what grape it is made from or who made it.
traditional method	A term used to describe the production of a sparkling wine. It indicates that the second fermentation (essential to the production of fine sparkling wine) has taken place in the bottle. This is the most expensive method and one that by law must be utilised in Champagne.
ullage	The air space between the wine and the cork. As a bottle ages this will increase, a large amount of ullage in a bottle that is relatively young might indicate a wine that has been stored badly.
unfiltered	One of the finishing processes before a wine is bottled is filtration, ensuring a wine arrives to you crystal bright. However heavy filtration detrimentally affects the taste, thus non-interventionist winemakers now advocate only light or no filtration. These bottles will typically throw sediment at a young age.
un-oaked	Certain grape varieties, such as Chardonnay, have in the past suffered from being over-oaked. There is thus now a trend towards bottling these wines without oak. The wines are fresher and lighter as a result.
vieilles vignes	A French term meaning 'old vines'. These produce the most concentrated grapes and thus the best wine.
vigneron	A French term for a winemaker.
vinification	The practice of making wine.
viticulture	The practice of growing vines.
weingut	A German term for a wine producing estate.
yeast	One of the essential ingredients in the winemaking process. It feeds on the sugar in grape juice to produce carbon dioxide and alcohol.
yields	The amount of grapes (in weight) harvested from a given piece of land can affect a wine's final quality. More generally equals a lower standard. This yield is often measured in hecto-litres and in Europe is controlled by each country's wine regulations.
vin doux naturel	A French term for a sweet wine that has been created by adding a spirit to partially fermented grape juice. This halts the fermentation process, leaving extra quantities of sugar in the final wine.

ACKNOWLEDGEMENTS

I would like to thank the following people and places without whom I would never have been in a position to write this book: Penny and Teddy for presenting me with some well-chosen cases on my 21st birthday and thus introducing me to fine wine; those at Bibendum restaurant for being brave (or mad) enough to give me my first job serving wine, in particular François for afternoon drinks and long nights; Matthew Jukes for never-ending lunches and advice; Nicolas Stanley who took me on at the Tate; all those who I have worked, or do work closely, with – in particular Duncan, Jackie, Anita, Matt, Elliot, Derek and Keith for their support over the last nine months; the Tate in general for having the foresight to do things differently; all the suppliers and vineyards I work with, whose passion for this fabulous liquid is infectious; friends outside work who listen to my wine ramblings and help out with samples; Jim, Cess, Griff, Claire, Tree, Will and Clare who modelled during the food shoot; Martin for the stunning photography and putting up with the above drunken, hungry friends; Jeremy who wrote the recipes long-distance, and Pete for making them look so good on the day; my agent Arabella and her father Abner for their encouragement; all those at Century and Random House who made the book possible; Oliver for commissioning it and fermenting ideas. Lastly special thanks to Emily, who has performed the roles of sous-chef, taskmaster and editor with equal proficiency and good grace.